THE STRENGTHS APPROACH IN PRACTICE

How It Changes Lives

Avril Bellinger and Deirdre Ford

D1612300

START
students and refugees together

All payments to the authors from the sale of this book will be donated to Students and Refugees Together (START)

First published in Great Britain in 2022 by

Policy Press, an imprint of
Bristol University Press
University of Bristol
1–9 Old Park Hill
Bristol
BS2 8BB
UK
t: +44 (0)117 954 5940
e: bup-info@bristol.ac.uk

Details of international sales and distribution partners are available at
policy.bristoluniversitypress.co.uk

© Bristol University Press 2022

British Library Cataloguing in Publication Data
A catalogue record for this book is available from the British Library

ISBN 978-1-4473-5969-2 paperback
ISBN 978-1-4473-5970-8 ePub
ISBN 978-1-4473-5971-5 ePdf

Cover designer: Nicky Boroweic
Image credit: Alamy/David Woodfall
Printed and bound in Great Britain by CMP, Poole
Policy Press uses environmentally responsible print partners

This book is dedicated to our friend and colleague Brigitte Riebartsch (22 March 1957–16 December 2020). Brigitte epitomised the strengths approach throughout her life and work. A fiercely professional social worker with deep integrity, she cherished life in all its rich diversity. As the Socrates Erasmus lead for the Esslingen Fachoschule, Germany in the enduring partnership with Plymouth University, UK she created countless opportunities for staff and students to extend their horizons. Brigitte believed in START, trusting us with students from the beginning. Through her role and her friendship Brigitte had a profound influence on the growth of START as an international learning organisation. We miss her.

Contents

List of figures, tables and boxes

About the authors

Avril Bellinger (previously Butler) is a registered social worker, grandmother and allotmenteer. She founded START, is the current Chair of Trustees and is an independent international volunteer. A passionate believer in the strengths approach, she remains active in promoting social justice through practice and education. Although no longer in paid employment, she holds an honorary post with Plymouth University as Associate Professor in Social Work. Publications include creative autobiography, feminist research, learning in practice and appreciative inquiry. She co-edited *Practice Placement in Social Work* (2016, Policy Press) with Deirdre Ford.

Deirdre Ford, a registered social worker, practised in multi-disciplinary teams supporting people who have learning disabilities and mental health problems. She has taught on social work and related programmes at Exeter and Plymouth universities. She continues to publish and support practitioners in adult social care as a Research in Practice associate. Deirdre has been a trustee of START since 2004. Publications include *Social Work Models, Methods and Theories* (2nd edn, 2012, Russell House, co-edited with P. Stepney).

Acknowledgements

'START is more like a family not just an organisation. Everybody is now part of my past, part of my life.'

Jokow

This comment by Jokow in Chapter 9 captures our feelings in START's twentieth year. We cannot begin to acknowledge all of the people who have passed through START in this time and made it what it is. We cannot fully appreciate in these pages the work, the gifts and the impact of all the people who have left their legacy in the organisation. Like a family, however, from time to time we receive news of people as they get on with their lives. Across Europe former students contact us, wanting to keep in touch and sometimes to involve us in their current work. It is a constant pleasure and privilege to be part of this ever-growing and ever-changing family. The stories in Chapter 9 reveal something of the complexity of people's lives. This book would not have been possible without you. We want to express our heartfelt appreciation to all.

A number of people were critical to START's inception, in particular: Rowena Cerrino, first student, caseworker and manager; Viv Horton, social worker, international volunteer and trustee; Louise Houston, practice educator; Belinda O'Flynn, Ethnic Minority Achievement Service; Professor Mary Watkins, formerly Dean of the Faculty of Health, University of Plymouth.

As we go to press, the extraordinary team who continue to 'carry the torch' for the strengths approach at START are Susie Dent, Isaac Kelly, Hana Skenklova, Azeb Mengisteab and Kathy Rago. Thank you – not least for your consistently positive approach to every difficulty encountered, whether in individual casework, government policy or global pandemic. Thank you to all staff, trustees and volunteers, past and present. Thanks also to Plymouth City Council, a Welcoming City and City of Sanctuary.

We appreciate the generosity of so many students who have 'gone the extra mile' at START, specifically those who have agreed to the inclusion of their work in these chapters. Thank you to Kim Embra, Shreena Ghelani, Elena Gnant, Lucy Holmyard and Phyllis McNally for sharing your scholarship. START has thrived from partnerships with universities both in the UK and internationally. Thanks especially to Plymouth, Esslingen and Lillehammer.

Finally, thank you to Laura Vickers-Rendall and colleagues at Policy Press for enabling us to share this work and to the anonymous reviewer whose careful feedback helped us to improve it.

Preface

> To refuse to participate in the shaping of our future is to give it up. Do not be misled into passivity either by false security (they don't mean me) or by despair (there's nothing we can do). Each of us must find our work and do it.
>
> Lorde (1984: 141)

Give me strength: a personal invitation to action

It was autumn 1971. I remember being on duty, as a 21-year-old trainee social worker in the newly formed social services department in Hounslow, close to Heathrow airport. One of my responsibilities was to arrange accommodation for a homeless Asian family expelled from Uganda by Idi Amin. I witnessed the man's distress and horror at being allocated a single shabby room in a Victorian hostel alongside some of the poorest, white British families. He described to me the spacious house and gardens he had left to save his family's lives and questioned whether this was the only accommodation available. I checked with colleagues and was met, not with sympathy, but with anger and hostility because, they said, 'He should be grateful!'

Throughout my career I have been shocked by people's capacity to place themselves above the possibility of such disasters happening in their own lives. I wonder whether this triumph of entitlement over compassion arises paradoxically from a sense of inadequacy and powerlessness. The examples given throughout this book of the strengths approach in action show its power to rekindle compassion, and to create opportunities for humanity to flourish.

In Europe, the response to refugees has become increasingly hostile. Refugees who were living in the 'Jungle' camp in Calais are now the targets of police aggression; police are destroying their tents and moving people on wherever they find a place to shelter. All over Europe there are people who have fled for their lives, risking dangerous sea crossings with their children and family members, avoiding the authorities and being treated like criminals. In Rome, the right-wing government arbitrarily closed the largest Italian refugee centre after an anti-terrorist raid. On 6 December 2018, the municipality of Rome closed down the Baobab transit centre for refugees, which had been run completely by volunteers who had decided to step forward in place of negligent authorities. The Civil Liberties Union for Europe reported that the centre played a fundamental role in providing a safe haven for people on the move and asked authorities to guarantee proper structures to welcome migrants in transit. Even before the closure, people had been sleeping on the streets in sub-zero temperatures, supported only by individuals and non-government organisations (NGOs). No such guarantee was given. In 2020, on the Turkish-Greek border, people escaping from the humanitarian disaster in Syria were encouraged by Turkey to try to cross into Europe in a cynical political attempt to pressurise the European Union. In the absence of an agreed European policy, Greek border guards, guns loaded with live ammunition, fired tear gas to repel the desperate people (Rankin et al, 2020).

I can hardly believe that, in the space of five years, government and public attitudes have hardened against refugees to the extent that they have. In 2015, Europe received over a million people seeking asylum mostly from Syria, Afghanistan, Iran and Eritrea. In contrast to the UK, Germany and other European countries responded to this humanitarian crisis by building shelters and employing social workers and other staff. By 2018, the numbers of refugees arriving in Europe had reduced dramatically because of multi-national agreements that people managing to survive the Mediterranean crossing should be returned to appalling conditions in Libya and that anyone seeking to rescue people from drowning as they attempt the crossing should be treated as law breakers (Bertelli, 2019). How can it be that to save the life of a child, woman or man is a criminal act? I am appalled to witness how effectively and quickly governments have moved to 'other' refugees and represent them as less than human in people's minds. As numbers rise again, national responses are defensive rather than humanitarian.

I know many people who do what they can in the face of such inhuman regulations, and believe that we can always find opportunities to make a difference, however small. As Susan Sontag (2004) says in her analysis of our responses to images of suffering – we need to be able to take action or we will become desensitised. The organisation, Students and Refugees Together (START), described in this book is one such action to improve the lives of people who have experienced forced migration and found themselves in Plymouth, United Kingdom. Informed by the strengths approach, I initiated it because it was something I could do with the resources available at that time. It has shown that the strengths approach, consistently applied over 20 years, is a powerful force for change.

I have always felt ambivalent about my profession of social work with its focus on the here and now of people's lives and on building relationships that enable people to live those lives as fully as they wish. We do this in a context of a social and political analysis critiquing the conditions that produce those difficulties in the first place, but it is essentially person-centred. A focus on the individual seems to me an inadequate response to such global influences – a sticking plaster on a deep and enduring wound. However, I know that I am not a politician or even an activist in the generally accepted meaning of protest and campaigning, while I applaud those who are able to do that vital work. My resolution of this ambivalence about what I really ought to do, is to do whatever I can, where I am, with what I have. The power of the strengths approach is that it frees us to see what opportunities and resources are already available to us and to put our energy into harnessing them.

In 2000, the city of Plymouth in the southwest of England, where I worked as a social work lecturer and placement organiser, was not used to responding to people of other languages, religions and ethnicities. I had visited a charity for women who were single parents in Kazakhstan. There the absence of a welfare floor meant that homeless people froze to death on the streets, young women had few alternatives to sex work and many people were selling single cigarettes to make enough to live on. I was forcibly struck by how it would be if I were to find myself with my two daughters in a country where I couldn't even read the alphabet. I felt lucky to be returning to a country where no one was left destitute and where the social security system ensured that no one should starve or be homeless for long if they accepted help. I naively believed that the state's role was to care for people, particularly those unable to care for themselves, and that following the rules would lead to fair treatment.

By 2001, the law had changed with the result that the Home Office were contracting with local authorities and private companies throughout the country to provide accommodation for people waiting for a decision on their asylum claim, a process known as dispersal. I was at an International Women's Day event when the city's Labour Member of Parliament (MP), Linda Gilroy, announced that Plymouth was to be a dispersal area for people seeking asylum in the UK. This meant that families from all over the world were being dispersed to Plymouth without any choice while they waited for a decision on their asylum claim. At that time, Plymouth had a black and minority ethnic (BME) population well below the national average (0.6 per cent) and a variety of reports had shown it to be a difficult place for refugees to be (Jay, 1992; Dhalech, 1999). Even mainstream services like health and education were unfamiliar with providing interpreters. As a social work educator, I had long wanted to encourage students to feel part of a global community and to realise their own potential (Butler et al, 2003) and began to explore ways in which students could work alongside refugees in whatever services were established.

The only money coming into the city council for the dispersed families was a small amount to support school-age children's access to education. All other support, such as access to health and social care, was meant to come from the privately contracted housing providers and, in practice, was negligible.

The head of the city's Ethnic Minority Achievement Service (EMAS) at that time, Belinda O'Flynn, appointed a specialist teacher to work with the families and schools. This teacher, who lived in Plymouth, quickly became the person families went to for help with a whole range of issues. Belinda and I lived in the same village so when she expressed her worry about the increasing demands on the teacher, I thought this could become an opportunity to benefit everyone and suggested social work students could do their professional placement working with the families.

That summer, I invited students to help create a new service. In September, three brave students were introduced to families by the teacher. They quickly deployed their professional skills and ingenuity to help families access their entitlements. A university practice educator supervised their professional learning and provided a room in her house as a makeshift office. The EMAS teacher and social services referral coordinator met the students each week to check what they were doing and to direct their efforts. As student placements finished, others took over the work until the summer when the service itself stopped because there were no students. In this way, a virtual organisation was created over the first two years in which 14 students worked with 21 families (35 adults and 68 children) (Butler, 2007). Since then, the organisation has matured and retained its core philosophy of a strengths approach.

In 2018 START had two co-managers, seven staff and welcomed about 20 students per year (more than 280 students overall). Services are provided to refugees in Plymouth and West Devon. START now works with a professional fundraising organisation to ensure financial stability and has been highly successful in attracting funding from both charitable bodies and government contracts.

START's model of students as the majority workforce, although unusual, is quite a simple idea based on the strengths approach which could be replicated with other groups and in other areas. I hope the material in this book will encourage others to build on the strengths of students and people who are denied state services. This book is not simply a historical account of the development of an extraordinary organisation, nor is it intended primarily to persuade others to replicate such a charity. It is not an instruction manual but rather a collection of stories that illustrate the strengths approach in action. Deirdre Ford (my co-author) and I have seen ourselves as curators rather than instructors, choosing and presenting practice examples, research, historical accounts, theory, policy, narratives and provocations to bring the strengths approach in practice to life. We believe that it is possible to make things happen in any situation if we are brave enough. The features that brought START into being and continue to support it are transferable to other situations. It is opportunistic, values-led, collaborative, creative, innovative – not simply oppositional. It is educative, supports collective action and is organisationally flexible and responsive.

So really this book is a challenge to those feelings of inadequacy and powerlessness mentioned initially. It provides examples of how a strengths approach can be applied to any situation and of the consequences of applying it to learning, organisational management and law and policy for example, as well as to casework with individuals. Each chapter concludes with a set of practice points that are drawn from our experience and which apply beyond social work, beyond the UK and beyond work with refugees.

Our intention in writing this book is to provoke, inspire and encourage you to find your work ... and do it.

Avril Bellinger (formerly Butler)
Founder of START
May 2020

Introduction: The strengths approach in a global emergency

The strengths approach (Saleebey, 2009) is a way of thinking about social problems that harnesses the strength and potential of people, their communities and environment, even in conditions of the most depleted social capital. In times of austerity and the dismantling of the welfare state, it has much to offer anyone seeking to maintain hope and optimism.

People are conditioned to identify problems, target them and propose solutions in the belief that the answer always lies in taking more control. In contrast, the strengths approach requires a departure from positivist thinking and a stance more aligned to that of deep ecology (Naess, 1973):

- acknowledgement of the depth and severity of the challenges;
- respect for all parts of the system, from microbe to constellation; and
- trust in the potential for true sustainability.

The strengths approach offers a way of thinking and acting that goes beyond mere mitigation. It is a holistic practice that, as illustrated in the chapters of this book, is indeed sustainable.

In our own practice as social workers we have found that the strengths approach has often been misrepresented and superficially applied in a manner that belies its value base. While it has been incorporated into the lexicon of theories taught on professional courses, the strengths approach has been significantly marginalised in favour of more empirical, positivist methods that focus on problems and pathology in order to find cause-and-effect responses. The current focus on it in UK policy and practice, however, has prompted many writers to rediscover its considerable influence in other theories, methods and models of intervention. At worst, it is the latest approach to be appropriated and colonised in serving the neoliberal agenda as a cost-cutting panacea, similar to the fate of concepts like resilience or solution-focused models. It is increasingly urgent, therefore, to reconsider the strengths approach and really understand it.

Being prepared to face the reality of our condition is fundamental to the approach. Much of that reality gives cause for hopelessness. Humans continue to devastate the planet with wars and extractive commercial activity. Compelling, well-founded critiques of UK welfare services encompass the impact of capitalism, neoliberalism, austerity and the removal of the welfare floor for growing numbers of people. Mark Carney, former governor of the Bank of England who gave the BBC's Reith Lecture in 2020, charts the move from a market economy to a market society. He observes that the market is without morals and therefore incapable of resolving difficulties that necessitate human judgement. Yet capitalism is regarded as more important than human welfare; austerity is falsely represented as a cure for the country's economic difficulties when in practice it has compounded homelessness and destitution in wider society. Carney (2020) criticises the way economic growth is valued more highly than wellbeing – that health, social relationships and psychological wellbeing are almost set in opposition to economic health. Inevitably practitioners become discouraged and disparaging of services that fail to provide the support needed by the people they work with, or the time to develop meaningful relationships with them. In contrast the strengths approach has the potential to render practice effective rather than simply efficient, to enable people to thrive, not just survive. So what? Does the strengths approach really work?

This book is not a textbook or a book simply about refugees or about social work. It seeks to render the strengths approach accessible to anyone wanting to apply it to their own circumstances. The strengths approach should be seen as a position, a way of thinking and, most of all, a practice.

Its effectiveness is demonstrated comprehensively by a critical review of the history and work of a remarkable NGO. START has embraced the strengths approach as its core philosophy since its inception 20 years ago and epitomises its power in practice. START is employed as a case study in the book, detailed in Box 0.1, to celebrate strengths as a 'whole systems approach', one which informs organisational culture and values as much as operational systems and interventions. Each chapter shows how the strengths approach has been applied to different aspects of the organisation's operation and concludes with generic learning points. Many chapters contain original research by students, as part of their studies, and by the authors. These diverse perspectives are augmented with the voices of refugees, students and others derived from routine evaluations, end-of-contact feedback and personal correspondence. All observe standard ethical practices and provide unique and practical examples of how the strengths approach changes lives. However, these examples should not restrict ideas of how it could be applied.

Box 0.1: The case study

START is an NGO in the southwest of England. It has the dual purpose of supporting the education of students on professional placements and, equally, that of supporting refugees (people granted leave to remain in the UK) to access their rights and realise their ambitions. One of the students, Elena Gnant, gives the following account of the organisation:

> The Board of Trustees is a group of volunteers who support START in different ways. They oversee and support the administration, public relations or fundraising activities. The board members also often take part at START activities and many of them are the founders of START who promoted the organization within their communities and raised funds and awareness.
>
> There are two managers in the START office. One is the main administrative, fundraising and marketing staff

member and one is a community work coordinator, student supervisor and caseworker. They have regular supervisions with the other five paid staff members and they are always there for questions as they mostly work in the same office room. The managers also regularly attend the board meetings of the START Board of Trustees to keep the communication flow between all the different members of the organisation.

The currently five paid staff members with origins in Eritrea, Nigeria, Czech Republic, Great Britain and the USA are responsible for different tasks such as being caseworkers and student supervisors. One of them is additionally an Arabic interpreter, another one is a work and employment assistant, a Syrian and Afghan lead worker – one of them is mostly representing START to the community and conducting refugee awareness trainings, etc.

The students are the main work force at START and throughout my placement time, I had two co-students from France, three from Germany, two from the Netherlands, one from Hungary and nine British students. There is a capacity [for] more than ten students at once. The students came from different study backgrounds such as some (International) Social Work Bachelor and Master students but also Occupational Therapy or Global Health and medical students. The students co-work with a supervisor from the paid staff supporting [them] with the day-to-day work, caseload and become caseworkers with increasing responsibilities. Through regular supervisions and openness, they are able to always ask questions and seek for support, information, reflection or opinions.

The volunteers are a group of enthusiastic and interested people of all ages and different countries who support the different activities and services of START. Some of the volunteers are refugees themselves who went through many of the processes and are therefore able to share their knowledge and experiences but there are also many young and older volunteers from the host community taking part at the different START activities. (Gnant, 2018: 4)

START's community activities
Although initially a casework service for people with leave to remain (comprising more than 2,000 refugee households to date), START has developed a range of community activities that remain core to its work:

- a Cultural Kitchen;
- a Women's Group; and
- two allotments (community gardens).

Other activities are a Job Club, attended by an average of 53 refugees each week seeking support and advice in looking for work. This has also opened up huge opportunities for students and volunteers (both refugee and non-refugee) to work together. Volunteer recruitment and support are now core aspects of START's work. A strong Service User Forum gives a voice to people to whom the organisation belongs. Agencies, schools, police and other groups throughout the city benefit from refugee awareness training courses run by workers and refugees.

The START walking project was aimed initially at encouraging refugees to discover the countryside around Plymouth, to access cultural exchange and English language learning. A book of nine walks, published in 2013, established 'STARTwalking' as one of the regular community activities which featured on national radio (https://www.bbc.co.uk/programmes/b08k4bxw).

All of these services have grown out of the initiative and energy of refugees, students and staff who have seen gaps in the support offered and possibilities for filling them. The range enables people to access support in whatever way they choose. Equally, they can move between receiving help and helping others without difficulty. The whole environment encourages confidence and community-growing; it also gives students experience of working in a variety of settings.

START has gained recognition in the following ways:

- NHS Social Care Awards 2005 – regional winner;
- SWAP Learning and Teaching Award 2011 – 'Innovation in Practice Learning Opportunities';

- Social Care Institute for Excellence 2015 'Good Practice with Refugees' publication;
- Radio 4 'Ramblings' programme with Clare Balding 2017 which featured STARTwalking;
- shortlisted for the Good Help Award, NESTA 2018.

In 2017, having been nominated by our regional Member of the European Parliament, START was awarded a European Citizen's Prize. This is given to 'citizens, groups or organisations who have displayed exceptional achievements and commitment to areas promoting stronger integration, cultural cooperation and links to the European spirit' (https://www.europarl.europa.eu/news/en/headlines/eu-affairs/20171009STO85664/parliament-honours-winners-of-2017-european-citizen-s-prize).

This commitment to integration and cultural co-operation is exemplified in the conclusion to Elena's student report:

> I personally developed to appreciate life and the world itself in its fragility and diversity a lot more whilst realizing my living situation and practising a small part of my hope and conviction to be able to be there for each other, respect and support each other as humans. Many experiences gave me a professional calmness and understanding as well as an interest into learning more and an energy to work creatively towards a sustainable, peaceful and socially just future. (Gnant, 2018: 18)

The structure of the book

Chapter 1 sets the record straight regarding the origins and theoretical development of the strengths approach, its practice, critiques and misuses. This chapter celebrates the breadth and reach of its utility way beyond human services to encompass its application in confronting societal, environmental and existential challenges – in short, any area of life and work.

Employing the work of an organisation that supports refugees as a case study is significant if refugees are seen as a litmus test for society. The way they are treated indicates how, or whether, we value people, our relationships to humans and non-humans. It reflects how other groups might be affected in future, as governments realise what they can get away with. Chapter 2 gives a chilling account of how law and policy can be used to deprive people of their human rights by stealth, neglect and incompetence. Its unique application of the strengths approach to law is relevant for any discipline that engages with law and policy to challenge social injustice.

Throughout the book we share Mark Carney's (2020) distinction between value (that which can be expressed as a financial measure) and values – recognition of a public good. Chapter 3 brings a fresh approach to organisational development which celebrates the capacity of organisations to be values-led in a monetised environment. It records the history of the organisation's development; how a strengths approach supported START to become resilient and more effective through challenging times. It combines research from a business studies perspective with rigorous theorising to demonstrate how the strengths approach can be applied protectively.

While much of the book was written before the global COVID-19 pandemic, the latter accentuated many of the themes and messages conveyed by its chapters. At the time, START was working to support refugees in conditions imposed by the UK government's response to the COVID-19 virus. People continued to make their way to the UK to claim asylum and were dispersed to the city without prior health checks. Others were being moved from temporary accommodation to enable the city council to meet its obligations to homeless people. Under the strain of the pandemic and online working, employees across the western world typically experienced loss in all its forms, both personally and professionally, including vicarious trauma, isolation and burnout, IT fatigue and information overload (Ford and Nosowska, 2020). At one stage, START's staff group of seven were working from their respective homes to provide an essential service (using mobile phones, online facilities and volunteers) to more than 80 families in the city. Their resilience in these conditions affirmed the vital importance of maintaining a strengths approach whatever the circumstances. A gradual return to office working and accommodating students was managed through the collaboration and consensus decision-making illustrated in Chapter 4, which addresses the strengths approach to management and governance. This chapter, inviting resistance to the pressures of New Public Management (NPM) as a tool of neoliberalism, shares the strategies used to maintain a flat structure through co-management and active promotion of a learning organisation culture. It is underpinned by research exposing the dangers of the uncritical adoption of computerised recording systems.

A strengths approach requires an overarching system of leadership and governance that encourages diverse local responses consistent with shared goals and values. Chapters 3 and 4 illustrate this on an organisational scale. Such a system values responses for their relevance, rather than for their compliance with a pre-set formula or their ability to be replicated. The COVID-19 pandemic reminded us that collaboration in all aspects of the system is at the core of the strengths approach. Everyone's perspective, experience and resources are relevant if we are to avert the consequences of global crises.

Chapter 5 addresses the subject of finance and sustainability. This might seem paradoxical in a book that consistently asserts money is not an end in itself, but it respects the fact that organisations need funding to function. Grounded in the commercial reality of capitalism, it positions START as in equal partnership with funders rather than as a subservient beneficiary.

All disciplines are dependent on the quality of research in their area. Chapter 6 examines the nature of research, explaining how research is essential to an organisation like START and why a strengths approach to research is a prerequisite. The potential for research to be exploitative is balanced by an example of original research using a strengths approach. Accepting that all research is imperfect, this chapter asserts it is always an intervention. The strengths approach can support research that is co-production in which the process is more important than the product.

Another unique feature of this book is the model of educating placement students who become the majority workforce, supporting people otherwise excluded from society. The voices of students are spread liberally through different chapters.

Chapter 7 shines the spotlight on students as resources rather than burdens on the professional community. It disrupts 'common sense' beliefs about how students learn by offering a theoretical model alongside previously unpublished research. It shows that a strengths approach to student learning enables their skills to be made available quickly and powerfully. It celebrates the power of academic activism in any discipline to make a difference in society.

In Chapter 8 a strengths approach theorises community, 'commons' and reciprocity. It frames community as a process not a product. Detailed examples of how to grow community with refugees and students are provided – how to create commons rather than delivering services, and the difference in practice between the two. The transient nature of both populations accentuates this difference and its wider application more clearly. A particular theme in the book is the importance of initiatives by people who are knowledgeable about their locality. Every area requires a unique response that draws on the expert knowledge of people on the ground. As the UK moves away from the privileged, structured and ordered community services for everyone enacted through the welfare state, an ever-growing range of people are left without help of any kind, even for necessities. Instead of feeling helpless, however, we can learn from rural communities in the global south – think small, act local, and do what we can with what we have, where we are. The power of micro-credit is well-documented (Kavanagh, 2012) as is that of self-help groups (Chatterjee and Sarangi, 2004; Suguna, 2006), changing the lives of the poorest people by harnessing the resources they already have. The story of START provides evidence of what such an approach can achieve in the 21st-century UK.

Under COVID-19 valuable learning has accrued from the extraordinary measures adopted by the staff team at START to show how to support a community in crisis while maintaining the sustainability of an organisation. As time passes, our perspective on the pandemic will change. It will still be a reality, but science's response to the threat with vaccines is much more than a fortunate outcome for humankind. Vaccine research, manufacture and distribution exemplify global co-operation and the form of competition signalled in Chapter 8 by Harvie's

(2004) 'convivial competition'. This is so different from 'business as usual' where companies and countries try to gain economic advantage over each other by being first. One lesson reinforced by the pandemic is that we are all interdependent. 'What is needed is an interdependent community, not independent individuals' (Carney, 2020).

Finally, the stories of five refugees in Chapter 9 remind us of human needs beyond shelter and food. These narratives show that help should not be a transaction in which dignity is exchanged for what is needed.

Conclusion

The strengths approach is an effective response – there is always something that can be done. Fortunately, it is not necessary to wait for a system to be fixed in order to use the strengths approach. Micro-level activism is not the whole answer, as change is needed at all levels of society – but every action matters. We cannot know the longer-term outcome of what we do. For example, and local to us, the influential journal *Resurgence and Ecologist* grew out of the individual vision and collaboration of peace activist Satish Kumar, founder of the Small School in Devon, and has over the past 50 years evolved into an international movement (https://www.resurgence. org/). We make no claim that the adoption of the strengths approach will solve every problem. We do know, however, that it brings energy and hope. The strengths approach has never been more relevant than in a global crisis which forces us to realise the interdependence of all humans and non-humans on this fragile planet. The chapters in this book show how the strengths approach can provide a map to guide us through the most challenging terrain. It is not the intention that the book should preach about the strengths approach or take the moral high ground. Clearly, we all are embedded in the system and are, therefore, complicit. This account, however, is an example of what is possible if we invest in the one life we have and fully commit to realising our aspirations.

1

A strengths approach to human need

Hope is not like a lottery ticket you can sit on the sofa and
clutch, feeling lucky ... hope is an axe you break down
the door with in an emergency; because hope should
shove you out the door, because it will take everything
you have to steer the future away from endless war, from
the annihilation of the earth's treasures and the grinding
down of the poor and marginal. Hope just means another
world might be possible, not promised, not guaranteed.
Hope calls for action; action is impossible without hope
... To hope is to give yourself to the future, and that
commitment to the future makes the present inhabitable.

Solnit (2005: 5)

Introduction

We have never needed a strengths approach more than we
do now – when a climate emergency and the COVID-19
pandemic compete for public attention with global economic
interests; when populism is fed by frustrated individual
ambitions and the entitlement of the few triumphs over the
common good. A strong incentive for writing this book stems
from the resurgence of far-right populism, racism, homophobia,
hate crime and division with the concomitant danger that ideas
like the strengths approach are eroded and diffused. But it is in
the power of such ideologies to change society for the better,
not least because their consequences are so radical in shaping
the way society functions. Just as the forces of greed and power

are constantly re-made and repositioned, so, too, can practices that are mutually beneficial be re-made, reinstated and re-articulated. This book is a small contribution to the re-telling of that story.

This chapter introduces the strengths approach, its generic character as a whole systems response and its wider manifestations. Drawing on our specialist knowledge from the discipline of social work, we present its historical roots and applications. We explore an important component of the approach – that of our relationship with one another and with the environment. We critique the way it has been colonised in welfare services by government in mitigation of the neoliberal project. The scholarship presented here is also a defence against claims that the strengths approach lacks evidence of efficacy or that it shies away from problems.

Critics, cynics and, sometimes, those new to the strengths approach, charge it with being vague and elusive, lacking clear 'how to' protocols for practice. To counter these misperceptions, the chapter introduces two practical applications, notably the power of narrative and an approach known as Human Givens. These practice frameworks apply across a spectrum of disciplines and contexts, working with individuals, communities, organisations and more widely.

The power and efficacy of the strengths approach in action is exemplified throughout the book by our experience of working with refugees through START to support them as they seek to make their home in the UK. As outlined in the Introduction, START was founded on the approach which has informed all of its activities consistently over two decades. START is simply an illustration, however. Our intention here is more ambitious – to fire the imagination for anyone to adopt a strengths approach in any circumstances.

Terminology

This book favours the term 'strengths approach' because it implies action. The phrase is often used interchangeably with that of 'strengths perspective', reflecting questions about whether the concept is a philosophical lens, an ideology or a method. Terminology is significant; the phrase 'strengths-based' (that is, based on strengths) is commonly used in contemporary health and social care practice but can indicate a diluted or highly selective appropriation of components of the strengths perspective, rather than a commitment to a whole systems approach.

History of the strengths perspective in human services

In the field of social work, the term 'strengths perspective' represents a long-held tradition, notably that of building on people's strengths and capabilities to empower them to achieve. It has been a fundamental building block of the profession since the latter developed in the late 19th century. Its presence is traced in the early formulations of social casework developed by Mary Richmond (1922), who challenged the preoccupation with moral deficiency, and notions of the 'deserving' and 'undeserving poor' that persist to this day. Subsequently, Bertha Capen Reynolds, regarded by many as a founding force of strengths-oriented social work (Kaplan, 2002), aimed to empower people who sought help and to mobilise their strengths: 'Our first question to someone who comes to us for help should not be ... "what problems bring you here today?" but rather ... "you have lived life thus far, tell me how you have done it"' (Reynolds, 1951: 125). As a START worker at her exit interview on retirement said: "I'm not saying you should cut corners for them but, again the strengths approach, recognise that they are not beggars. They had things. They are capable. And work with that capability to build them up. It's letting refugees themselves be part of the solution." Helen Harris Perlman (1957) and Florence Hollis (1964) maintained this focus on people's strengths in social casework. Humanistic developmental psychologists, Erik Erikson, Abraham Maslow and Carl Rogers, with their emphasis on innate problem-solving skills and self-actualisation, also heavily influenced social work in recognising strengths. The commitment to empowerment is analogous to conscientisation and animation, implying 'a redistribution or recapturing of power, both personal and social' (Sullivan and Rapp, 1994: 93).

Schwartz's (1971) interactional framework offers another practice theory focusing on an individual's capacity rather than *in*capacity (Shulman, 1993). It takes the stance that problems are the result of misaligned interactions between individuals and organisations rather than deficits within either of them. Structures and organisations are set up to reach out to people who need them and the practitioner's job is to remove the obstacles that prevent successful interaction. This is no small task when the immigration service or benefits agency seem designed to obstruct, or when colleagues are critical or difficult to work with. The strengths approach never lets you off, however. The questions have to be asked 'What are the strengths in this situation? How can I use them to make a positive difference?'

Numerous writers have charted the impressive history of the strengths perspective in social work. This culminated in the work of Ann Weick, Dennis Saleebey, Charles Rapp and their colleagues at the University of Kansas who researched mental health practice in the mid-1980s and critiqued its deficit-oriented practices, epitomised by the *Diagnostic and Statistical Manual of Mental Disorders* (Weick et al, 1989; APA, 2013; Rapp and Sullivan, 2014). Over the last three decades, the strengths perspective has developed as a theoretical framework which reasserts the profession's values – values compromised by the preoccupation with individual pathologies and problem-oriented practice that have dogged practice for much of the last century (Weick and Saleebey, 1998). With a focus on pathology, the identity of the individual is fixed by diagnosis and labelling so that they 'become their problems' – a process of internalised oppression. For example, families using all their ingenuity and skill to escape conflict and persecution, and who further risk their lives by making hazardous journeys to seek asylum in another place, are often simply constructed by social policy and practice as a 'burden' on the host country (Butler, 2005). Their agency and achievements in surviving are completely disregarded. In contrast, the strengths approach maintains that 'the strengths and resources of people and their environments rather than their problems and pathologies should be the central focus of the helping process' (Chapin, 1995: 507). As a worker at START said: "It was bringing my own take on the service users. They have abilities and potential and a future. It's about helping them to achieve that. Sometimes they don't even know, and it's helping them to realise the strengths and abilities they have. Working with them to develop their aspirations." The strengths approach is the embodiment of the ethical principles that shape professions, expressing 'some of the deepest values of social work' (Weick et al, 1989: 350). The International Federation of Social Workers' 'Statement of Ethical Principles' explicitly guides social workers in 'Identifying and developing strengths – social workers should focus on the strengths of all individuals, groups and communities and thus promote their empowerment' (IFSW, 2012: Section 4.1.4).

Similarly, occupational therapy embraces the approach which resonates with its own core values (Kivnick and Stoffel, 2005; Dunn et al, 2013: 2): '[Occupational therapists] take an asset-based approach, analysing and utilising the strengths of the individual, the environment, and the community in which a person lives and functions' (Royal College of Occupational Therapists, 2017: 2/Section 1: 2). The strengths approach is also deeply rooted in hope and a determination to confront the truth of difficulties without being defeated by them. A student social worker at START, when asked how she responded when there was nothing she could do to help a family, replied, "There's always something you can do." Just being alongside someone and caring about their situation is in itself an intervention. In the student's response is the understanding that simply being with someone increases their capacity for problem-solving. We are social animals and need relationships to thrive. A strengths approach encourages us to build relationships, realise potential, seize opportunity, reject adversarial reactions and, above all, maintain hope (Tse et al, 2016).

Since its inception, START has explicitly employed the strengths approach to underpin its mission. The approach shapes the culture of practice in the organisation so that staff and students alike consciously frame all aspects of their work in terms of strengths. They celebrate and harness the skills and resources of refugees alongside the assets to be found in their communities. This mirrors the strengths approach of progressive policies in countries welcoming refugees who argue for inward migration due to declining populations and the needs of their economies (Stone, 2015; Scottish Government, 2018).

Defining the strengths approach

There is a wealth of literature about strengths, yet it is not easy to find a clear definition. The strengths approach is both an orientation that seeks out the potential in people and their environments, and a commitment to action based on hope (Solnit, 2005). It has been defined as 'an appreciation of the positive attributes and capabilities that people express and ... the ways in which individual and social resources can be developed and sustained' (Weick et al, 1989: 352). This dynamic, and constantly evolving approach is usually framed by a set of underlying principles of which the following is an example:

1. Every individual, group, family and community has assets and resources to be used in reconstructing and redirecting their lives.
2. Every individual and collectivity has the inherent capacity for wholeness, regeneration, healing and transformation.
3. Every person and group has a fund of innate wisdom and health to draw upon in times of crisis and challenge.
4. Everyone has the capacity for rebound and righting the trajectory of their development in the face of adversity and trauma.
5. All individuals, families, communities, and cultures have rhetorical, metaphorical, narrative tools to refashion and reformulate their understanding and interpretation of their situation and condition. (Weick and Saleebey, 1998: 27)

For those determined to define the strengths approach, it evades simple categorisation. It is simultaneously an ideology, a philosophy, a value system, a theory, an approach and a set of methods. Most significantly, it is a call to action. In human services it represents a cultural shift from that of deficit and disease to one of hope and wellbeing. It is the antithesis of siloed, targeted systems designed for cost-effectiveness and efficiency in which conformity and control are paramount.

Rather it embraces the complex systems in which humans and non-humans interact.

This book explores the consequences of using a strengths approach as a way of conducting oneself during *every* kind of interaction – personal and professional, teaching and learning, micro, meso and macro. Undoubtedly, it demands a whole systems approach, intrinsic to an organisation at every level and in all aspects of its functioning. It has the potential to change more than we expect. It is complex, dynamic and so much more than methods alone.

Strengths in practice

> No-one has ever realised their potential by relentlessly focusing on their problems.
>
> Lieberman (2014)

While almost anything can be regarded as a strength in certain circumstances, in this context, a strength is a 'personal or environmental attribute that has the potential to stimulate growth and solutions' (Kondrat, 2010: 39).

A construct to help practitioners uncover the strengths of an individual, group or community is that of 'CPR'. It was inspired by the medical practice of cardiopulmonary resuscitation where the person giving assistance effectively breathes for someone until they can breathe for themselves. This metaphor was used to develop the strengths perspective in mental health services where CPR involves believing in someone until they can believe in themselves (Saleebey, 2009). This notion of belief is fundamental to START's approach in its work both with refugees looking to settle in the UK and with students as they embark on professional careers. Box 1.1 is an illustration.

Box 1.1: An example of work at START

The student had a Sudanese refugee in front of him. The Job Centre expected the Sudanese man to do a CV and look for work. He said that he had never worked before, so the student didn't know what to put in the CV. He had the name, address and ... the man had never been to school. So ... he started asking him 'What do you do in your spare time? So, what did you do in Sudan?' And from what the man described it emerged that he used to rear cattle and sheep in his father's farm. And the student said 'What time did you start work?' 'Oh, very early in the morning. Hard work. We would go and take them for water and ...' 'Did you ever sell any of them?' 'Yes, my father was very rich. Sometimes we would go to market and sell'. 'Did you ever sell any of them?' 'Yes, I done good. I sell sheep and cattle.' 'And they pay you money?' 'Yes, they pay me money.' And in the end the student was able to craft this CV about his communication skills, customer service skills, cash handling. And then when he read back this CV to the service user (they had an interpreter) ... his face just lit up because he thought he had to go to school, to have a job in an office to have a CV, you know. But ... this student was able to pull out information from him and design his CV in a way that was true but played to the service user's strengths.

To shift the focus from problems or deficits to the discovery of an individual's strengths and to celebrate their achievements, the following seven kinds of questions are proposed:

- **Survival questions:** How have you managed to overcome and/or survive the challenges that you have faced?
- **Support questions:** Who are the people that you can rely on? Who has made you feel understood, supported or encouraged?
- **Exception questions:** When things were going well in life, what was different?
- **Possibility questions:** What do you want to accomplish in your life? What are your hopes for your future, or the future of your family?
- **Esteem questions:** What makes you proud about yourself? What positive things do people say about you?
- **Perspective questions:** What are your ideas or theories about your current situation?

- **Change questions:** What do you think is necessary for things to change? What could you do to make that happen? (Saleebey, 2009: 102–3)

These same questions can be adapted for use with groups, organisations and communities.

Relationships

For these questions and conversations to be effective, relationships and relational practice are crucial. In many respects the relationship developed between the individual and the worker *is* the service (Romeo, 2017). The strengths approach is mandated in UK policy as:

> a collaborative process between the person supported by services and those supporting them, allowing them to work together to determine an outcome that draws on the person's strengths and assets. As such, it concerns itself principally with the quality of the relationship that develops between those providing and those being supported, as well as the elements that the person seeking support brings to the process. (Social Care Institute for Excellence, 2015)

Saleebey (2009) is among many writers who celebrate the power of the caring relationship as a force for change and healing. There is ample research evidence regarding the significance and effectiveness of relationships in practice, not least Shulman's (1978) study of satisfaction in families whose young people were before the juvenile court and the subject of a social history report prepared by a social worker. Shulman found there was no correlation between the level of satisfaction in the service and the outcome for the young person. Rather, satisfaction stemmed from the quality of the relationship with the practitioner – the way they related to the young person and their family. The findings are corroborated by subsequent research, not least that of Beresford et al (2008), about service user views regarding the primacy of their relationship with palliative care social workers. The important components identified by the participants were relationships founded on trust, respect, reciprocity and mutuality – all hallmarks of the strengths approach. In essence these are partnerships, 'with each party bringing something of value to the transaction' (Weick and Saleebey, 1998: 36). They challenge traditional power relations as professionals adopt a collaborative approach to work with the individual or community seeking support. The same study concludes that professional boundaries need to be flexible. Participants consistently described their workers as 'friends', leading to some useful consideration of 'friendship' in the context of professionalism. Satish Kumar (2019) takes this further and calls for humans to become friends, not just of each other, but of the environment:

> You might call me an idealist. Yes, I am an idealist. But ... 'What have the realists achieved? Wars? Poverty? Climate change?' The realists have ruled the world for far too long and have failed to achieve peace and prosperity for all. So, let us give the idealists a chance, and let friendship be the organising principle of our life and our world. (2019: 107)

This chapter began by asserting that the strengths approach is founded on hope. Studies reveal how people value relationships with workers that are hope-inducing. As relationships with others, their communities and cultures develop and are strengthened so, too, is hopefulness (Rapp et al, 2005). The significance of relationships in this respect cannot be overstated. In the broader context of health inequality, Michael Marmot (2010) has demonstrated repeatedly how social networks and social capital impact positively on mortality rates. Relationships are essential to the quality of life and wellbeing of people, their families and communities (Blood and Guthrie, 2018).

Over two decades, START has built relationships with refugee networks, students and their universities, agencies in the city, the local community and national bodies including the Home Office to make a positive impact on the way systems work. Relationships can take time to build effectively (Glasby et al, 2013), a fact which does not sit comfortably with the targets, performance indicators and other constraining factors attendant on NPM. Writers such as Gillian Ruch (Ruch et al, 2010: 22) have commented incisively on these instruments of neoliberalism and managerialism in terms of the consequences for relationships between people. Under marketised forms of welfare and the perception of people seeking support as 'commodities', relationships are reduced to impersonal, dehumanised transactions of the 'buyer-seller' (Engelbrecht, 2010: 48). Complexity and the affective dimensions of practice are met with denial and risk aversion. This climate for practice was further compounded by the UK government's adoption of austerity in response to the global financial crisis of 2008. The 'perfect storm' has created 'relational austerity – practice that is increasingly authoritarian rather than authoritative, and combative rather than compassionate' (Hingley-Jones and Ruch, 2016: 296).

Meanwhile the 'Big Society', the political ideology favoured by former Conservative Prime Minister David Cameron with its emphasis on communities, volunteerism, charities and social enterprise, found expression in the reform of adult social care and privatisation. The strengths perspective, together with relational practice, was enshrined in statutory guidance governing the UK's Care Act 2014. At the time of writing, local councils continue to invest heavily in training and initiatives to change the culture of practice and their organisations in order to comply with the requirements for 'strengths-based practice' and collaborative partnerships with people seeking support. Sadly, this guidance is not accompanied by the conditions needed for it to flourish, notably time, adequate staffing, reduced workloads, a complementary management culture – in essence, a whole systems approach involving service users and managers, shared by all professions. This leaves time-poor individuals working in low-warmth/high-blame environments to try to implement strengths-based practice in their daily work. Such policy and legislative changes (in child and family services as well as adult social care) have restored the language about the centrality of relationships and the strengths perspective. This presents a significant opportunity to seize the rhetoric and work with people in a manner that celebrates their capabilities, skills and achievements. However, relationships within organisations also need to be characterised by reciprocity and co-production as do those with external agencies. Without a whole systems approach, the legislative framework is simply lip-service.

Universal application

So far our review of the history and literature surrounding the strengths approach might suggest that, predominantly, it lends itself to health and social care practice with individuals. Nothing could be further from the truth. We see it evidenced in initiatives as diverse as Satish Kumar's account of the 'Small School' in Devon, Rowena Cade's construction of the Minack Theatre in Cornwall, Josh Littlejohn and Alice Thompson's creation of the 'Social Bite' in Scotland and Katie Paterson's 'Future Library' art project in Norway as well as many other examples beyond human services where imagination, creativity and hope triumph over 'business as usual'. Such approaches deliver surprises and unimaginable benefits.

Organic agriculture is a particular example of the strengths approach in practice. Becoming proficient in techniques and practices that are complex and adapted to local conditions requires high levels of scientific knowledge, specific skills and openness to continuous learning. The results, as we have seen in the UK and beyond, are remarkable in changing people's livelihoods. To give an example of the strengths approach in practice from our own experience, Avril has collaborated with a Ugandan NGO, Kulika, for the past 15 years and seen the remarkable effects of their work in a challenging rural environment (http://www.kulika.org/). For example, a subsistence farmer had to supplement his income by hawking goods in Kampala because he could not afford chemical fertilisers and pesticides to increase the productivity of his farm. He participated in an intensive 11-month training course in sustainable organic agriculture enabling him to recognise and harness the natural resources that were already there. He now has a highly successful business producing organic banana juice.

The training transformed his life and the farm where he lives which now produces sufficient income for his nine children to complete their higher education. He fulfils his commitment to Kulika by training others in his local community.

Parallels can be drawn in the UK with the challenges recorded by Isabella Tree (2018) of convincing the establishment and her neighbours of the benefits of 'wilding' the family farm at Knepp. Working holistically *with* nature for over 20 years has been transformative, resulting in environmental and economic sustainability. If such transformation is possible working with what we already have then why aren't governments prioritising this approach? Isabella Tree's account shows how hard it was for Knepp to access grant funding for what they were doing. Similarly, in Uganda, the government continues to promote chemical fertilisers and pesticides while the organic approach relies on charities raising money for training. These examples of the strengths approach in action are neither cheap nor fast and demand long-term commitment. They require a policy change and a shift of focus for what is a whole system approach. Resources are needed to enable the transformation but the outcomes cannot be predicted. Perhaps most significantly, the results of both of these examples are that the people concerned are more powerful. They have more control over their lives and are much less susceptible to global commercial agendas. However, as long as money rather than wellbeing is at the heart of government agendas, regrettably it is unlikely that the strengths approach will be embraced systemically.

In confronting a global climate emergency and collapse of welfare systems, it is essential that we find different ways of responding. Stories like that of Knepp, where a failing agricultural business has been turned into a sustainable, environmentally-rich estate, illustrate the potential of the strengths approach in action. The landowners trusted in the principle cited earlier in the chapter that 'Every individual and collectivity has the inherent capacity for wholeness, regeneration, healing and transformation'. By relating this to the land, they stepped back from trying to maintain control through normal agricultural practices, but instead used all the knowledge available to them worldwide, recognising that there is a 'fund of innate wisdom and health to draw upon in times of crisis and challenge'. According to their account of the past 20 years, the principle that 'Everyone has the capacity for rebound and righting the trajectory of their development in the face of adversity and trauma' would appear to be true for the physical environment too.

Criticisms of the strengths perspective

Mel Gray (2011) offers a scholarly critique of the strengths approach, arguing that it places too much emphasis on the individual and their community without attending to structural and economic realities. Howe (1992: 47) demonstrates how social workers consistently have had to reconcile individualism and collectivism: working with people's internal worlds and external circumstances, recognising themselves as agents of social change and activism while engaged in some degree of social regulation. These positions are not binaries; all professionals must negotiate these confusing, 'swampy lowlands' (Schön, 1991) of theory in practice during each professional encounter (James et al, 2020). In practice, the strengths approach is not limited to the micro perspective but rather recognises that all situations are complex and that micro, meso and macro systems are interrelated. We would therefore agree that 'The neoliberal embrace of the core philosophical foundations of the strengths perspective requires that the perspective goes back to basics to rethink ways of distancing itself from the harsher aspects of contemporary welfare policy' (Gray, 2011: 6).

The enthusiasm of successive governments for strengths-based approaches is just such an embrace. It is imperative that the strengths approach is not misunderstood or conflated with strengths-based approaches serving political agendas in the desire for 'quick fix' solutions. Successive movements have certainly been co-opted and domesticated by governments in this manner (witness the Recovery Model developed by people experiencing mental health problems). What matters is that the approach is a manifestation of the whole organisation's values – not just in name alone (Scerra, 2011).

So is a strengths perspective naive? The strengths approach is criticised as if it glosses over the truths of environmental and social disasters to offer an escape from grim reality. It has been accused of positive thinking which 'simply reframes deficits and misery' (Saleebey, 1996: 302). For over 30 years these accusations have been refuted by evidence of its potential to improve people's lives but it is clear that, in a deficit-orientated culture where profit-motivated 'provision' is seen as the answer, the strengths approach struggles to compete with dominant narratives. Protagonists repeatedly state that the strengths perspective does *not* ignore structural realities. On the contrary it requires the worker to have a forensic appreciation of the factors causing the difficulties. Is it this exposure of the real causes that provokes this defensive critique? 'The identification of strengths is not the antithesis of the identification of problems. Instead, it is a large part of the solution' (Graybeal, 2001: 234). The strengths approach helps us to see the world as it is and not to be defeated by it. It involves reframing to employ the language of possibility and opportunity. It requires us to discover the qualities and skills, motivation and aspirations people have, and how these can be harnessed to promote change so that people can find better ways to resolve conflict (Saleebey, 1996).

Perhaps the real challenge is that the practitioner cannot retreat to a place of cynicism or blame but must actively look to find possibility in all individuals, systems and structures. Faced with the alternatives of cynicism and burnout, or a determination to find something that works, we would encourage workers to place the strengths approach at the core of their practice. It presumes hope, even in the face of overwhelming difficulties.

Many writers point to a lack of empirical evidence to support the use of a strengths approach (Lietz, 2009; Manthey et al, 2011; Tse et al, 2016) as if valid comparisons could be made using conventional evaluative research for discrete methods of intervention. Such criticisms fail to recognise, however, that the strengths approach is a long-term, whole systems intervention in which outcomes are neither quick nor possible to predict. Moreover, if existing measurements of success are grounded in the way things are, then radical improvements that are too complex to fit into those measurements cannot easily be registered – a conundrum that is explored in Chapter 6.

As the chapters in this book reveal, the strengths approach, far from being limited to the individual and their immediate community, encourages us to recognise the potential in local authorities and organisations, in law and policy, in social movements, in cultural norms and environmental conditions. It is indeed a whole-of-systems approach and so is examined in this book across the spectrum.

Human Givens

To provide a solid foundation for the strengths approach, we draw on the lens of alternative psychology and a positive framework for understanding human behaviour and relationships, applicable to any situation regardless of place or scale. Developed by UK psychologists Joe Griffin and Ivan Tyrrell, Human Givens (Griffin and Tyrrell, 2003) bears similarities to the work of Abraham Maslow but is so much more. It is a non-pathological, holistic approach to support the capacity for growth which engages intellect (thought), emotion, body and environment. Human Givens regards all aspects of human functioning – mind and body – and the environment as fully connected. It embraces spirituality and is deeply rooted in the whole of life. Although grounded in psychotherapy and counselling, it can be deployed at micro and macro levels; its practices are equally effective in social, organisational and even environmental psychology, as in therapeutic interventions with individuals in distress (Neal, 2018). The Human Givens approach is not limited to perception or internal functioning of mind. Similar to Schwartz's (1971) Interactional Model, it emphasises the capacity for positive and health-promoting relationships between people and their environments. Any action takes place within the whole context. It is not just about one service user group or one particular method. Understood in this way, it is a strengths approach which has no limits, in which environmental consciousness and practitioner bond together.

While emphasising the uniqueness of each individual and situation, there are some universal 'givens' essential to health and wellbeing, which have a direct impact on people's self-esteem and resilience. They involve meaning, agency, role and engagement. They are:

- the need to give and receive attention;
- the need for community and connection beyond the immediate family;
- the need for autonomy or a degree of control;
- the need for purpose or meaning; and
- the need for flow (utter absorption in a worthwhile activity). (Griffin and Tyrrell, 2003: 351)

For people to remain healthy both physically and mentally, these fundamental emotional needs have to be met in balance. With these in view, Human Givens' practitioners, having established rapport and gathered information about a particular situation, will work to make the best use of resources available in order to achieve a solution. Reflecting the strengths approach, they help to promote innate resources: memory, imagination and problem-solving abilities, self-awareness, the ability to dream and other qualities, as well as those in the environment (Griffin and Tyrrell, 2003: 93–4). It is this fusion of needs and resources that comprise human givens.

To take the first given as an example, 'attention' in these terms is not what society currently values through the celebrity culture and social media. Rather it is the experience of being heard and seen by others, and in return being open to hear and see others in an environment that is not highly charged emotionally. This will be familiar to practitioners in moments of learning and teaching where trust and openness of mind foster growth and the development of who we are.

For people who have experienced forced displacement, however, their experience of attention will be that it is risky and, indeed, highly charged emotionally. It is therefore critical to create an environment of trust and reciprocity if people are to become able to give and receive attention in return in a positive way. We witnessed this in action when we visited a German former student now working with refugees in a 'camp' in Stuttgart. Her manner was unhurried, friendly and attentive as she spoke to people and although part of her job was to ensure the building was maintained, at no time did this seem her priority. Reflecting on her work, she told us that her main aim is to find a good balance between building up relations with the people on the one hand and keeping the house order on the other. The work with the people is specified through their special and individual needs and questions.

It can be difficult to achieve such a balance when the demands of daily life distract us; sometimes we need others to help us understand what we see. In her book *Wilding*, Isabella Tree (2018: 13) gives prominence to a visit by Ted Green, a tree expert who explains what the ancient oak is telling them. It seems that this moment of attention was a catalyst for the radical change of direction that followed. Sometimes we fail to attend to what is happening around us because we know that the consequences of our actions would be equally disconcerting for the related systems and structures. However, as was the case in Uganda and at Knepp, systems and structures are not achieving positive results either for people or for the planet, so we argue that the risk is worth taking.

The Human Givens approach removes blame, both from the individual and the environment. Under this framework it is unhelpful to see 'unmet need' as anyone's failure. Uniquely, Human Givens views gaps in services as absences, not as something pathological, and it explores positive ways of filling those spaces in each situation. Gaps or absences, whether in the lives of individuals, groups or communities, are seen as challenges to be solved. Critical reflection is essential. Viewing social problems through this lens does not interpret refugees as a burden, nor see them primarily as people whose rights are being denied by social structures; in other words, society is not the focus for its failure to provide. Human Givens would not see refugees as inherently needy, but as people who have agency and resilience, who, with support, can achieve balance for themselves. Naming strengths is the first step in enabling them to be deployed. It affirms the agency that individuals have while resisting the construction of refugees as victims. It refutes the homogenising of people who are easily stereotyped and reduced by such processes.

Re-storying the narrative

Human Givens practitioners use therapeutic story-making to enable people to fill the gaps in their lives that are causing distress. Narrative work is central to a strengths approach. This is as true in a wider social context as it is in work with individuals: 'Culture is the means by which we receive, organize, rationalize, and understand our particular experiences in the world. Central elements of this cultural patterning are story and narrative. That is, we find or impart meaning largely through telling stories and weaving narratives, the plots often laid out by culture' (Saleebey, 1994: 352). Stories, then, are the way we make sense of our lives whether through literature, religion, history, economics, scientific discoveries or international news reports. Even memory is the construction of a story about what has happened – one that we tell ourselves and others. Stories change and evolve with each telling, sometimes in order to reflect the truth more fully, sometimes to convince people of different truths. Based on this understanding, narrative therapy (White and Epston, 1990) has been a significant influence as a collaborative, non-pathologising approach. Its aim is to separate the problem from the person by deconstructing dominant narratives that conflate identity and the problem. People are recognised as experts in their own lives with skills, abilities and beliefs that can help them to re-story their relationship with difficulties, including those compounded by the social divisions created by intersectionality.

The kinds of stories we can or cannot tell are shaped by the culture in which we live, exemplified by the substantial scholarship emerging from groups that have been oppressed and silenced. This is powerfully illustrated by children's literature, for example, in which BME protagonists are still largely absent, and true of anti-racist writing in general made visible yet again by the Black Lives Matter movement. Dominant narratives are rooted in culture, which, in turn, dictates available plot lines and the meanings associated with them (Laird, 1989). The rise of populism internationally, fuelled by social media, is evidence of the power of stories. Humans use narrative to bring themselves into being – to make sense of experiences, both positive and negative.

The possibilities of meaning-making exist in the places where culture, myth and story intersect. We are socialised into meaning and truths from a very early age and are unlikely to become aware of their origins, specificity or limitations until we are immersed in a different culture or engage in critical reflection. As an example, the BBC's announcement of a change in language to 'climate emergency' rather than 'climate change' opens a space for more urgent stories to be told even though the science has been clear for decades. 'Without a story, meaning, conviction, and possibility fail. Only when we endow a circumstance, event, or situation with words and a plot line does it become relevant' (Saleebey, 1994: 354). In contrast, witness the explosion of LGBTQ+ and feminist writing around the turn of the century. Likewise, the extraordinary political impact of thousands of people in the UK who, feeling ignored and silenced, were given words and a 'plot line' through the Brexit campaign (Peston, 2017; Carter, 2019).

So, if the stories we tell are grounded in the cultural truths we inhabit, and we are limited to those that are congruent with dominant narratives, it can be difficult to make space for stories of aspiration, hope and resilience, whether global or individual, unless they are specifically sought. People who become refugees in the UK have been schooled by the immigration process to tell a particular story of persecution and victimisation without deviation or variation, if they are to be granted a place of safety. That process is rooted in cultural norms that construct refugees as victims at best and, at worst, as manipulative intruders or even terrorists. Visitors to START sometimes want to focus on stories of escape and trauma – the question 'How did you get here?' is not uncommon. Interest in stories of flight, however, constructs people as refugees whereas our concern is to help individuals construct themselves as people. Our task is to support them in re-storying themselves in the context of the UK – a story of their present and future.

In our experience, students of the caring professions, especially international students, are ideally placed to seek out those stories. Starting from a commitment to social justice, they listen very attentively in order to try to understand what matters to people. If we are 'brought into being' by the stories we can tell, then the mutual cultural ignorance of refugees and students creates very fertile ground for stories of aspiration, hope and capacity beyond the anticipated range of options. This 'no man's land' becomes a dramatic space where students and refugees can cross Vygotsky's 'zone of proximal development' in the same way that David Oddie (1997) describes in his book, *The Barefoot Actor*. Here the use of role play and drama supports children through performance to achieve learning that they and others thought impossible. This mirrors the process of students listening to refugees. When students are supported to perform the role of social worker or occupational therapist or psychologist using a strengths approach, they achieve more than they had imagined possible.

In a place like START where nearly everyone is a 'foreigner', conventional British cultural norms are inoperable. All have to be alert because they cannot know what to expect of each other. A strengths approach reaches for stories of hope and aspiration, of resources and achievement, newly constructing refugees as people with a future as well as a past while listening carefully to elicit those stories. Students, in turn, realise the power of that exchange and no longer limit their self-narration to being 'just a student'. Rather, they recognise their own potential and claim an autonomy based on authenticity (Butler et al, 2007). A strengths approach involving the use of narrative can change everyone's future. When systems no longer work, it can support the imagining of different stories and possibilities, ones that meet our needs as humans, in harmony with the environment. As Ann Weick writes: 'There is special power in reflective sharing of experience … Stories are a form of knowledge and some would say, the only knowledge we have' (1994: 22).

Learning points

- Giving attention and active listening are vital in seeing both difficulties and potential.
- Being honest about how bad things are and what would make them better is a good start and generates hope.
- Focusing on what works is likely to produce more success than focusing on what doesn't.

- Never place a limit on the aspirations of others.
- The more clearly we can articulate the future we want, the more likely it is to happen.
- Real change takes time, patience and conviction.

2

A strengths approach to law and policy

> Some would say it would be better to challenge and break
> the law. Instead of advising on dispersal, mount pressure
> to stop NASS from dispersing! Instead of evicting from
> emergency accommodation, refuse to subcontract such
> accommodation and then resist all evictions attempted by
> … landlords! Instead of advising on the NASS scheme,
> advise on how to campaign for the restoration of full
> benefits not linked to immigration status! Instead of
> colluding, disrupt! Instead of becoming a slave-master,
> unite with the slaves!
>
> Cohen (2006: 141)

The manipulation of law and policy by governments to
perpetuate power and social injustice (seen in every totalitarian
regime before, since and including the Third Reich) is one
of the toughest challenges confronting the strengths approach.
This chapter is unique in exploring what a strengths approach
to mobilising law and policy will involve. It aims to show
through the examples how maintaining a strengths approach to
legal frameworks can, in itself, subvert a government's aims to
undermine human rights by such harmful means and promote
social justice.

Understanding law, its purpose and function

Law is a core component of practice for professions like social
work and is a way to achieve social justice at the level of collective
action as well as that of the individual. In the contract between

33

the individual and the state, it plays a key part in the regulation of power. Students and practitioners alike approach it with more than a degree of ambivalence, however – it is complex and constantly changing, not 'set in tablets of stone'; it is not neutral but subject to interpretation; it can be contradictory in some areas and outdated in others; it is heavily influenced by political ideology, interest groups, public inquiries, the European Union, the media and moral panics.

It is characterised by inaccessible language and terminology rendering its use elitist; it is a blunt instrument incapable of covering every eventuality in a given situation. In risk-averse societies, it is increasingly deployed to impose 'uniform solutions at the expense of private space' (Sumption, 1999: 6) – with peers expressing concern at the 'tsunami' of new legislation in the UK, for example – as governments attempt to legislate their way out of trouble. When an act of parliament receives royal assent, it can be a matter of years before it is implemented. On the other hand, it is sometimes forged hastily in the wake of a disaster to give an illusion of control and certainty in situations of complexity and intractable difficulty. In seeking to apportion blame, people demand that 'there should be a law against it'.

People in receipt of human services may experience its prime functions as those of regulation and curtailment of liberty, with some justification, especially in the field of immigration controls. Critics, meanwhile, warn that the proliferation of procedures accompanying law and policy fetters professional judgement and discretion. To add to its complexity, law takes many forms, notably criminal and civil law, common law, statutory instruments, regulations and codes of practice. Historically, English law has indeed tended to be regulatory and procedural, providing a remedial, compensatory response to the problems and perceived deficits of welfare recipients (Williams, 2004; Braye et al, 2006). In itself, it does not guarantee the right to services. It is argued that the advent of rights-based legislation in the UK, however, most notably the Human Rights Act 1998 and the Equality Act 2010, with an attendant concern for international convention rights, has shifted the focus towards ethical considerations, rights and values in the enactment of law and policy (Williams, 2004). For a profession like social work, which constantly has to balance compliance with legal mandates against the requirements of professional codes, this has been a much-needed, though fragile, development.

Example 1

> The profusion of common, or case law in social care especially, exemplifies the regularity with which rights-based legislation is successfully applied to combat injustice. For example, In the case of *R (MD) v Secretary of State for the Home Department [2014] EHWC 2249 (Admin)* the claimant, a refugee, travelled to the UK to join her husband for family reunion. Under Article 5 of the European Convention of Human Rights (ECHR) she was found to be unlawfully detained when the Home Office wrongly cancelled the entry clearance to join her husband. Detention for 11 months caused the claimant to suffer severe mental health problems and it was judged that her treatment while unlawfully detained (which included frequent segregation and the use of restraint by male guards) subjected her to inhuman and degrading treatment in breach of Article 3 of the ECHR.

Ever since these statutes received royal assent, however, they have been the targets of fierce opposition by successive right-wing governments in the UK. Claims are made that Article 8 of the Human Rights Act 1998 (the right to private and family life) for example, has been used as a 'charter for terrorists' and by 'illegals' to avoid deportation. Enshrined in recent government manifestos are plans to replace the Human Rights Act 1998 with a 'British Bill of Rights' (Stone, 2016) and its future is uncertain.

Social work in the UK is increasingly regarded as a regulatory arm of the state, co-opted to undertake surveillance in 'policing the boundaries of welfare' (Humphries, 2004: 93). It is seen to be culpable in implementing neoliberal policies that control, discriminate and exclude certain groups in society. For all of these reasons, it is vital that anyone working in human services, especially, critically examines and reflects on law and policy, including their own attitudes to the law and its functions. In this chapter we argue that critical reflection is the basis of a strengths approach to law.

In understanding attitudes to law, social work has been assisted by a seminal study commissioned by the Social Care Institute for Excellence and conducted by Suzy Braye, Michael Preston-Shoot and colleagues (2005). The study provided the first systematic knowledge review of law teaching in social work (and gave rise to subsequent publications by the authors regarding the relationship of other non-lawyers to law, for example, medical students). Here they identify different attitudes or rather, orientations to law – technical-legal, ethical, rights-based and procedural. They argue that it is not enough to regard law as simply a matter of knowledge acquisition or procedural compliance. Rather they maintain that all orientations are necessary in combination for the exercising of professional judgement and what is termed *legal literacy*. Braye and Preston-Shoot (2016: 2) define it as 'the ability to connect relevant legal rules with the professional priorities and objectives of ethical practice'. Legal literacy is another crucial element of a strengths approach to law.

The functions of law are well rehearsed in western democracies and, at times, hotly debated, but, in general, consensus gathers around it as a means to maintain order in society, a form of social control to protect rights and liberty, and to resolve disputes. Less evident in the wider literature is the typology proposed by Braye and Preston-Shoot (2016: 27–33) which identifies its functions as:

- the regulation of power structures;
- social engineering;
- shaping attitudes and behaviours;
- promoting ideology; and
- finding solutions to social problems.

Examination of these functions engenders deeper, more nuanced understanding and opens up the debate about the role of law in society. They are especially prevalent in immigration policy that constructs people seeking refuge as a public order problem rather than a humanitarian concern.

Law and professional judgement: exercising discretion

The UK government has articulated a vision for the profession of social work as one that involves working with 'complexity, uncertainty, risk and conflict within a complex legal framework' (Department of Health and Social Care, 2016: 1). In environments characterised by these conditions, professionals are required to conduct assessments, form professional judgements and make decisions about the best course of action. Inevitably they will be dealing with 'wicked problems' (Gawande, 2012) where there is no linear chain of cause and effect. Attempts to control risk and then to attribute blame when tragedies occur in fields such as child protection have led to over-bureaucratised, procedural policy responses that, in excess, may constrain the critical, analytical thinking essential for good professional judgement (Munro, 2011). Professional judgement necessarily involves individual autonomy, accountability and, above all, the exercise of discretion.

Just how effective a profession is in managing complexity and making decisions is made visible by the work of a political scientist Michael Lipsky. Lipsky was writing in America in the 1980s in conditions similar to those in which we find ourselves today: challenging situations, over-worked staff and under-resourced services. He coined the term 'street-level bureaucrats' to refer to public employees who 'interact directly with citizens in the course of their jobs and (who exercise) discretion in the execution of their work' (Lipsky, 1980: 3).

Street-level bureaucrats are police officers, teachers, social workers, nurses, judges, IT officers and public administrators such as those working in employment services. In order to make sense of, and implement social policy, street-level bureaucrats use discretion. They have to work out practical versions of public policy so that they can find 'real-world solutions to get the job done' (Lipsky, 1980: 3). They practise the art of discretion through everyday interactions with service users and their families. Discretion in itself is neither good nor bad, but the way in which it is exercised can have very negative or positive consequences. Workers under pressure may simply apply the rules and hide behind them in a mindless, heartless way, as portrayed in the film *I, Daniel Blake* (Loach and Obiols, 2016). At its best, however, discretion involves using creativity and skills to find and operate in the *spaces* between principles and rules. Braye et al (2006: 136) encourage practitioners to be conscious of 'the space that the legal rules create for (them) to exercise knowledge-informed discretion'. It enables practitioners to work with uncertainty and limited resources, and to respond to individuals and communities in a holistic way not necessarily sanctioned by neoliberal policy. Mindful of their own values, discretion is about how workers implement policy. Not surprisingly, a significant factor in a professional's willingness to implement policy rests on whether it will be meaningful to the service user. Policy has to be tailored to unique needs and diverse circumstances.

The wealth of literature about discretion is considerable and trans-disciplinary. An early critic of discretion in social work was David Howe writing in 1991. Howe considered that with increasing regulation, targets and managerial control (compounded by politicians, the media and public opinion), professionals no longer had the autonomy to exercise discretion. He perceived that the spaces to do so had shrunk. Writers such as Tony Evans (2010) argue to the contrary. Evans maintains that increasingly complex work and a plethora of policy-making mean that workers have to decide which policy to apply in any given situation. Often the rules surrounding implementation do not correspond to the specific situation at street-level so they have to be interpreted in order to make policy 'on the hoof'. Practitioners may be operating under different sets of contradictory rules. They have to contend with new situations for which policy has not been developed. Thus, it might be argued that the proliferation of rules and procedures has, paradoxically, created *more* spaces for discretion. We return to this possibility with practice examples in confronting injustice.

In view of the complexity of practice in welfare services, understanding and exercising discretion are essential components of a strengths approach to law and policy. It is vital that people working in this, and in any field, recognise their own power and responsibility when operating as 'street-level bureaucrats'.

People seeking asylum and refugees: UK law and policy

Immigration law in the UK is particularly labyrinthine and draconian – intended, according to Steve Cohen (2002), to make it so hard for people to negotiate that they either fail or give up. He was one of the first of many activists who describe it as 'inherently racist' (2002: 191). More recently, David Olusoga has shown through archival research how racism has been enshrined in law and affected the Windrush generation (Olusoga, 2019). A reasonable response would be that of extreme anger at the levels of injustice in the system and a refusal to co-operate. This either places people against the law, like, for example, the immigration lawyers who opposed a piece of legislation (subsequently repealed) and refused to act under it (Cohen, 2006: 14–142). Or they are outside the law with acts of subversion: a family of six were waiting for a decision on their claim for asylum in the UK when it was rumoured that they were due to be arrested early one morning and deported. Aid workers quickly mobilised to offer them a 'mini-break' away from their accommodation to frustrate that possibility and buy time to challenge deportation. A third option is provided by the strengths approach which enables people to work *with* the provisions of the law to achieve a positive result.

START works mainly with people whose claims for asylum are successful in as much as they are granted long-term, but limited, leave to remain with refugee status. Staff and students collaborate with agencies skilled and qualified in giving advice about the asylum process and support to those still waiting for a decision on their claim. Examples in this book, therefore, are mostly of people who have negotiated the UK's Kafka-esque immigration system with a degree of success. In view of the quantity and complexity of law and policy in this field, accounts in this chapter are highly selective and illustrated by casework undertaken by staff and students at START. The examples highlight injustices confronting refugees in the UK which can occur to such an extent that they experience secondary trauma in the very countries purportedly offering sanctuary (Eggers, 2006; Marlowe, 2010). Table 2.1 charts the history of the legal framework governing immigration through key statutes and

Table 2.1: Selected statutes and their impact

Selected statutes	Impact on refugees
Aliens Act 1905	Set up barriers to the entry of Jews fleeing pogroms in Eastern Europe, particularly those who were ill or destitute.
Commonwealth Immigration Act 1962	Introduced immigration controls for Commonwealth citizens by removing their automatic right to live and work in the UK.
Commonwealth Immigrants Act 1968	Instituted a limited voucher system for Commonwealth nationals who wanted to live and work in the UK.
Immigration Act 1971	The right to live and work in the UK was restricted to people with citizenship, people who had lived in the UK for five or more years and those with a father or grandfather born in the UK. Commonwealth citizens became no different legally from other foreign nationals.
British Nationality Act 1981	A person could now be deprived of their citizenship if the home secretary is satisfied it would be 'conducive to the public good' and they would not become stateless as a result.
Immigration Act 1988	Restricted the right of entry of dependants and made deportation easier by restricting the right to appeal.
Asylum and Immigration Appeals Act 1993	This act distinguished between immigration and people seeking asylum. It introduced the UK's right to control or refuse entry to people deemed to be making 'unfounded' claims and those who had arrived from a third country. A separate process for people claiming asylum was introduced including finger-printing for identification.
Asylum and Immigration Act 1996	Introduced the offences of 'illegal entry' and 'harbouring'. People could be returned to a 'safe third country' without their claim being considered. It also linked virtually all non-contributory benefits including child benefit, to immigration status.
Immigration and Asylum Act 1999	Removed the right of asylum seekers to claim either state benefits or support from local authorities. It created a parallel, separate system of support administered by the Home Office – National Asylum Support Service (NASS). Accommodation was contracted with private providers. Financial support was provided for people whose claim had been refused but who could not be returned.

Table 2.1: Selected statutes and their impact (continued)

Selected statutes	Impact on refugees
Nationality, Immigration and Asylum Act 2002	Removed the right of asylum seekers to work. Removed welfare support if people had not made application 'as soon as reasonably practicable on arrival' or for other reasons. The Court of Appeal overturned this ruling in 2004 as being in breach of Article 3 of the Human Rights Act 1998.
Asylum and Immigration [Treatment of Claimants] Act 2004	Reduced rights of appeal. Back-dated benefits for successful claimants were replaced by an integration loan. All support, including housing, could be withdrawn for people whose claim was exhausted. This included families with children.
Immigration, Asylum and Nationality Act 2006	Introduced penalties for employers who could not prove that employees had the right to work. Immigration appeals were further restricted. Immigration officers were allowed to confiscate travel documents and the Secretary of State to remove citizenship from dual nationals if 'deemed in the public good'.
Borders, Citizenship and Immigration Act 2009	Increased powers of UK Border Agency. Extended the period of temporary leave before refugees are given a permanent right to stay. Changed the definition of where detainees can be held and allowed indefinite detention.
Immigration Act 2014	Increased control on landlords to ensure people have a right to rent and introduced the healthcare surcharge. Placed further limits on the right of those in detention to apply for immigration bail. More strictly regulated appeals against removal and deportation orders based on Article 8 (ECHR).
Immigration Act 2016	Introduced new sanctions on illegal workers and 'rogue' employers, preventing illegal migrants in the UK from accessing housing, driving licences and bank accounts. Introduced new measures to make it easier to enforce immigration laws and remove illegal migrants.
Immigration and Social Security Co-ordination (EU Withdrawal) Act 2020	Removes the right of EU nationals to free movement in the UK after 30 December 2020.

their purpose. It exposes the function of law as a political tool that promotes an ideology in respect of refugees, one that has been maintained consistently by successive administrations. For both Cohen (2006) and Olusoga (2019) the function is one of immigration control in which law and policy negatively construct the status and indeed identity of people escaping conflict and disaster.

This litany of immigration controls exposes law as a social construct that mirrors prevailing discriminatory narratives. It is a tool through which ideologies are sustained, together with power relations that determine the status and interests of certain groups (Dalrymple and Burke, 2006: 92). It is accompanied and fuelled by myths about people and moral panics. Its mechanisms are used without warning to 'erase' rights and citizenship, as the following section reveals. Jelka Zorn's research with people deprived of citizenship following the collapse of former Yugoslavia is a chilling analysis of the way law can be used:

> The people erased from the Registry of Permanent Residents (RPR) were suddenly left without any rights: the right to a residence in Slovenia (in their homes with their families), the right to cross the state borders, and all other economic, social and political rights. The implementation of the erasure concerns the suspension of basic human rights, the annulment of the principles of a legal state and the production of a redundant people. (Zorn, 2005: 135)

Definitions, categorisation and labelling

Language shapes our reality. Labels such as 'asylum seeker', 'refugee', 'illegal immigrant', 'terrorist', 'invaders' have been devised to negatively construct people and allow inequitable treatment to be deemed socially acceptable (Green, 2020). Simply imposing the term 'asylum seeker' on an individual rather than describing them as a 'person seeking asylum' diminishes their personhood (Kitwood, 1997) and reduces their humanity in the minds of those hearing the label. As is evident from the legislative changes listed earlier, the specific group of people termed 'asylum seekers' were moved out of mainstream society in terms of rights and services. They became invisible except through media representations or specialist provision. The act of being labelled contributes to loss of self-esteem and the internalisation of oppression: 'It was not just their formal legal integrity that was shattered, but also their sheer existence, health and even lives' (Zorn, 2005: 138). As individuals concede to the attributes accompanying such labels they become 'self-fulfilling prophecies' characterised by problems and pathology rather than by their true identities, skills and achievements. A small example of how quickly people assume an identity is that of a newly arrived Syrian parent who asked whether routine inoculations administered to their child were given solely because they were refugees. The following categories and labels are employed carelessly and interchangeably so that society and the media do not differentiate between them. Routinely, labels are wrongly and deliberately assigned to create moral panics (Cohen, 2006: 24). It is important, therefore, to apply these terms with care and understanding.

Migrants: Migration, the movement of persons from one country or locality to another for whatever reason, has occurred throughout human history, and is a feature of the natural world especially. For example, German students showed us evidence in Tübingen's Schlöss museum of migration by *Homo sapiens* 47,000 years ago prompted by climate change. It is government responses, however, that turn migration into a problem (Yuval-Davis et al, 2019).

Economic migrants: People who have moved to another country for employment. If accepted, they are granted a work permit enabling them to live and work there. For example, the Gujarati parents of the Home Secretary, Priti Patel (at the time of writing) emigrated to the UK in 1960s from Idi Amin's Uganda and established a chain of newsagents. (Had they tried to emigrate later they might well have been refused owing to the later restrictions of the Immigration Act 1971.) Some jurisdictions such as Scotland actively welcome inward migration to strengthen the workforce, while the UK in general continues to be heavily reliant on migrant workers in many sectors of the economy, not least the National Health Service, social care and farming. Economic migrants are commonly encouraged to fill gaps in a national workforce but without strategic planning for their long-term human rights. When people settle, unless they apply for citizenship – a very expensive process – they can find themselves exposed to changing political agendas. This became clear with the UK referendum vote in favour of leaving the European Union; economic migrants from Europe were suddenly uncertain about their longer-term futures. The uncertainty was intensified by the 'Hostile Environment Policy' in 2012, explored in more detail later in this chapter, which had a severe impact on people who had been economic migrants with full rights to work and live in the UK.

Illegal immigrant: Anyone who has entered the country or remains in the country without proper documentation. Included are:

- economic migrants who are undocumented and without work permits;
- people who are being trafficked;
- people who are fleeing oppressive regimes who have not yet claimed asylum;
- people affected by modern slavery.

Illegal immigrants have only a short period of time in which to make a claim for asylum before they will be deported. Once people are labelled 'illegal' in this way they are not protected by the laws accompanying citizenship. Many people in this situation are unaware of the process or its timescale and find themselves treated like criminals in a fascist state – detained without trial in immigration removal (deportation) centres for an indefinite time (Taylor, 2018).

People seeking asylum: An 'asylum seeker' is a person who:

- flees their homeland;
- arrives in another country;
- makes themselves known to the authorities;
- exercises their legal right to apply for sanctuary.

There is no such thing as an 'illegal' or 'bogus' asylum seeker. Under international law, anyone has the right to apply for asylum in any country that has signed the 1951 Refugee Convention and to remain there until the authorities have assessed their claim. Although not a requirement of international law, Britain has insisted that refugees claim asylum in the first safe country they reach. Home Secretary Priti Patel has also suggested dispatching people seeking asylum in the UK to the island of South Georgia thousands of miles away for processing, as well as proposing military intervention and wave machines to counteract migrants attempting the hazardous crossing of the English Channel in rubber dinghies (Birrell, 2020).

Refugees: A refugee is a person who:

> [o]wing to a well-founded fear of being persecuted for reasons of race, religion, nationality, membership of a particular social group, or political opinion, is outside the country of his nationality, and is unable to or, owing to such fear, is unwilling to avail himself of the protection of that country. (The 1951 Convention Relating to the Status of Refugees)

The Refugee Convention is the primary source of the framework of international refugee protection. Created in the aftermath of two world wars, the Convention was originally limited in scope to Europeans fleeing events occurring before 1951. The 1967 Protocol amended the Convention to give it universal coverage. The subsequent development of international human rights law has strengthened it. These documents clearly spell out who is a refugee and the kind of legal protection, other assistance and social rights a refugee is entitled to receive.

The UK is a member of the Executive Committee of the UNHCR, the UN Refugee Agency which oversees the UNHCR Refugee Rights Convention 1951. Article 12 establishes:

- the right not to be returned to their country of origin if their safety cannot be assured, known as 'non-refoulement'. Article 33(1) prevents signatory states from returning individuals to

their country of origin where their life or freedom would be threatened on account of their race, religion, nationality, membership of a particular social group or political opinion;
• the right to be accorded in many respects the same treatment as the citizens of the country in which they are given refuge;
• the right to have their personal status acknowledged and the rights that come with it, particularly rights related to marriage;
• the right to access the labour market, education and healthcare.

The construction of refugees as 'asylum seekers' or 'illegal migrants' allows the state to withhold these rights from people who are legally classified as refugees. As can be seen from the implementation of the UK government's Hostile Environment Policy, a change in procedure can render people unwittingly vulnerable to infringement of their rights, removal of liberty and even deportation to a country unknown to them.

Political agendas

> Political rhetoric helps to set the tone of debate, and it should not seek to simply follow the lead of press coverage or perceived public opinion ... A key move ... should thus be to valorise the word 'refugee' and to return to it the rights, dignity, and responsibility that it has long been associated with.
>
> Darling and Passarlay (2017)

Changes in immigration law exemplify the racism critiqued by Cohen (2006) and the manner in which policy responds to, and is influential in, public opinion. In the aftermath of the Second World War, Enoch Powell, MP actively recruited people from former colonies in the West Indies to work in the UK to staff hospitals, factories and drive buses. They were given the right of residence and they paid taxes. Subsequently, in April 1968, the same MP denounced mass immigration from the Commonwealth in an infamous speech now known as 'the rivers of blood'. Referring to the civil unrest allegedly generated by the presence of non-white immigrants, he quoted Virgil in saying: 'As I look ahead, I am filled with foreboding: like the

Roman, I seem to see the River Tiber foaming with much blood' (Powell, 1968). The pervasive legacy of this speech inciting racial hatred cannot be underestimated.

Changes are made not only by new legislation such as the Immigration Act 1971 forged in the aftermath of Powell's speech, but also by stealth – the removal of entitlements through bureaucratic means. Amelia Gentleman's account of the treatment of the 'Windrush generation' is chilling (Gentleman, 2019: 9).

The 'Windrush generation' were economic migrants who came from the Caribbean between 1948 and 1971, invited by the British government to fill post-war skill shortages in hospitals and transport, for example. The term is now used to refer to Commonwealth citizens who came before the Nationality Act 1971 (implemented in 1973) and settled in the 'mother country' with full leave to remain. Many of the children of those migrants had travelled on their parent's passport and the only documents to prove their entitlement to remain in the UK – the landing cards – were destroyed by the Home Office in 2010. As a consequence, and because of pressure to meet net migration targets, from 2012 people who had lived and worked in the UK for decades were suddenly treated as illegal immigrants and required to prove their right to remain. Of the thousands of people without a passport or other definitive proof of citizenship, many lost jobs, homes, were denied healthcare, imprisoned and even deported to countries they had never known (Gentleman, 2019; Corradi, 2020).

The Hostile Environment Policy deprived people of their rights by intention and also by ineptitude. As a result of administrative errors, highly skilled, long-term migrants legally living and working in the UK were deemed illegal under paragraph 322(5) of the Immigration Rules which covers a threat to national security. People who had lived in the UK for a decade or more and whose children were born in the UK were given 14 days to leave the country (Hill, 2018). Their situation is echoed in Zorn's observation: 'The individuals erased from the RPR on 26th February 1992 never received any official document or notification. They learned about it individually, in various (chance) situations' (2005: 139).

A strengths approach to law and policy in practice

> [E]nvisage the law as one space to exploit for individual and social change.
>
> Braye and Preston-Shoot (2006: 386)

Here we reflect on the variety of ways there are to respond to injustice and inequality by adopting a strengths approach to law and policy. In using illustrations from START we would emphasise the transferability of these examples to other groups and situations.

At times, the public are fed a diet of exaggeration and untruths via the media to justify the harsh treatment of certain groups in society. A key element in the process of excluding and discriminating against sections of the population is that of myth-making. Myths are designed to shape dominant discourses and underpin the rationale for oppressive policies. They have a long history in respect of refugees, portraying them as 'benefit scroungers' who can be violent and who 'take our jobs' (Humphries, 2004: 98). Myths incite moral panics; witness, for example, the false argument promoted by the then UK government adviser Dominic Cummings in favour of Brexit: 'More than 700,000 Turks will flock to the UK if we stay in the EU' (Cooper, 2016).

It has long been recognised, and especially in this era of 'fake news', that an effective means to highlight and combat discrimination is the provision of factually correct information. For example, the media routinely state that the UK is overwhelmed by refugees when, in fact, they represent 0.26 per cent of the population (Refugee Action, 2021). Knowledge is power and an effective way to safeguard human rights. Given what is at stake, it cannot be stressed enough how important this is.

Inevitably, information will need to be constantly revised and updated. We would strongly urge anyone adopting a strengths approach to ensure that their practice is informed by up-to-date knowledge to combat fake news and celebrate the real achievements of the people with whom they work. The websites of organisations like those shown in Table 2.2 are useful in maintaining currency to challenge myths, stereotypes, propaganda and plain lies.

Table 2.2: Sources of information

Refugee Council	https://www.refugeecouncil.org.uk/
Refugee Rights Europe	https://refugee-rights.eu/
Refugee Action	https://www.refugee-action.org.uk/
UNHCR – the UN Refugee Agency	https://www.unhcr.org/refugees.html
The Migration Observatory	https://migrationobservatory.ox.ac.uk/
Refugee Studies Centre	https://www.rsc.ox.ac.uk/
Amnesty International	https://www.amnesty.org/en/

A strengths approach recognises that law, as the global pandemic has revealed, is not necessarily a panacea to find a way through difficult situations. On a brighter note, it is important to look for the spaces for creativity and opportunity in its application. If law is viewed through a strengths perspective rather than simply as a set of rules, it extends, rather than limits, what can be achieved. Attitudes towards the law may need to change – to regard it as a resource not an obstacle, a tool for practice. It can be a powerful influence for the good of both people and planet – for example, the Well-being of Future Generations (Wales) Act 2015 requires every decision made by the Welsh government departments to address the wellbeing of the population 'in a manner which seeks to ensure that the needs of the present are met without compromising the ability of future generations to meet their own needs' (s.5 (1)).

Critical reflection on law and policy is essential, scrutinising the relationship between the state and the law, and the extent to which the state is bound by the law, not least in respect of resources. Localism, for example, must not mean abandoned by the state. Critical vigilance must be maintained as new legislation is made. The climate for criticality and practice is challenging not least because of the constantly changing, increasingly dense web of laws, policies, statutory instruments, regulations and procedures governing immigration in the UK. Following the best principles of knowledge management (Leung, 2009), START's culture as a learning organisation encourages everyone to learn continually, assuming responsibility for their own learning and contributing to the learning of others. When helping students to learn about law especially, staff attend to students' assumptions and fears about it. They help students develop critical competence in tandem with techno-rational knowledge underpinned by an ethical framework (Braye and Preston-Shoot, 2006). By its very nature, the organisation also celebrates interdisciplinarity. All parties, particularly international students, model enquiry and external scrutiny of UK policy which fosters criticality (Ford et al, 2005).

Example 2

An undergraduate social work student successfully challenged a housing association in respect of a Sudanese family of five. The two-child cap imposed on housing benefit prompted a housing association to judge that the family could not pay the rent so would not allocate them a house big enough for their needs. The student's intervention overturned this decision by advocating for the family and their resourcefulness which caused the housing association to review their policy.

Legal literacy is fundamental in any context, making best use of legislation rather than simply allowing it to control. Knowledge underpins legal literacy by recognising and locating core principles enshrined in law and policy that are congruent with the strengths approach, together with their implications for practice. Most significant are those that promote respect, empowerment, self-determination, autonomy and choice. Other specific examples found in UK legislation include:

- paramountcy in respect of the welfare of the child (Children Act 1989);
- duty to promote the individual's wellbeing (Care Act 2014);
- all persons using services must be treated with dignity and respect (Health and Social Care Act 2008 (Regulated Activities) Regulations 2014);
- a presumption that a person has mental capacity unless proven otherwise (Mental Capacity Act 2005);

- the 'least restrictive option' must be sought (Mental Health Act 1983; Children Act 1989);
- interview 'in a suitable manner', having regard, for example, for age, understanding, hearing or linguistic difficulties (Mental Health Act 1983);
- proportionality, whereby actions that restrict rights must be proportionate to the outcome sought – not excessive in the circumstances (Human Rights Act 1998; Mental Health Act 1983).

Principles such as the five governing the Mental Capacity Act 2005 are equally congruent with a strengths approach (see also the Family Law Act 1996 and the Crime and Disorder Act 1998) as are principles enshrined in Codes of Practice as well as other forms of statutory guidance, notably administrative law.

Legal literacy involves the ability to uphold these principles in any given situation. It requires us to be thoroughly conversant with rights-based mandates. In the UK these include the Human Rights Act 1998, the Equality Act 2010 and international frameworks, most notably the Universal Declaration of Human Rights 1948, the UNHCR Refugee Convention 1951, the UN Convention on the Rights of Disabled Persons 2006 and the UN Convention on the Rights of the Child 1989.

Example 3

> Similar to the case law cited at the beginning of this chapter, A. was granted limited leave to remain in the UK; his wife had tried to join him on a visitor's visa, but this had expired so that she had 'No Recourse to Public Funds'. With legal support, START workers deployed Article 8 of the Human Rights Act 1998 to fight her deportation.

It is also important to look beyond the scope of different pieces of legislation and think laterally to apply other statutes; for example, in respect of refugees, the Modern Slavery Act 2015, domestic violence legislation and laws to combat hate crime. Practitioners should be open to the scale of knowledge and develop confidence in their ability to search for it.

Example 4

> Having been detained in hospital under the Mental Health
> Act 1983, B. was discharged home to her flat without any
> support, in contravention of the aftercare provisions of s.117
> of the Act. One of START's co-managers worked with B. and
> her social worker to challenge this successfully.

Sources of legal knowledge might include forging relationships with lawyers to advise on family reunion, for example, or tenancies under housing law. Alliances with campaigning groups (for example, the Citizens Advice Bureau to pursue social insurance iniquities through the courts; the Child Poverty Action Group to challenge injustice and support collective action) also characterise legal literacy.

Example 5

> A co-manager at START worked with the Child Poverty Action
> Group to appeal successfully against a decision to refuse a
> mother's claim for a £500 Sure Start Maternity Grant for her
> second child. The grant was only available for a first child as
> families were expected to reuse all they bought with it for
> subsequent children. C. had fled to the UK with her pre-flight
> child and had been unable to bring any baby items. Her claim
> for her second child born in the UK was refused on the basis
> that even as a refugee she was still not eligible under Social Fund
> Maternity and Funeral Expenses (General) Regulations 2005. The
> appeal was upheld as the grant was deemed to be in the ambit
> of Article 8 ECHR and so refusal could amount to discrimination
> contrary to Article 14 on the basis of her refugee status. This
> decision has secured the entitlement of refugees subsequently
> (https://cpag.org.uk/welfare-rights/resources/test-case/
> refugees-pre-flight-children-and-access-sure-start-maternity).

The strengths approach requires us to seek the means to challenge the law when it is in opposition to professional ethics, and to hold the state to account, as in *Urgenda v The Netherlands, 2015* (The Climate Docket, 2019).

Protagonists of a strengths approach need to be vigilant to avoid complicity in implementing discriminatory policies (Humphries, 2004). Remedial law used alone to 'protect people' may result in poor practice. Clarity in what should be achieved by the application of law and policy for a particular situation is vital. In 2002, families whose asylum claim had failed had no recourse to public funds and so were destitute and homeless, unless detained. As a consequence, local authorities were expected to accommodate the children as they were deemed to be at risk. Individual authorities used the Children Act 1989 (Section 17) to pay for families' food and accommodation while the Association of the Directors of Social Services and the British Association of Social Workers campaigned successfully for a change in the rules.

The right to appeal is commensurate with a strengths approach which is also served by establishing and supporting service user forums for group advocacy and collective action. All at START have learned the value of helping people to acquire legal knowledge and understand their rights in law so they can advocate for themselves. As experts in their own lives they can gain the confidence to work with discretion effectively in order to access their entitlements. Characteristic of the strengths approach, their focus and energy can be directed at negotiating the spaces rather than being pathologised by or simply blaming the legal system.

Example 6

> START were working with a family with two children. They were wrongly informed by an officer of the Benefit Agency that the family were not entitled to universal credit (social insurance) due to austerity. Workers shared detailed information about the benefit with the family who were then able to challenge the decision themselves.

START has also supported refugees to access higher education and train for the legal profession. Under the global COVID-19 pandemic and lockdown constraints on case workers, refugees have had to be more self-reliant and pursue their rights with support at a distance with some positive results. Law can make space for hope; helping people to understand they have agency in upholding their rights engenders hope.

Example 7

> START successfully challenged the decision of a university which tried to impose overseas students' fees on a law student whose family were seeking asylum, as well as on other students who were refugees with limited incomes.

Learning points

- Be vigilant in exercising critical reflection on law and policy.
- Understand the relationship between the state and the law.
- Develop legal literacy and knowledge of the law, especially principles and rights-based mandates congruent with a strengths approach.
- Encourage a positive attitude to legislation; look for opportunities for creativity in its implementation.
- Understand the nature and power of professional discretion.
- Enable self-advocacy and collective action by people directly affected by legislation in a particular context.

3

A strengths approach
to organisational development

> Since trust has to be placed without guarantees, it is
> inevitably sometimes misplaced: others let us down and we
> let others down. When this happens, trust and relationships
> based on trust are both damaged. Trust, it is constantly
> observed, is hard earned and easily dissipated. It is valuable
> capital and not to be squandered.
>
> O'Neill (2002: 6)

How does a strengths approach apply to organisational
development? As an alternative paradigm to conventional
theorising, this chapter introduces the concept of social
innovation defined in Box 3.1. We begin with an account of
entrepreneurship – using existing resources in a new way –
and record how academic activism led to the creation of an
NGO. Charting the development of the latter reveals how
frequently people sought to pigeon-hole it within conventional
organisational types. The effects of growth on the organisation
are revealed and an account is given of how the strengths
approach enabled it to mature through a period of financial
difficulty. A critique of the neoliberal notion of social enterprise
is also offered in this context.

A transferable model of social entrepreneurship derived
from our early experiences at START then illustrates the way
a strengths approach to organisational development can result
in social innovation. Drawing on research using a business
administration lens, we consider how social innovation can
produce organisations that are suited to their particular locality

in size and composition, responsive to national and local agendas, *and* energising and educative for all concerned. A vital component of the approach is trust.

Entrepreneurship

Box 3.1: Definitions

Entrepreneurship is the activity by a person or persons that identifies existing resources or potential and brings them together in a new way.

Social entrepreneurship is the activity by a person or persons that identifies existing resources or potential and brings them together in a new way with the specific intention of social benefit.

Enterprise is an organisation whose activity is designed to produce profit (sometimes at the expense of both people and planet) as in the activities of large, profit-driven multi-national corporations.

Social enterprise is the organisation or structure resulting from social entrepreneurship which has money at its core. Profits are used to improve social benefits for individual and community wellbeing, exemplified by fair trade companies.

Social innovation is the organisation or structure resulting from social entrepreneurship that has wellbeing at its core. Although money is necessary for its functioning, individual and social wellbeing are always primary, and profit is not a goal. Money is used to support value-based activity in which the wellbeing of people and planet are paramount.

Since its inception in 2001, START has been something of an organisational anomaly. It began as a virtual organisation which had no formal structure, other than a steering group of representatives from the university, city council and health authorities. It was commonly misrepresented by people as being part of the university, or the city council, or one of the larger national charities. In response to this confusion and attempts to normalise it, Avril wrote a paper in 2005 reviewing existing organisational models and identifying the defining characteristics of START (Butler, 2005). Using the strengths approach to challenge the construction of refugees and students as 'burdens' – on society and on placement agencies respectively – she describes both groups as 'significant social contributors in transition'. She says:

> One characteristic that refugees and students have in common is that they are both groups with substantial resources, identified by their social context. As groups in transition, they bring a high potential for creativity and change through the formation of new alliances. Whilst the contextual needs of both groups are recognized, an emphasis is placed on capacity-building through learning together. (Butler, 2005: 149)

At this stage of its development, Avril identified START as a 'micro-activist' organisation. An 'activist' organisation provides 'a space for the development of oppositional interpretations of interests and needs, where the voices of those who are excluded from the dominant discourses can be heard' (Kenny, 2002: 292). In these early years, START was designed to place the service to refugees on the same level as the education of students. It was an environment in which neither group was privileged at the expense of the other. The constant flow of both students and refugees meant that the organisation remained open to radical approaches in which social casework is connected to other forms of social action (Goldsworthy, 2002).

Latterly, Avril has reviewed the survival of the organisation through the lens of a student-led placement project, comparing it to one in Victoria, Australia (Bellinger and Testa, 2016). This concludes that START's status as an NGO, independent of both university and city council, has been an important aspect of its survival, together with its combined ambitions of service to refugees and student education. The concept of students learning with and from people excluded from society is not new. The UK settlement movement founded in 1884 was premised on the idea of students living and learning alongside people in poverty to their mutual benefit. The settlement movement has been a major influence on the development of professions like social work in the voluntary sector (Manthorpe, 2002) both in the UK and the US (Koerin, 2003).

The record of work achieved by START students in the first two years with no resources other than themselves, was impressive: one student saved a woman's life by accompanying her to a GP surgery where previously she had been perceived as attention-seeking and a nuisance. The woman was sent away – only to be diagnosed with neglected septicaemia and admitted immediately to hospital following the student's intervention. Another student acted as a birth partner for a woman from Afghanistan newly arrived in the city and who had no one else in the UK to support her. Making arrangements for the care of her own family, the student stayed with the woman throughout the night until the baby was born. By her own account, she was profoundly moved by the experience. The project's steering group had been able to draw in small amounts of grant funding to pay a graduate of START as a temporary continuation worker in order to maintain a service to families in the summer of 2003, and the following year she supported new students. Evidence of the students' interventions was sufficiently powerful to secure a contract with the local authority and a successful Big Lottery bid resulting in a dramatic increase in funding from less than £10,000 to £120,000 per annum in 2004 (explored further in Chapter 5).

The next two years were occupied by work to produce a Memorandum and Articles of Association, registration as a company and charity, converting the steering group into a board of directors and trustees, and the production of policies and procedures. We had to recruit six full-time staff, find office accommodation, furniture and computers in order to develop as a fully-fledged organisation with a public profile and expectations of performance against a variety of externally imposed targets. In essence, we had become successful social entrepreneurs, defined by Martin and Osberg (2007: 39) as:

someone who targets an unfortunate but stable equilibrium that causes the neglect, marginalization, or suffering of a segment of humanity; who brings to bear on this situation his or her inspiration, direct action, creativity, courage, and fortitude; and who aims for and ultimately affects the establishment of a new stable equilibrium that secures permanent benefit for the targeted group and society at large.

The concept of social entrepreneurship will be revisited later in the chapter. Meanwhile, this rapid transformation from a fragile project to a more mainstream registered charity was both exciting and sobering. We were no longer engaged in something new and different that could disappear at any time. We had entered the world of regulated organisations with responsibilities to grant bodies and contract commissioners.

It is a paradox that an organisation committed to social change has to comply with existing organisational models and business structures in order to gain recognition. Social innovations need space to grow but existing structures could have the effect of closing them down and reducing them to something already known. The experience of identifying charitable objects for START was educative in this regard as twice the Charity Commission rejected the language used to express our intentions before it was finally accepted. Equally the development of a Memorandum and Articles of Association provided a legal framework in which the organisation constituted itself. There are a number of models that new initiatives can adopt such as Community Interest Companies, Charitable Incorporated Organisations, co-operatives and charities, but the range is limited and once an innovation has become stable, it must choose from these available formats.

The graduate who had been employed to maintain a service over the summer of 2003 suddenly found herself in the position of co-managing a substantial organisation. Reflecting on this experience in 2006, she wrote:

Not only has the service user group gone through a transitional process [to achieve refugee status], I also have had a steep transitional opportunity firstly as a student in 2003 through to the manager in 2005. I feel that START has given me the opportunity to launch ... Those values, skills and knowledge I learnt have been transferable to management and START as a learning organisation has provided me with the opportunity to further my studies directed in business management to enable me, the staff and the board of directors to take START forward as a creative organisation working outside the box. (Butler et al, 2006: 62)

A sudden abundance of funding, pressure on performance and achieving the targets set by funders, public visibility and the need to meet expectations caused the organisation to shift its focus inwards. Ironically, this resulted in staff adopting a more conventional attitude towards students as something of an inconvenience to the organisation, a preoccupation with how it was seen in the city and anxiety about positioning START as a service provider alongside other agencies. In a climate of competitive funding for charities, a report by Dame Suzi Leather and Andrew Hind (Charity Commission, 2010) powerfully illustrates the inherent contradiction of organisations being expected to collaborate with each other while competing for steadily reducing funds. Over the same period, media constructions of refugees fuelled a shift in policy from one of social integration to managing the public burden that refugees were deemed to represent. Refugees were used as a political tool to show the government's concern for its citizens and control of borders, so that funding for START became increasingly difficult to access.

These years were also challenging because growth had been so fast. Instead of healthy incremental change, the organisation had 'shot up' overnight. Looking back, we liken it to the story told by Tim Smit about the beginning of the Eden Project in Cornwall. There the trees and plants in the domes were grown from seed and, because they were not competing with an existing canopy, they grew tall and fragile very quickly. The Eden Project had to employ people who would go around and shake the trees to encourage them to develop resilience and strength.

Strength and maturity

In 2007 when the Big Lottery funding came to an end, the organisation had an equivalent shaking. The dramatic reduction in the budget meant that half the staff had to be made redundant. This was a very painful process; it did, however, give all involved (students, refugees, staff, trustees) the opportunity to refocus the organisation calling on the principles of the strengths approach to inform our practice as cited in Chapter 1:

1. *Every individual, group, family and community has assets and resources to be used in reconstructing and redirecting their lives.*
   We recognised the resources that individuals had brought and the experience of being part of the initial project and subsequent organisation. This shared history allowed us to identify the values and practices that we wanted to preserve.
2. *Every individual and collectivity has the inherent capacity for wholeness, regeneration, healing and transformation.*
   Although the organisation was forced to reduce the staff costs by half in order to survive, we saw this as an opportunity to reflect on the core principles of START and to see the future as *different* but not *less*. By prioritising the two aspects of student learning and service to refugees we were able to build a picture of a smaller, but more focused, organisation.
3. *Every person and group has a fund of innate wisdom and health to draw upon in times of crisis and challenge.*
   People were trusted to have all the information available so that each could make the right decision for themselves. While the standard procedures of notifying people of risk of redundancy were observed, the new structure was designed together *with* those at risk rather than imposed upon them by the trustees.
4. *Everyone has the capacity for rebound and righting the trajectory of their development in the face of adversity and trauma.*
   As individuals made the decision to stay in the new structure or leave, we shared their distress and celebrated their achievements. In the end there was no need to have

competitive interviews for the new posts as redundant staff were able (and supported to) find other work to progress their careers. Individuals were empowered to talk to one another and in one instance, amicably negotiated their future with a potential competitor for a post.

5. *All individuals, families, communities, and cultures have rhetorical, metaphorical, narrative tools to refashion and reformulate their understanding and interpretation of their situation and condition (Weick and Saleebey, 1998: 27).*

On reflection, we managed this difficult process by talking together about what START's essential attributes were, what attributes service users and students valued, and how we could preserve those. Students and refugees were again centre stage as potentially high contributors in transition. The role of staff and trustees was to create the conditions in which that potential could be realised. These processes were made possible by the close relationships that had been forged between refugees, students, staff and trustees. Regular meetings and informal contacts meant that everyone's voice was sought and could be heard so that all ideas were incorporated in the new arrangements. Little by little, we created a renewed vision together that brought the best of the past into the future, sharing ideas, concerns, proposals and passion. This process reflects the common principles inherent in both the strengths approach and appreciative inquiry which are explored further in Chapter 6. The equal status of student learning and refugee support (Butler, 2005) was reaffirmed as a fundamental aspect of this vision.

It is our view that none of this reorientation and revitalising would have been possible if START had been part of a larger institution bound by rules and structures that could not take account of local conditions and the unique circumstances of people and place. The small scale and local specificity of START were significant factors in its resilience. Indeed, we have continued to reflect critically on this position and remain convinced that, in scaling up, vitality and direction can be lost (Cottam, 2019). Throughout strategic planning sessions held by START we have consistently revisited the organisation's fundamental purpose. With its strong theoretical foundation of the strengths approach and clearly articulated values, we were persuaded initially by the traditional idea that growth is good but then, in contrast, resolved to maintain a manageable size and local reach. Contracts in adjoining counties have confirmed that START has no wish to extend or to franchise but rather to work out of a single base in Plymouth. In promoting the model of student labour extensively there is no intention to seek financial profit but rather to encourage other innovations with a social impact.

Why START is not a social enterprise

Having survived a major transformation and wanting to avoid becoming a conventional mainstream service organisation that provided occasional student placements, we looked for concepts that would help us to position the organisation and secure its funding for the future. The government's response to the financial crisis of 2008, together with low interest rates, was to cut welfare services yet again – at the same time grant funding for charities was rapidly diminishing. There was significant encouragement from local authorities and central government agencies for charities to reconfigure themselves as businesses. Indeed, we recall that funding for reconfiguration was made available and for a brief period even loans were offered as part of that drive to embrace capitalism.

In that climate and the early years of the new millennium, the concept of social enterprise became the vogue. We, therefore, imagined that we should identify START as a social enterprise. We were disappointed with the outcome of our explorations, however, and bewildered by the reality of 'social enterprise'. At an inaugural meeting of the newly formed Social Enterprise UK and engagement with others active in social enterprises, we realised the emphasis was on making money. Our motivation surrounding the welfare of people escaping conflict, together with the values of the strengths perspective, did not fit with the profit motive of conventional social enterprises. Our commitment to the strengths of individuals and the organisation was difficult to translate in those settings. One of our trustees invited a nationally renowned social enterprise consultant to visit START who was most impressed by the holistic nature of the work. He recommended that, if we were to move from being one of the 'bottom feeders' to being one of the 'big fish', then we should *sell* our processes to other agencies rather than work directly with refugees and students. This drive to find a socially responsible product that could be sold seemed alien to all of us involved in START. It represented a gross shift of priorities from social justice work to income generation. It also transpires that the belief in social enterprise as a solution to difficulties was inherently flawed. As Stott and Tracey (2018: 6) warn: 'the weight of expectations placed on social entrepreneurship to overcome others' "failures" is at best unhelpful and at worst counterproductive, not least because sustaining social enterprises appears to be inherently difficult'.

Business models tend to assume that growth is necessary and positive for organisations – we have resisted this over time, remaining alert to the neoliberal assumptions underlying such models and choosing carefully what fits with the organisation's values and integrity. Although START has now bid for, and won, contracts with local authorities to deliver time-limited services in Cornwall and parts of Devon, the core work remains in Plymouth and there is a very cautious approach to any extension of the organisation itself.

START and social entrepreneurship

> Social entrepreneurship [is] the process of creating and growing a venture to tackle social challenges.
>
> Stott and Tracey (2018: 5)

START's mission is to 'work in partnership with families, individuals and community and mainstream organisations to facilitate the transition of refugees from people in need to self-reliant contributors to their local community, whilst providing high quality practical placements for students of social work, occupational therapy and other health professions'.

In common with most UK NGOs, START is now registered with the Charity Commission with the following objects determining its remit. START will:

- **SUPPORT** and relieve financial hardship among those seeking asylum and granted refugee status, particularly in the provision of housing. To signpost and promote access to education and training opportunities.
- **ADVOCATE** and assist asylum seekers and refugees to live within a new community or to move to a new geographical location.
- **PROVIDE** various facilities for recreation and other leisure time occupations for individuals and groups.
- **ADVANCE** the education of students in training by providing learning experiences, which contribute to their personal and professional development.

We came to regard this micro-activist organisation as an example of the outcome of experimental social entrepreneurship. It is important here to differentiate between social enterprise and social entrepreneurship. As noted earlier, social entrepreneurs are people who identify a social difficulty and seize an opportunity to use existing resources in a different way in order to meet that difficulty (Dees, 1998). According to Dees, a central aspect of social entrepreneurship is that the activity is aimed primarily at solving a social problem and not at financial gain. The social problems identified in 2001 resulted from the lack of support for families seeking asylum who were being dispersed by the Home Office to Plymouth, and also the difficulty in finding good quality placements for students where they could work with people from diverse countries of origin. As detailed in Chapter 7, START provided a service to 21 families (35 adults and 68 children) by engaging the labour of 14 social work students over the first two years, offering support that was otherwise unavailable. This was achieved on a shoestring, without significant financial outlay. START clearly did not fit the model of a social enterprise. As previously explained, entrepreneurship is the activity of seeing new possibilities in existing systems and finding ways to exploit them. Entrepreneurship may be founded on diverse principles and values, on a scale in which money and profit have primary importance at one end and where sustainability and wellbeing (of people and planet) are paramount at the other. In this global capitalist society, money is accorded a status far beyond its original function as a tool. It can be difficult to retain focus on human and environmental wellbeing and sustainability in a culture where their value has been replaced. Social entrepreneurship, however, exploits possibilities for social rather than monetary outcomes. What follows is a model of social entrepreneurship that results in social innovation rather than a social enterprise because wellbeing, not money, is at the core.

In 2003, following the satisfactory completion of that initial project, Avril articulated a different transferable model of social innovation that could both respond to people's unmet needs and also contribute to the education and training agenda through the provision of placements. The following account therefore focuses on a service model delivered primarily by student labour. Inevitably, it overlaps with the literature about practice education and setting up placements for students of different disciplines. Here the account is primarily concerned, however, with the organisation – how to provide a service in response to human need. Chapter 7 offers more detailed information about developing practice placements in themselves.

Social innovation: the social justice model

There are some groups of people in society that are described as 'hard to reach'. Mostly, they have consistently experienced difficulty in accessing the services to which they are entitled and instead occupy a kind of hinterland where it is believed that they 'look after their own'. This phrase was much in use in the 1970s and 1980s in an attempt to explain why migrant elders did not use the existing care services, for example. But it is too simple to blame the community themselves for their failure to engage with mainstream services when the obstacles to doing so are almost insurmountable. We also know that help-seeking behaviour creates vulnerability and often misunderstanding, not to mention disappointment – or worse. Groups such as young people leaving care, travellers, people dependent on drugs or alcohol, people with chronic mental ill-health, BME groups and people in long-term poverty all have difficulties negotiating mainstream services.

When groups have had negative experiences, when help-seeking behaviour triggers an authoritarian or punitive response, people reasonably withdraw and look elsewhere for help. Within their own circles, stories circulate of possibility and dangers, and the reputations of agencies and individuals are established. Seeking help is deeply personal and requires a degree of trust in the person or organisation approached. Even unsolicited help will be viewed with suspicion by people whose encounters with 'those in charge' are negative. Given the experience of people seeking asylum in the UK of an immigration service that is hostile and suspicious, arbitrary in decision-making and quick to seize on inconsistencies – even in the spelling of a name – people are unlikely to feel confident in asserting their rights to services. The gap between access to services and reality for people in this situation is so wide that a 'bridge of trust' (Butler, 2007) is needed to enable people to cross the chasm to their entitlements. Individuals already trusted by the community can sometimes act as that bridge and vouch for the trustworthiness of others who are committed to social justice.

Stages of the social justice model

The **first stage** of the model depicted in Figure 3.1 is the identification of unmet need. This is not as straightforward as it might seem. The way current services are set up frequently results in service users being passed from one agency to another. Needs may be identified as outside one profession's remit but not sufficiently acute to meet the eligibility criteria for another. (In the past the unfortunate term 'silo' has been applied to indicate that services are discrete, and access is guarded.) As commissioning of services increasingly relates to outcomes (changes in people's circumstances) rather than outputs (quantity and quality of work undertaken) so people with complex needs and enduring difficulties are more likely to be excluded because they are not a good fit. While the scope for proactive preventive work is clearly recognised by a range of professionals, the resources to intervene effectively are not available.

Figure 3.1: The social justice model

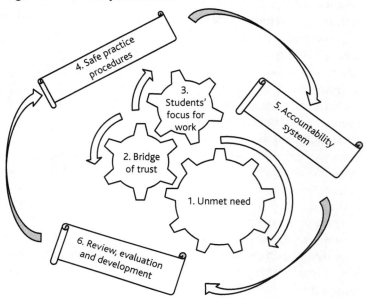

> Referrals to the project come from agencies and individuals who identify refugees with unmet needs, not eligible to be met by other agencies. This gap in service may be because needs are not expressed in ways that will enable a response or because they are too complex. Disaggregation of services and an emphasis on measurable outcomes (Clarke, 2000) means that services tend to be highly targeted and inaccessible for people who cannot articulate their needs within the specific service contract framework. (Butler, 2005: 4)

The commitment of staff to social justice can be undermined by frustration and burnout as they are constrained by such structural barriers (McFadden, 2015). If it is possible, however, to bring together some of those concerned professionals to begin to shape a response, it can be protective of their own resilience as well as creating potential in difficult circumstances.

At this early stage, it is essential that the needs identified are those expressed by the people themselves in line with the strengths approach. A principle of this model is that it is fully person-centred and not professionally defined.

The **second stage** is concerned with how students can be exposed to the reality of the work and be allowed to do it. As we have observed, people who are socially excluded and disenfranchised often will have learnt to be wary of people offering help. To counter this lack of trust, students can bring openness and optimism together with a willingness to work in truly responsive and flexible ways – provided they are supported to do so. At the same time, someone who is known and trusted by service users needs to provide that 'bridge of trust' into the student service. Their professional background, if any, does not matter – it is vital that they have the trust of service users together with an investment in their wellbeing that goes beyond their particular role boundary. People's trustworthiness derives from their humanity rather than from the role they occupy. It stems from their integrity, honesty and humility rather than espoused values or rule-bound behaviour. The person who acts as a bridge of trust for students to cross will need to provide ongoing information and support. It may be that individual workers who feel personally overwhelmed by the needs they recognise but cannot respond to, can resolve their own dilemmas by supporting students to do the work that they cannot.

The **third stage** of the social justice model is defining the scope of the work. Clear limits need to be set on what students should do to ensure they are not replicating services already provided such as legal, benefits and housing advice, or working beyond their competence. The emphasis in this work is on early intervention, prevention and supporting people to access the services to which they are entitled. Characteristically, students are very keen to be helpful and, in the absence of agency resources or procedures, have to rely on their knowledge and relationship with the person seeking help. Without assessment forms and 'normal provision', students must listen carefully to what people are finding difficult and support them to achieve it. This will be different in every situation and students have time and attention to give, providing a genuinely holistic, person-centred response. For some students this meant sharing meals in people's homes, going with them to the public library and working with extended friendship networks. Most professional programmes have clear guidelines that include competency or capability standards and placement policies. Using these alongside a strengths approach, rather than a deficit model, provides a framework for students to recognise what they should, and should not, do.

The **fourth stage** of the social justice model that creates a service using student placements is to set up systems of accountability. In a neoliberal bureaucracy where NPM results in a plethora of reporting systems designed to gather data and ensure compliant practice, we know that the result is not necessarily the high quality, consistent service that is intended. There are many critiques of the unintended consequences of quality assurance systems (van Thiel and Leeuw, 2002). As Onora O'Neill says: 'We set detailed performance targets for public bodies but are complacent about the perverse incentives they create' (2002: viii). This model of an independent, multi-agency student service means that accountability for the quality of service is much more clearly recognised as being to the service users rather than to a particular agency. Services are truly user-led, not service outcome-driven, and the service user's satisfaction is the principal measure of success. These themes are developed in Chapter 4. Everyone makes mistakes and trust is more likely to be maintained if they are acknowledged and used for learning than if they are covered up as if they had never happened.

Stage five of this process is to focus on the development of procedures for safe practice. These student-led services do not fit neatly into any existing service protocols and so they need to have tools and processes set up that are fit for purpose. This is much more challenging than simply undertaking formal risk assessments and following standardised safeguarding and lone working procedures. Students must be supported to make judgements about risk and vulnerability that are primarily focused on the service user's wellbeing. This does not mean 'playing safe' or putting organisational considerations first. Saffer et al (2018) assert that overly protective, risk-averse practice can jeopardise a person's human right to exercise choice and control. It can lead to dependency on the organisation and hinder their progress as they strive to regain citizenship. At its worst, it can undermine the very qualities and skills that enabled people to escape conflict and survive.

At START, students learn about risk enablement. Carefully considered risks can enable individuals and help improve their wellbeing. Positive risk-taking is a way of working with risk that promotes enablement: 'Life without risk would be life without living. It is only through accepting a level of risk in our daily lives that we are able to do anything at all' (Sorensen, 2015). It is important to remember that the 'positive' in positive risk-taking refers to the outcome, *not* the risk.

Data ownership and use have acquired enormous public significance (GDPR, 2018). A virtual organisation such as the one proposed here gives students an opportunity to be in at the beginning and consider fundamental questions that can assist them in recognising the power of information throughout their careers. For example, in the early days of START, students had to think about ways to let future students know what they had done, and what the result had been. They developed a system of brief record cards that were held by service users themselves. This meant they were clear about recording, its purpose and the ownership of information.

Successful projects may generate data that can be used to develop new services, as noted later in this chapter. Such data might also be employed to help to change obstructive practice in other agencies. Students must therefore learn to record appropriately, respect the rights of service users and avoid duplication of services.

An essential **sixth stage** of the social justice model is that of review, evaluation and development. While the progress of individual students is usually monitored and assessed by staff from a particular academic programme, the service itself needs to be kept under review. The quality and availability of the service provided to users must be weighted equally with the quality of learning for students. Service users, students, the individual acting as the bridge, other concerned practitioners and educational staff should be party to review and development to ensure that the service has not drifted from its original purpose.

Any concerned group wanting to create a service in tandem with a local academic institution can adopt this organisational model. It provides a recipe for student learning and service provision in a way that emphasises the strengths of all involved rather than the deficits and gaps in service. Clearly there are some basic challenges for anyone embarking on such a venture: not least office accommodation for students and associated health and safety issues; insurance; and access to resources such as telephones and internet. It is also a model that exposes vulnerability, not only of the people needing support but also of the students and professionals engaged in something innovative. Motivation is key as is trust in the potential of all parties. Creating resources in a vacuum requires personal investment by all alongside a willingness to recognise and manage risk. After all, one of the core principles of the strengths approach is that we should not limit the aspirations of others – or indeed, of ourselves.

Although this book draws heavily on the example of START, there is no reason why this social justice model of student learning as a way of responding to social exclusion cannot be utilised with other groups if people are determined. There are so many communities who are disenfranchised by the increasingly draconian criteria for state services whereby people must experience severe difficulties in order to qualify for a service. One consequence of this state of affairs is that professional education becomes increasingly specialist and theory-driven. Moreover, it should be recognised that academics preparing students for the 'helping professions' are caught between the demands of the institution for academic output (preferably that which attracts research funding) and complying with employers' expectations of work-ready practitioners. We would argue, however, that job satisfaction for academics with a commitment to social justice comes from the academic activism that Catherine MacKinnon describes as 'engaged scholarship'. In her analysis of the study and teaching of law she observes: 'Engaged scholarship at its best is both grounded and theoretical, actively involved in the world of its subject matter, and for that reason, able to think about it in fresh ways' (MacKinnon, 2010: 12). Thus, while we make no claim that developing a social justice model is easy, or that academic activism will necessarily be welcomed by the academy, it does provide rich learning for all involved and contributes to knowledge in fundamental ways. More importantly, it is a means to offer humanitarian assistance to individuals and families who are in desperate need and increasingly rendered invisible by oppressive government policy.

START and social innovation: a research study

The status given to learning within START has consistently included an openness to research activity that complies with the values and principles expressed in Chapter 6. There are many ways in which research contributes to the work of START. As a learning organisation, START welcomes feedback and evaluation to improve the developing service; data are needed to secure funding and to report to funders; students require examples of research studies for their work and are encouraged to develop a research-minded approach to their practice. Most importantly, the voices and concerns of refugees and students must have a platform and contribute to the knowledge available to professional and academic communities.

One notable example of research is that undertaken by Phyllis McNally, who, for her MSc in Business and Management, completed a dissertation entitled 'Developing a qualitative research framework to define social innovation' using START as a case study (McNally et al, 2020). As a former student at START and temporary staff member before beginning her programme, Phyllis was determined to investigate the characteristics of the organisation that were so different from others where she had worked. Using a business and management orientation, she adopted a qualitative approach in which she triangulated data from documentation, leadership and management interviews, as well as a focus group session with service providers and service recipients. Further insight was established through participant observation and auto-ethnography.

Many governments have reacted too slowly or with outright hostility to the volume of refugees coming to Europe. Dwindling finances, low quality services, misguided practices and wasted resources have all strained patchy welfare support. Phyllis argues that work with refugees must therefore enable social innovation because radical solutions are needed. The results of her study highlight that the active engagement of refugees in social welfare provision is essential. This bottom-up approach is a fundamental aspect of social innovation – if not its very foundation. Phyllis' work demonstrates how social innovation can offer a template for future education and practice that has international value and is equally relevant to other groups who are failed by existing resources.

Phyllis reviews the various definitions of social innovation and identifies two key ways in which it differs from social enterprise. First, it is primarily concerned with social justice and wellbeing rather than having money at its heart. Second, true social innovation can only be generated from the bottom up, as noted, rather than from the top down.

The strengths approach is fundamental to an organisation that rejects hierarchies, experts and control. Phyllis concludes:

> A priority at the organisation is the avoidance of any possible exploitation and great care is taken to ensure arrangements impact in equal measures on students, the community and the educational institution (Bellinger and Testa, 2016). The strain to maintain a balance through a strength approach may be the attribute determining START's social innovative capacity. (McNally, 2018: 25)

For an organisation to maintain a commitment to a bottom-up approach to social justice, it must be small, adaptable and open to change. We have already argued that START was seen as a micro-activist organisation (Kenny, 2002). Key features of START's organisational resilience are that it is small and locally controlled. Lynn Keevers et al offer a useful definition of what they call 'locally-based community organisations'. These 'do not distribute profits to members; [but] have autonomy in local decision-making; have voluntary participation by members; are self-governing organizations; are community-serving and pursue some "public good" within a particular geographic area (Salamon and Anheier 1996)' (Keevers et al, 2012: 6).

START provides services in response to social injustice in the community. The categorisation of START as a 'locally-based community organisation' is critical in recognising what sets it apart from many local branches of national charities, private companies or other structures. Decisions are all made collectively and in response to local conditions. With a high degree of trust throughout the organisation, significant decisions are delegated to those with most information about the situation and confirmed by the trustees. As described by Atul Gawande (2010) in *The Checklist*, emphasis is placed on START's embedded principles and goals and on good quality communication, with responsibility for action delegated to those 'on the ground'.

Conclusion

At the time of writing (2021), there is a move, nationally and locally, towards increasing the size and remit of third-sector organisations to promote ease of commissioning and contract compliance, with an emphasis on consistency, collaboration, partnerships and economies of scale (Bovaird, 2014). We have seen the rise of organisational cultures that pressurise workers through targets, threats of insecurity and scapegoating as people are expected to produce more for less (Green, 2004; Gill, 2009; Giroux, 2014; McFadden, 2015). Such a development is an obvious consequence of the neoliberal agenda in which three myths are perpetuated:

- that consumption brings fulfillment;
- that growth solves problems; and
- that choice is a universal human right. (Whiteford, 2016: 15)

Although, currently, received wisdom regards organisational growth as a sign of health, we would concur with the environmental economists who argue that constant growth is neither sustainable nor desirable (Pettifor, 2019). Writing in *Resurgence*, Donella Meadows observes:

> The first commandment of economics is Grow. Grow forever. Companies must get bigger. National economies need to swell by a certain percentage each year ... The first commandment of the Earth

is Enough, Just so much and no more. Just so much soil. Just so much water. Just so much sunshine. Everything born of the Earth grows to its appropriate size and then stops. (2002: 17)

START is now in its 20th year. Over time, it has gained national and international recognition. Replicating this model or using these ideas to begin something similar does not need a practical blueprint so much as the wisdom that stems from self-help groups, from rural Uganda in this instance:

- be inclusive;
- be patient, grow step by step, learning together;
- recognise difficulties as an opportunity for learning and growth;
- celebrate achievements;
- work as a team towards a shared vision. (Horton, 2018: 4)

All of these imperatives reflect a strengths approach. This is about people and planet, not money – social innovation, not social enterprise. Social innovation itself is about wellbeing, not financial gain, and its power comes from the people themselves.

Learning points

- In any organisation, social innovation for sustainable change must be led by those most closely affected by the issues addressed.
- Maintain trust in people's capacity for regeneration, healing and transformation.
- Look locally for individuals and practices outside the mainstream and build alliances based on values.
- In times of crisis particularly, give the quiet stories your full attention – they contain wisdom about survival.
- Small, locally controlled organisations can be inclusive and responsive to local conditions and thereby contribute holistically to a global response.
- Mistakes are inevitable. In a learning culture they are shared openly so everyone can learn from them.

4

A strengths approach to governance and management

> Under conditions of true complexity – where the knowledge required exceeds that of any individual and unpredictability reigns – efforts to dictate every step from the centre will fail. People need room to act and adapt. Yet they cannot succeed as isolated individuals, either – that is anarchy. Instead they require a seemingly contradictory mix of freedom and expectation – expectation to coordinate, for example, and also to measure progress towards common goals.
>
> Gawande (2010: 79)

A strengths approach to governance and management is a philosophical core providing an anchor in stormy seas. The strengths approach has enabled our own organisation to be responsive to constant changes in circumstances and to be nimble-footed while retaining financial probity, policy compliance and quality assurance, as well as remaining true to its values. The approach described by Atul Gawande as essential is difficult, but it is possible to sustain. In our view, there are three preconditions:

- trust that everyone in the organisation will do the best they can to deliver the shared goals;
- respect for different specialist knowledge and attention to detail;
- constant communication between team members to ensure that they all own strategic decisions.

These features underpin a strengths approach to governance and management based on mutual respect, shared goals and a system of supervision that encourages everyone to contribute. Responsibility is shared collectively but individual accountability is never abdicated.

In this chapter we review the neoliberal context for practice and specifically the influence of NPM. We discuss the elements that are part of a systemic strengths approach to management and governance, namely non-hierarchical structures, leadership and supervision. This is followed by a detailed examination of the way electronic systems, as an instrument of NPM, can undermine an organisation's core practices and how the strengths approach can be applied in mitigation.

The political context

> Neo-liberalism concerns itself with markets and profits rather than social justice and human rights; with individualism rather than the promotion of community and citizenship.
>
> Bellinger et al (2016: 204)

The current climate for many western democracies has been explored extensively by political analysts and commentators. In setting the context for the strengths approach, it is important to remember that, as stated in Chapter 1, the ascendancy of the New Right in the 1980s with a corresponding retrenchment of the welfare state, resulted in a managerialist approach to health and personal social services in the UK which is now endemic (Clarke and Newman, 1997). Fuelled by neoliberal concerns about the spiralling and unrestrained costs of welfare provision, as well as the cult of individualism with minimal state intervention, a managerialist approach places a heavy reliance on market principles and the operation of quasi-markets. This latter term refers to what became known colloquially in practice as the 'purchaser-provider split' which, in the 1990s, signalled the separation of state funding from the provision of services. In accordance with a market culture, competition for service contracts was introduced ostensibly as a means to improve standards and 'consumer' choice (Gorman and Postle, 2003).

Despite the perceived failure of the quasi-market to produce better quality services, and of Blair's 'Third Way' to stimulate private sector involvement (Jordan and Jordan, 2000), competition nevertheless, with internal markets and contracting, remains a central pillar of government policy. This trend towards disaggregated provision under central control is captured in the expression 'New Public Management'. NPM is based on an assumption that welfare bureaucracies in the public sector are notoriously inefficient and need tighter managerial control in order to deliver better services. To recap, NPM comprises techniques from the private sector aimed at making services more efficient and effective through:

- increased managerial control of professional behaviour;
- a detailed framework of practice, specifying targets and performance indicators to measure and shape practice;
- a greater demand for transparency so that services show they are spending public money wisely;
- a paper, or electronic trail documenting professional activity. (Munro, 2010: 1144)

NPM is characterised by 'hands-on' private-sector management styles concerned with the regulation and surveillance of service providers. In such an environment, the work of individuals is scrutinised to ensure compliance with outcome delivery. However, as Munro (2004) observes, this surveillance comprises the audit of internal quality control systems rather than of the service itself: 'providers are expected to show evidence of self-regulation, through record-keeping, protocols and information processing systems. The public sector then audits these internal systems of control, rather than studying the actual performance of the organisation' (Munro, 2004: 1079). NPM places emphasis on pre-set output measures rather than process, as well as on explicit and measurable standards of performance with corresponding performance indicators. It involves 'Value for Money' auditing to assess 'economy, efficiency and effectiveness', and latterly, 'Best

Value' governed by accountability, transparency, continuous improvement and ownership (Hood, 1991; 1995).

Public accountability

In the context of a funding and reporting system that can operate to the detriment of organisational responsiveness and sensitivity to service-user need, there is an inherent contradiction in user-led services being provided through output-driven funding (Vare, 2008). As priorities of funders change, they may not align with people's immediate needs. Audit and quality assurance processes can also drive organisations in particular directions unrelated to their original aims. For example, while it can appear to be an advantage to a small agency to receive significant government funding, there is a danger that NGOs become agents of government, no longer responding to local need, but rather to political agendas, a critique identified over 30 years ago when the Greater London Council funded 'grass roots' organisations (Carter, 1986) and reinforced more recently by Keevers et al (2012). Both authors make a helpful distinction between 'locally based community organisations', explored in more detail in Chapter 3, and centrally controlled services operating in dispersed units as in local offices of large national charities. It is like the difference between a small, independent business and a franchise of a national chain.

This is not to say that local or individual responses are all that are needed. Such a view plays into the individualising approach of the neoliberal project, deflecting responsibility and blame onto those experiencing its worst consequences. As public provision is withdrawn, however (Macdonald and Morgan, 2020), large-scale organisations commissioned to deliver national contracts repeatedly fail (Bowcott, 2015; Johnstone, 2018; Taylor, 2020). The UK's inability to establish an effective 'Test and Trace' system for COVID-19 infection was a case in point. The well-established local authority public health officials repeatedly asked central government for resources to do their job (Ham and Tuddenham, 2020; Merrick, 2020). Instead, the government created a new structure and awarded valuable contracts for a national scheme to private sector companies. In spite of much political rhetoric with promises of a 'world-beating' system and a 'moonshot' scale of testing (Halliday, 2020), this vital provision remained in disarray. In the UK, the lack of consultation and communication with health leaders, devolved governments and others is endemic (Unison, 2020).

A further conundrum is experienced when funding from central government is administered by a local authority, for example. This is an increasingly common feature of public service provision as functions are devolved while central control is maintained (Gorman and Postle, 2003). When quality assurance mechanisms are used to manage resources that are administered by a third party, those resources become subject to the requirements of two different systems. In practice, we have found these to be incompatible and, at times, contradictory, imposing reporting demands that are incoherent (O'Neill, 2002). A strengths approach recognises that this incoherence, however, offers both challenges and opportunities created by the gaps between the systems.

In circumstances where change is constant it may be tempting to assert control by setting tight criteria for accessing a service, defining the extent of any intervention and when it will end, framing success in the language of funders and allowing them to dictate the activities undertaken as time-limited projects, a response clearly articulated by Woolford and Curran (2012). In part, this shift towards tighter administrative scrutiny of professional activity is the product of a 'risk-averse' society leading to what Munro (2004) describes as the 'protocolisation' of risk assessment and management and a culture of blame when tragedies occur. It could be inferred that the intention behind these processes is directed towards protecting government from blame rather than actually protecting the public. Power (1997) discusses the 'audit explosion' that has occurred in the UK. He warns of the dangers of these 'shallow rituals of verification' derived from the belief that the new accountability will in itself improve public services. Such practices are counterproductive as professionals aim to satisfy the regulators by concentrating on targets. As a result, attention is drawn to the requirement to reduce the number of complaints made against a service for example, rather than to outcomes and the quality of service provided.

Numerous criticisms are levelled against performance measures that, although reliable and easy to record, fail to capture the elements which people supported by services regard as of particular value. Relationships between the worker and service user are identified by many as a particular casualty of managerialism (Holman, 2001; O'Neill, 2002; Carey, 2003). The perverse incentive created by bureaucratic demands of targets, budget-led administrative tasks and ultimately league tables, undermines the proper aims of professional practice. For example, Donna Baines (2010) undertook research with 66 workers in Canada and Australia to explore their experience of working in the non-profit sector in a climate of neoliberalism. In so doing, she drew on her previous research in British Columbia where the election of a strongly neoliberal government resulted in dramatic cuts to public funding. She argues that the wider context of targets, outcome delivery and surveillance inherent in NPM means that, increasingly, individuals have difficulty in working in ways that accord with their own, or indeed with the organisation's values. Moreover, the culture of neoliberalism appears to limit workers' vision to individualised concerns of interpersonal practice, pay and conditions, as opposed to wider strategic or political visions of how service structures could be improved. She says: 'Research suggests that global pressures and restructuring in the sector have curtailed possibilities for values-based, participatory culture in the non-profit sector (Weisbrod, 1998; Van Til, 2000) making it increasingly difficult to sustain or initiate liberatory and/or empowering services' (Baines, 2010: 930).

At START, we have discovered that accurate reporting against specified numerical targets can be more important to funders than explaining the depth, quality and real consequences of the work. Indeed, it came as a shock to realise that over-reporting can be seen as equally negative as under-reporting because it challenges the system calculations. It seems that meeting targets precisely is more important than exceeding expectations. Over-reporting is also risky because it encourages funders to expect more for less in subsequent contracts, acting in the same way as 'breaking the rate' in factory piecework. Understanding these political and structural influences has allowed START to maintain a critical position – to avoid being swept along on a tide of compliance, remaining open to innovative solutions to each challenge. For this to be possible, the management and governance must indeed operate with that 'contradictory mix of freedom and expectation – expectation to coordinate, for example, and also to measure progress towards common goals' (Gawande, 2010: 79).

A strengths approach to governance and management therefore commits everyone, at all levels of the organisation, to recognise the insidious and pervasive nature of neoliberal thought and culture and to respond creatively to preserve social justice.

Governance

The separation of function between governance and management is universally understood but not easy to maintain. In the UK, charitable or third-sector directors or trustees are responsible for governance – for evaluating, directing and monitoring the strategic direction of the organisation and ensuring that it remains true to its objectives and values while operating within its available resources. The UK's Charity Commission and the National Council for Voluntary Organisations have undertaken substantial work to respond to the failure of governance and erosion of public faith in the sector. Complaints by the public about aggressive fundraising following the death of Mrs Cooke (Morris, 2016), publicity about alleged serious mismanagement of funds as Kids Company went into sudden liquidation in August 2015 (Meade, 2016) and the exploitative behaviour of an Oxfam representative in Haiti and failure of the organisation to respond appropriately (Gayle, 2018) have resulted in new codes of practice and self-assessment materials for charities.

The main role of trustees is to:

- ensure that the organisation's values, aim and objects are maintained;
- ensure financial probity;
- critically consider proposals for a way forward; and
- hold the responsibility for the outcome of those decisions.

Managing this responsibility can be challenging, particularly when measuring progress towards goals through targets, whether predetermined outcomes or quantitative calculations on the basis of monetary value, cannot provide a meaningful measure of an organisation's work. Even goal-setting is problematic. In 2007, START recruited two new trustees who had not been part of the original steering group and neither of their backgrounds was in social care. An illuminating consequence of this extension of perspectives was the production of a business plan for the organisation. The document contained the conventional sections of mission and objectives, a brief history, the financial situation, staff structure and a strategic plan. Opportunities and risks were catalogued and the future anticipated. However, the exercise was never repeated in that format because of the impossibility of predicting *any* element with any degree of confidence:

- People seeking support can come from anywhere in the world where there is conflict, and each person's situation is unique.
- Constant changes of law and policy, dispersal and housing availability, mean that the flow of referrals to START, always erratic, can stop altogether if no one is granted leave to remain, or rise exponentially as happened when the Home Office implemented the Case Resolution Scheme (GOV.UK, 2010) for people who had been waiting for a decision on their claim for asylum, some for many years.
- Staff resources are similarly unpredictable as students are the main workforce and the timing, length and part- or full-time nature of their placements are dictated by their academic institution.
- In common with other charities, START's funding sources are also unpredictable – some contracts depending on hours worked or numbers of individuals, others requiring specific project activities. The lead-in time for applications can be anything between two weeks and nine months, depending on the source.
- Public attitudes to refugees are in flux as politicians use immigration control as a means of gaining electoral support, while the media conflates the labels 'asylum seeker', 'refugee', 'migrant worker' and 'terrorist'.

In these circumstances, a conventional business plan is impractical – an attempt to give an impression of control where there is only unpredictability and complexity. At the time, it felt like a paper exercise that consumed important resources. It was more accurate in its representation of history rather than a plan for the future based on realistic projections of workflow and funding.

It is important to be honest in recognising what we have control over and ensuring it is the best it can be, while staying with the uncertainty embedded in what is beyond our control. We have relied on the strengths approach as an enduring core value to inform each decision and process, feeling our way 'in the dark' and staying open to surprise, discovery, learning and change at every level of the organisation. The flow of both new refugees and students also ensures constant questioning of the organisation as well as reasserting the integrity of the strengths approach in responding to the needs of both groups.

Key principles that enable an organisation to meet standards of public scrutiny and flourish in response to local needs and potential are embedded in Simon Western's careful study of leadership in the Quakers. He offers valuable insights about three principles of practice that accord with the strengths approach. These are:

- Solidarity, meaning we stand as equals not in hierarchical relationships.
- Mutuality which he describes as a 'non-transactional relationship' in which we care for each other and the planet.
- Engagement in that we accept our responsibility to care and act. (Western, 2019: 282)

In adopting these principles, we fully recognise the challenge in demanding such a deep level of accountability at the same time as sharing responsibility for the resilience and longevity of the organisation with everyone involved. In this case, individual responsibility is not reduced through being shared with others. Rather, each person feels 100 per cent responsible for the success of the work and commits themselves to it accordingly. This is true across the spectrum from trustee to volunteer.

At START we have been sensitive to tensions that can arise between employees and trustees when their respective functions are not fully understood or agreed upon. The temptation to intervene operationally too much – or too little – is a challenge for trustees in any situation, particularly in a young organisation keen to make progress where everyone is forming new relationships. Over time, we have developed structures such as:

- a Scheme of Delegation that articulates the processes needed for all decisions and who can make them;
- a structure of supervision at all levels of the organisation to ensure people feel supported in making decisions, where they can review and learn from them; and
- an openness and accessibility between everyone involved.

Trustees are encouraged to participate in community activities – cooking and clearing up alongside refugees and students, for example, where spontaneous conversations can take place. Such is the informality in these relationships that sometimes a new student or volunteer even tells the founder about the organisation and how it came about, without realising who she is! Rather than correcting the account she celebrates the ownership that people feel. Mutual respect and trust are at the core of these processes.

We have learned from each other and from examples like that cited by Atul Gawande (2010) of the different responses to the disaster in New Orleans following Hurricane Katrina. In this instance, the government responded to the crisis as a threat, behaving defensively and seeking to control people – with disastrous results. The retail outlet Walmart, in contrast, encouraged local managers to use their initiative to provide essentials for people affected by the floods. In the same way, trustees interpret their role as enabling those closest to the work to be able to respond to the unexpected with speed and confidence.

Management and leadership

Embedding mutuality and non-hierarchical relationships throughout an organisation can be challenging. In the early days, START was referred to dismissively by people in the city as 'Avril's baby', a common description of a project or enterprise that is seen to depend on the founder or one person. There is a danger in any social innovation that the organisation itself never separates from the charismatic leader who initiated it. In Kids Company, we have seen the devastating consequences of a national organisation with an annual income of more than £20 million that was suddenly forced to close. The organisation was almost 20 years old, employed more than 600 people in three cities and provided services to 36,000 young people, yet it was declared insolvent and placed into administration almost overnight in 2015. The government was a significant funder and had commissioned an investigation in 2014 regarding financial probity. The subsequent report recommended some financial system improvements but was generally positive (Littlejohn, 2014). The founder and chief executive officer (CEO), Camila Batmanghelidjh, was strongly identified with the charity and, in turn, the charity was recognised through that charismatic and influential person. The high level of cash flow and a lack of reserves rendered the organisation vulnerable to the catastrophic consequences of a loss of public confidence (National Audit Office, 2015). As a result, the services closed without warning, staff have waited years for a (reduced) redundancy payment and all the trustees were initially disqualified from acting as company directors for the statutory period (GOV.UK, 2017). A case under the Company Directors Disqualification Act 1986, brought against the trustees and CEO by the official receiver was not found (Judiciary UK, 2021). Nevertheless, however history judges the cause or responsibility for this devastating outcome, it does highlight the potential fragility of charismatic leadership.

An organisation characterised by a strengths approach recognises and celebrates, but also channels the passion and charisma of the social entrepreneur. It incorporates the equally important contributions of others through the kinds of relationships that are non-transactional, focused on the benefits to people and planet. In this way, leadership becomes an activity rather than a role and its purpose is to enable everyone to give of their best.

In common with all relationships, that between governance and management is dynamic. As circumstances change and understanding develops, so the way those responsibilities are managed must be open to critical review and change. Joint strategy days provide opportunities to review changes in practice and affirm specific areas of responsibility to avoid drift and duplication. A strengths approach is fundamental to maintaining the entitlement of everyone to contribute to the healthy growth and development of the organisation.

Co-management to support non-hierarchical structures

Apart from a brief period, co-management has remained the principal model for START. At the time of writing, START is managed by two co-managers of equal status who share the responsibility for all:

- day-to-day management;
- staff and student supervision (both direct and indirectly since all team members work with students);
- financial accounting;
- policy compliance;
- recording; and
- contract compliance.

The Scheme of Delegation sets out clearly when decisions must be referred to trustees although, in practice, most decisions have already been discussed informally. The co-managers also take the lead in strategic planning, both short and longer term, gathering information about what is happening from refugees, volunteers, students, staff and partner agencies, while exploring ways forward that accord with the organisation's values, and responding to financial or resource challenges.

The pervasive culture is one of mutual respect, exploration and consensus-building. The organisational structure is kept as flat as possible without any abdication of responsibility. The model of co-management has a number of advantages that reinforce the strengths approach:

- Any changes – whether macro, meso or micro – are seen from more than one perspective. Responses are considered for their short- and longer-term impact.
- There is a higher level of trust and openness to differing views which encourages wider sharing of information and ideas. The more people that are involved in problem-solving, the more the resources that are available.
- External agencies or individuals may put pressure on an individual manager to make a decision quickly. Having to refer back to another person at all times gives a breathing space and allows time for wider consultation if necessary. It allows managers a distance from the politics and dynamics of local networks.
- The different areas of expertise are recognised equally in that administration, knowledge of refugee law and policy, techniques of teaching students in practice and inter-agency liaison, for example, are not placed in a hierarchy of importance.

Barbara Harrell-Bond, founder of the internationally renowned Refugee Studies Centre in Oxford University, undertook a key piece of research regarding provision for Ugandan refugees in the Yei River District in 1986. She made the following points about organisations which encapsulate our reflections about START's approach to management:

> There are three major critical points that emerge … The first is that assistance programmes cannot be implemented effectively by agencies that are hierarchical and bureaucratic. Second, assistance plans cannot be managed by officials, whether outsiders or hosts, who are unwilling to engage in discourse with the people whom they aim to assist. And the third critical point that emerges quite clearly is that while assistance plans, projects and programmes cannot be 'rule-bound' because they must be flexible, that nevertheless, *rule-making* will be an essential part of the assistance. (1986: 331, emphasis in original)

Supervision

Communication is key to flexible, responsive and responsible organisations. Although informal communication is facilitated by open plan offices and regular meetings, a culture in which every individual has planned opportunities to share ideas, challenges, needs and aspirations is fundamental to maintaining engagement. The co-managers use regular team away-days to discuss and resolve practical challenges, alongside scheduled supervision sessions with each team member. They also attend the trustee meetings every six weeks and have scheduled supervision themselves provided by the chair and another trustee – a model of co-management supervision and support that reduces the risk of subjectivity and bias. Reflective, strengths–oriented supervision has been recognised as perhaps the greatest contribution the profession of social work has made to human services (Davys and Beddoe, 2021). It is a requirement of professional education that students receive supervision while on placement, not least to learn how to use and value it. Supervision that is regular, consistent and high in quality is regarded as a key component of practice: it is its life-blood. Given the complexity of the work and decision-making at every level it must be available to all employees (Morrison and Wonnacott, 2010). In the context of sizeable workloads, START's co-managers prioritise regular supervision for the staff currently employed, both individually and as a group. The functions of supervision are well documented but briefly comprise accountability, discussion, knowledge exchange and exploration of practice, theorising, critical reflection, concern for wellbeing and personal development.

START consistently uses exchange models of supervision that favour co-production and attention to power relations. All forms of supervision are minuted and copies made available to participants. As a community of practice START holds an extensive knowledge and understanding of reflective supervision, underpinned by the theoretical frameworks of writers such as Donald Schon, Alfred Kadushin and Lawrence Shulman. Close collaboration with universities that accompanies practice learning ensures that knowledge and research are maintained and updated. The tenets of strengths-based supervision set out by Davys and Beddoe (2021: 44) are mirrored in START's approach.

Technological platforms

Recognising the dangers inherent in such non-hierarchical dynamic arrangements, a strength of public accountability processes is that they impose a public-facing formal reporting structure. Earlier caveats notwithstanding, a significant aspect of firmly establishing START as a sustainable, self-sufficient and accountable organisation has been to fully acknowledge the importance of monitoring and evaluation in order to comply with funder expectations. Key performance indicators are embedded in monitoring feedback, narratives and the quality of relationships, but targets of service provision and student placement completion are measured using information technology to manage the relevant processes.

In our organisation we have resisted the anxiety-management responses evident throughout NPM. Simply complying with cultural norms is likely to result in unintentional collusion with the neoliberal project. Trustees and managers, those responsible for the health and resilience of an organisation, must be as alert to both risks and potential as those who deliver services.

The use of technology is a significant factor in NPM's processes. As technology assumes greater prominence in all aspects of life, it is important to recognise the risks it poses to the management and governance of an organisation committed to social justice. In accordance with the expectations of funding bodies, we have accepted the necessity of adopting computerised record systems, but not uncritically. In 2017, START was developing an electronic platform and, at the same time, having one imposed on it by a contract partnership. In order to do this work in a way that was critically reflective, internal evaluative research was undertaken with staff and trustees to learn from the diverse reactions to its implementation. Interviews were recorded and transcribed, and themes identified through co-production. Electronic platforms are now universal and a sign that organisations are keeping up in the digital age. Although presented as 'a good thing', the introduction of Universal Credit in the UK revealed that they do not always fulfil their promise and can significantly reduce people's access to social justice (National Audit Office, 2018). The damage they can do to organisations and to individuals is considerable.

Electronic record systems are generally referred to by the acronym CRM. In NGOs the term CRM is often used to refer to computerised record management systems but it actually stands for Customer Relationship Management. It originated as a system or strategy for managing client interactions, dealing with future and current customers, optimising and systematising relationships in order to increase sales and brand loyalty. Most people will be familiar with the issuing of store cards that enabled retailers to collect data about consumer preferences and habits, while encouraging consumer loyalty through discounts or points saving. It is interesting to note that the customer relationship being managed is with the shopper. This is a financial model that does not transfer easily into the care sector where the source of finance is different from the person accessing the service.

An uncritical adoption of such tools or techniques can have seriously corrosive consequences on the relationship between worker and service user. This is illustrated very clearly in work undertaken in Australia to assess the impact of a computerised system designed to measure outcomes in practice.

Keevers et al (2012) undertook a three-year Participatory Action Research project with a locally based community organisation which adopted an electronic platform. Their paper rigorously records the processes by which the relational aspects of practice are rendered invisible. They show that attention moves from what goes on between people to what services are provided by the organisation. They reveal that activities that increase belonging and reciprocity become less visible. The particular platform studied was Research-Based Accountability (RBA) (Friedman, 2005). Presented as a positive tool to support organisations in becoming more efficient in achieving outcomes, RBA is derived from protocols of financial accountability. In Australia and New Zealand it is promoted as a means to strengthen government's capacity to manage service provision across the purchaser–provider divide, to ensure the efficiency and effectiveness of government spending, and to increase accountability and transparency of public and community sector organisations (Keevers et al, 2012: 5). In short, it is a tool of NPM, an aspect of which is to erode the richness of language. In social work practice, process is understood as reflection on the components of interaction such as relationships, the 'journey' in social casework and the *how* of interventions. When NPM intervenes, process takes on a new meaning, that of an uncritical adherence to bureaucratic procedures. As Lyn Keevers et al observe, it is the shift of focus 'from matters of practices, doings and action, to matters of the correspondence between "results" and "reality"' (Keevers et al, 2012: 37). Conventional forms of computer-based monitoring and evaluation can remove human practices that are the lifeblood of locally-based community organisations.

There are many reasons why organisations adopt CRMs. In our own organisation respondents cited:

- efficiency;
- data management and protection;
- better monitoring;
- easier navigation to find information and pull off reports;
- organisational resilience;
- demonstrating impact;
- greater accountability and transparency;
- greater responsiveness to change initiated by funders; and
- better support to clients.

However, we should remember the commercial origins of such platforms, their deep roots in the neoliberal project (Chen and Popovich, 2003), and proceed with extreme caution. Canaries were taken into mines to alert the miners to the otherwise undetectable poisonous gases that would kill them. Here we identify some of the common fallacies that have similarly fatal consequences for social justice practices, illustrated by findings from our own research interviews:

Fallacy 1: Improved goal-setting and planning will result in better services

This statement appears to be indisputable, but it is founded in a positivist view of the world in which activities to promote social justice can be predicted, planned for and managed. However, the desired outcomes for individuals struggling with social injustice are constantly changing. As they reach a particular goal or overcome a specific difficulty, their perspective and identity change and they see their world differently. Good quality practice embraces and, in the case of refugees, encourages this fluidity as aspirations are renewed. However, such practices might only be recorded as free text. *How* things are done is holistic and nuanced, and much harder to record electronically than *what* is done and when:

> 'So, with the [partnership CRM] it's very hard to put in a review because everything is scattered about. If you want to review the work … on the [partnership CRM] it doesn't look like anything. There's a bit there and a bit there and a bit there.'

> 'From watching our partner develop their system we also learnt that failing to review the whole service, and the client journey, and build the CRM around this was a mistake.'

The difficulty of designing a CRM when the needs are not yet known was articulated quite clearly in the data:

> '[T]here might be a whole group of people we are supporting independently, having the same group of issues that if we asked the right questions, we could highlight that and respond in a more constructive way. The modelling is hypothetical. You're designing something without looking at it so what you're going on is what you know.'

Fallacy 2: Collecting data is a neutral activity that simply improves the efficiency of reporting to funders

Reports to funders dictate the data collected in the first place. This, in turn, can dictate the work. Our respondents spoke of the benefits of being made to record specific information:

> 'With a paper system you are solely reliant on the individual recording the information. A CRM can make it mandatory to record certain data.'

Clearly this is beneficial where the information is an accurate reflection of the person's situation, but this is not always the case.

> 'Because the headings on the [CRM] were put there for multiple contracts, it's bonkers. So just headings like income on the [CRM] doesn't mean income. It means the dates benefit started. So if you use it enough I'm sure you get your head round it but it's not called what you'd anticipate it to be called.'

> '[I]t looks like it's already predetermined everything.'

Fallacy 3: Quantitative data is stable and tells a more accurate story than anecdotal evidence or case examples

One of the principal benefits attributed to CRMs is the ease of pulling off reports for funders. A sophisticated platform may be capable of identifying themes and patterns which are useful both to the organisation and their funders:

> '[I]t also will enable us to monitor the delays for Universal Credit, for example ... but the reality of it is, when I've sat down before and tried to get the information off 20 files ... it quite frequently stalls because of the time and effort you have to put into it and you get side-tracked by the actual service you are delivering. I think with the CRM it should be much easier to do that.'

The data collection design needs to anticipate the information that will be needed from it for service monitoring as circumstances change.

> 'It quickly became clear that many off the shelf options were not suitable to our environment of giving advice and supporting service users with very complex issues, as well as recording one-off community activities.'

And this difficulty of identifying relevant questions in advance was highlighted by the fact that funders appeared to ask for data that did not necessarily reflect their aims:

> 'One of their tests is to ask how many people attend four times or more and the dates when they attended. This statistical data bears no relation to their stated aims of knowing that people have extended their social networks. When staff gave the example of bread-making and loom weaving being hugely oversubscribed because of informal networking at a regional event the information was seized upon, but there was no place for it on the platforms for statistical reporting.'

And finally ...

> '[Y]ou must be able to recognise the point at which your work can't be represented through their language. There comes a point where you can't manipulate what you do to fit a funder's ambitions. That's the point at which you don't want their money.'

Our respondents recognised the need to:

> '[D]esign something from a standpoint of understanding the interaction between two people, using that tool to enable you to do that more efficiently, and highlight the change better, or to

celebrate people's success better, to understand the root causes of some disadvantage better.'

Findings

We were clear from our research that it was important not to comply with the neoliberal agenda of 'domesticating' organisations – replacing their flexibility with a predetermined range of service delivery options that can be costed and tracked. As Keevers et al recognise, such a substitution 'aligns with state-government efforts to re-position social justice organizations ... not as locally-based and autonomous but as detached sub-contractors in purchaser/provider relations' (2012: 33). In an environment where the reckoning of algorithms is increasingly trusted in favour of human judgement (Malik, 2020), it is essential that our capacity to make judgements in the light of actual events takes precedence over the predictions of computer modelling on the basis of statistics.

Tomlinson (2018) describes the quality of the relationship we are seeking to preserve as an affective, empathic response to the difficulties people bring, rather than a formulaic cognitive response that inevitably follows a streamlining administrative approach. This fits well with the language of the strengths perspective in relation to organisations, which identifies key attributes, expanded on in the following list as practical strategies to curb the corrosive impact of neoliberalism and NPM. From our research and subsequent experience, we would encourage NGOs and other organisations to accept the necessity for change and to mitigate the negative consequences of tools like CRMs by adopting the following principles of the strengths approach:

1. **Suspend disbelief.** Reactions to change can be strong and emotional, leading to a rejection of the necessity for adaption and an inability to work with the potential it offers.
2. **Critical and protective factors**. Recognise the origins and primary orientation of CRMs as 'customer-facing' and 'funder-facing'. Ensure that the primary entry point is the service user's situation and how the organisation can support their access to social justice.

3. **Empowerment**. The quality of the CRM is crucial to its success – a bespoke system may be more expensive but trying to save money is likely to be a false economy.

4. **Ownership**. Review the service user's 'journey' from the point of referral to the NGO. Work closely with the CRM's commercial developers. Ensure the system is flexible and bespoke for your particular organisation. Involve everyone in the development of the CRM, including service users and students, so that everyone has ownership of it. Make sure they feel that they have control over the CRM rather than it being simply imposed upon them.

5. **Resilience**. Use existing paperwork as a framework for the platform while critiquing its purpose for information-gathering. Make sure that everyone using it is clear about what the CRM should achieve – what data is being collected and why.

6. **Healing and wholeness**. Regard the first version of the new CRM as a developmental stepping-stone, not the finished article. Recognise that any CRM is work-in-progress. Review and change it when it does not sufficiently support the work with service users.

7. **Dialogue and collaboration**. Consider how to manage change and the transition to the new system from paper files. Understand staff emotions such as resistance to the CRM and take staff with you. Remember that older workers may be fearful of changes in technology and support them. Likewise, younger workers may see the CRM as simplifying the activity and may need support to maintain a social justice orientation.

8. **Community**. It is important to revise and review the CRM constantly. Avoid the CRM becoming fixed as a system that is no longer fit for purpose. Make sure that the CRM is flexible and easy to change as the needs of service users and demands from funders change.

Conclusion

People responsible for the governance and management of organisations committed to social justice must remain vigilant to the corrosive consequences of 'business as usual'. As we have shown, even apparently neutral administrative or bureaucratic requirements can significantly affect day-to-day working practices. This critique of uncritical adoption of the tools of NPM is informed by principles of the strengths approach. In an age where personal information has become valuable data it is essential to ensure that people needing help are not data-mined for other purposes. This is particularly true for those without secure citizenship status. Just as in the beginning of START's existence when people held their own records, information about people's lives is theirs and should only be shared when necessary for the work to be effective. The primary relationship is between the service user and organisation where a confidential and creative space can be preserved. Technical sophistication means that the service user no longer physically holds their own records, and that aspects of the work must be reported to funders. The principle however remains the same. The strengths approach provides a reliable mainstay in preserving integrity of purpose.

Using a strengths approach to governance and management encourages and promotes good practice. It assists the organisation to gather the data needed by funders without limiting the work people are able to do. It helps to maintain an openness to social innovation and to learn *with* people receiving services. The approach demands a willingness to share responsibility fully without solely relying on the false security of quality assurance measures to engender 'confidence' in the service. Instead it requires the humility to know that risk cannot be removed, and that people do their best when they are trusted, supported and encouraged. To illustrate, Guy Singh-Watson of Riverford Organic Farmers writes eloquently about his learning as an off-site manager of organic vegetable production for his company in France:

> Managing a business 250 miles away, with only a very limited grasp of a different language, law and culture, has led me to question what effective management is. In the early years I would dash around on the first day of a visit giving instructions: 'water this, plough

that in, get those crop covers off'. During my visit last week, I looked, listened and contemplated my purpose. The less I visit, the better the team seem to do – perhaps because they have space to grow. I am astonished by their appetite for learning and innovation. I used to think that was my job, but now I find investments being evaluated, and new crops, varieties and growing techniques being tried; it's me who's doing the learning. Relationships and roles are fluid, almost anarchic, but decision making is fast and efficient. There is one small office which is usually empty; most decisions are made in the field, over a coffee or a beer at the end of the day. Could it be that the most important part of management is knowing when to get out of the way – and its most common failing the underestimation of people's capability to find fulfilment by managing themselves? (Singh Watson, 2018: 1)

Learning points

- Strategic planning emerges from discussion and consensus-building with people directly engaged in the practice. This recognises local challenges and potential to produce bespoke, not mass-produced, solutions.
- Recognise that, under NPM, hierarchy and bureaucracy are essential and protective features of external control. However, these are not functional internally; they do not replace the constant communication and judgement fostered in open, non-hierarchical structures.
- Best practice is the result of consensus built through shared responsibility.
- Decisions about purpose and practice should always be value-driven, rather than expedient.
- Leadership is not about convincing people you are right. It is recognising your limitations and listening to everyone.
- No matter the level of experience and seniority, all benefit from structured supervision to promote critical reflection, creativity and growth.

- Be honest in recognising what you have control over while staying with the uncertainty embedded in what is beyond your control. Stay open to surprise, discovery, learning and change at every level of the organisation.

5

A strengths approach
to funding an NGO

> Intra-dependence, mutuality, and enriched co-existence
> are hallmarks of both natural and social systems deemed
> resilient and thriving.
>
> Whiteford (2016: 26)

This chapter examines the nature of the relationship between
NGOs and the sources of their funding. We reflect on the
fact that money can have both positive and negative impact
and explore some of the possibilities for mitigating its risks.
The ways in which NGOs are funded are highly contextual –
manifestations of the time and place in which the NGO operates.
There are, however, some enduring and transferable truths about
how a strengths approach can influence the health and resilience
of any organisation that does not rely on a capitalist model of
income generation and profit.

Neoliberal societies revere money as *the* key resource for an
organisation. Money though, however welcome, always has
consequences, both intended and unintended. In a capitalist
world there is no such thing as 'clean money' and all profit
may be regarded as exploitation of the earth's finite resources,
of people's labour or both. Money does not come without
expectation – whether it is to show the donor in a good light
or in some other transactional relationship. Inevitably, funding
is accompanied by requirements for outputs and outcomes as
if community action for social change is nothing more than a
commercial transaction. But the resources of any organisation
are much more than money. A strengths approach recognises

the environmental potential and the capabilities of service users, communities, students and their labour, alongside unexpected alliances. We also know that, without adequate funding to maintain a supportive structure, access to those resources may be lost.

While financial sufficiency is important for an NGO's continuation, it would be a huge mistake to regard it as the most important element of its resourcing. For money to become its central concern is to remove the core and leave the work without a heart. We fully acknowledge that money matters; Chapter 3 describes the impact of both the sudden increase and then the loss of funding on the organisation's development. Nevertheless, money is the oil – not the machine itself.

The welfare state established by the UK government in 1948 sought to address the five evils of poverty, ignorance, sickness, homelessness and idleness. National assistance, free compulsory education, a national health service, social housing and employment offices were paid for through taxation – a substantial long-term investment in the wellbeing and happiness of the population and, accordingly, the status of the nation. Welfarism was understood to be a reasonable function of government. Regrettably, ill-fitting business models have eroded all of these services through budget cuts, demand for efficiency savings and privatisation (Armstrong, 2017). Social problems are increasing targeted by short-term funding initiatives like the Troubled Families programme, for example, designed to deal with the symptoms of social inequality rather than the causes (Sayer, 2016). The result of this is a fixation on short-term solutions to some of the most enduring problems while denying their history and reality. It is in spite of the positive impact of schemes such as gang intervention (Craston et al, 2020; MVP, 2020) which address root causes. This is like building a new flood defence while continuing to invest in fossil fuel extraction and promoting international travel. A strengths approach, in contrast, fosters creativity, social innovation and prevents complacency because a key feature is understanding fully the connections and complexity of any situation. Even tried and tested responses have to be revisited and made relevant to prevailing conditions. This is why we are not advocating a return to some misremembered perfect time in the past. Rather, we are pointing to the mistake of seeing everything in financial terms and in calculating short-term costs and benefits. 'When the last tree is cut down, the last fish eaten, and the last stream poisoned, you will realize that you cannot eat money' (Wasserman, 1983: 277).

NGOs are part of the fabric of most societies. They are commonly developed to fill gaps left by state and commercial services. Many have charitable status of some kind and a clearly stated aim. Traditionally in the global north, the beneficiaries of a charity are seen as 'needy' and deserving of support by the more fortunate. This moral transaction can be observed in many fundraising campaigns in which case examples of individuals in difficulty are presented as a way for people to be assured that their money is going to a 'good cause'. These campaigns also show the difference the charity's intervention has made to that person's life to encourage people to give generously and to feel they are making a difference. Such campaigns can be very powerful in shaping public opinion, epitomised by the Children in Need campaign portraying Africa populated by starving people and abused children as helpless victims (O'Connor, 2020). In this transaction, beneficiaries are expected both to improve their situation and to feel grateful to the donor. It is a deficit model; the beneficiaries are given help in a philanthropic or altruistic way that belies their agency and the interdependence of the social systems in which we all operate. In much the same way as the needy beneficiary is expected to be grateful for the support given, so many NGOs are seen as benefiting from the financial support they are given for which they should be grateful. In this culture, an application for funding becomes a version of the 'begging letter' sent by someone in dire straits to a rich relative.

Funding for NGOs can be both restrictive and competitive. Organisations are expected to work collaboratively to the benefit of their beneficiaries while fiercely competing for the limited funding. This can generate competition and mistrust among rival NGOs in the same field who should be working together. Amalgamation of smaller charities into a network or larger unit could be seen as the answer. However, as we have argued in Chapter 3, locally based activist organisations can be responsive to local conditions in ways that a larger, centrally controlled one cannot. In this neoliberal world, NGOs can find themselves lurching from one financial crisis to another, arguing that they must be funded because of a moral obligation and threat of public outrage if people are abandoned. As public attitudes to certain groups harden, however, this becomes more and more difficult.

In contrast, under a strengths approach, an organisation resists presenting its work as simply charitable giving or its beneficiaries as victims. Instead, the NGO understands that it is part of a complex system in which all parties are both giving and receiving – to mutual benefit. Funders, in turn, need to have confidence that the money they administer will be used for the purposes set out by their organisation, in accordance with the wishes of the original benefactors, and not squandered. Moreover, a strengths approach acknowledges the depth of the challenge or difficulty people are facing without pathologising them. People are resourceful; their capacity and competence are harnessed and they will be part of the solution provided they are fully engaged as partners. So too, are NGOs equal players in the social systems that enable resources to be used more effectively to benefit everyone. Presenting the organisation as a capable collaborator is more likely to ensure longevity than any number of sob stories!

Here we chart the 20-year history of funding that has enabled START to achieve its aims through changes in public attitudes and financial systems. Trends in culture and policy that influence funding streams are examined. We review the transition from sizeable grants and local authority service level agreements to competitive tendering, crowd-funding and working alongside charitable foundations to secure START's continuation. The pros and cons of engaging with professional fundraisers are explored, together with the importance of seeking multiple funders to maintain the organisation's integrity. We reflect on the paradox that, while social problems are entrenched and enduring, funding now is always short-term. (A five-year period for a grant is seen as a long time and amounts usually taper off over that period, as though solutions should have emerged

Figure 5.1: Development phases

and funding is no longer needed.) Most significantly, features of the strengths approach are identified that have enabled the organisation to thrive and develop resilience throughout this time.

The structure of this account is chronological, reflecting the natural evolution of an NGO from initial concept to mature organisation as shown in Figure 5.1:

• From 2001 to 2004 START's **early years** were characterised by minimal finances with in-kind support from larger organisations like the university, and local authority in the form of small, specifically targeted grants.
• From 2004 to 2007 **becoming legitimate** was a period of regularising the organisation and responding to political and cultural agendas.
• The period from 2007 to 2011 was one of **surviving change**. In Chapter 3 the process of cutting staff at this time is described specifically in relation to the strengths approach and how positive growth can come from serious difficulties. The emphasis in this chapter is on the financial aspects.
• From 2011 to 2020 the theme has been one of **diversification and expertise**.

Each of these phases is reviewed within the social, political and cultural agendas of their time and an account given of the origins, purpose and value of the income generated. The intention here is to support people in this field to take a critical view of how funding works and to negotiate its constant changes constructively. By taking such a critically conscious approach, we hope to stay ready to draw in sufficient finances to continue to meet the needs of refugees and students while maintaining philosophical integrity as long as we can usefully do so.

The early years: 2001–4

When we arranged for students to undertake their professional placements by working with refugees who had been dispersed to Plymouth, we had no expectation of raising money or having to manage it. The students could not be accommodated in an existing agency and the initial provisions were all 'in kind'. As outlined in Chapter 7, the practice educator organised an 'office' in her home together with a laptop computer borrowed from her employer. Stationery, postal and telephone services and internet access were provided by the university. Students could claim travel expenses out of the daily placement fees available for all social work placements. When the local authority allocated the students a rent-free office, a small grant from the Home Office paid for a telephone answering machine with fax and basic 'pay as you go' mobiles for the students. By the academic year 2002/3, the students themselves were looking for funding to continue the service through the summer and to fund community activities such as START's Cultural Kitchen. By September 2004, the steering group had raised £28,000 from national and local government, charitable grants and income generation. (Sources included Devon Community Chest, the Scarman Trust, a local Primary Care Trust, student fees and Cornwall County Council.) The steering group opened a bank account and a group member acted as treasurer.

Encouraged by our success in attracting funds, at the beginning of 2004, we made an application to the UK's Big Lottery for funding to recruit to three posts, using the support of Plymouth Community Partnerships, a body funded by the city council to enable the development and governance of NGOs. As we waited for a decision about the Big Lottery, we continued to look for funding. A chance discussion about a policy change alerted us to the central government-funded 'Supporting People' programme. This was a ring-fenced budget to enable people with vulnerabilities to maintain housing tenancies. It aimed to support older people, people with learning disabilities and people with severe and enduring mental health difficulties, among others. For the first time in the UK, refugees were identified as a group entitled to receive help through this programme (Jarrett, 2012). Seizing the opportunity, we made a proposal to the scheme's new contract manager for START to deliver the service, as support with housing was already a substantial area of student activity when people were given leave to remain. The person appointed to set up this new service had previously worked with Avril and recognised the benefit of having an existing service to consider in the commissioning process. Meetings were set up with the contract managers to enable START to bid for the contract.

Becoming legitimate: 2004–7

In the summer of 2004, START was awarded £65,000 per year for three years by the Big Lottery. It also secured a contract to deliver the Refugee Housing Support Service (RHSS) funded centrally by the Supporting People programme and delivered on behalf of Plymouth City Council. The contract value was £163,000 per annum and required START to deliver a total of 800 hours to 100 refugees per month. In addition to the dramatic changes and activities described in Chapter 3, we note here some of the financial challenges to which we had to respond. The first was the need to recruit both staff and trustees who could manage these administrative demands. We had been convincing in the lottery bid and contract negotiations that we would be able to deliver on a new and much bigger scale at the same levels of quality and efficiency. We had evidence from the students' work and from academic papers about the organisational model of utilising student placements but no track record of managing this level of money. The Big Lottery worked closely with us over timing for the start of the grant but the Supporting People contract was different. The rules about financial probity for a central government fund administered by the local authority were inflexible. Although we had established a legally constituted charity and company with an experienced treasurer alongside other officers, START had to find an organisation that would act as guarantor before the money awarded could be released. Fortunately, a senior member of the university executive was aware of START's work and fully supported it, signing the necessary papers to underwrite the contract if START failed to deliver.

The year 2004 was a time of substantial political change when New Labour was preoccupied with social engineering. Their emphasis was on social integration (Ager and Strang, 2004). Charities were a significant player in New Labour's welfare provision and controlled through regulation. As noted, however, a further paradox was that they were expected to work alongside each other in a collaborative way when funding and the processes to secure it are competitive. After the first year of delivering the RHSS, the commissioners put the contract out to tender indicating that partnership bids would be more likely to succeed. Collaboration was developed with Plymouth Access To Housing (PATH) whose roles with the homeless population and deposit guarantee scheme meant there were already good working relationships with START. In retaining the role of contract lead, START sought to protect its values and organisational integrity. The partnership bid was successful but it should be recognised here that the work funded through the contract was very restrictive. Only activity that could be directly associated with Supporting People's construction of maintaining housing tenancies could be funded. Working directly with children or young people was outside this category, as was any health or community-related activity. Possibly because it was a central government ring-fenced fund administered by the local authority, council officials policed it very diligently and questioned many of START's activities that fell outside their provision. A combination of funders was therefore essential to maintain a holistic and needs-led service and the Big Lottery outcomes were complementary to those of RHSS. We fully understood the expectation that START would identify a portion of its activities as belonging to a particular funder as 'their project'. Other organisations with which we were familiar recruited to a project, delivered it and ended it when the money ran out, leading to issues of staff turnover and mission creep. Staff funded by a particular project in this way left the service when it finished despite the relationships they forged with service users. In contrast, START was committed to delivering an ongoing, holistic, needs-led service, driven by service users and students rather than by funders. This principle is explored in more detail in Chapter 4, but here it should be registered that each funder wanted to see START's core work as their own and had to be reminded of the written agreements that articulated their claim. Activities and outcomes not commissioned by a particular funder could be appreciated as 'value addition' or 'soft outcomes', but it was essential that the organisation maintained high quality information-gathering systems and could report to funders with accuracy and integrity.

In 2005–6, the success of START attracted other funding including awards from Children in Need, Sport Relief, Local Network Funding and European funding for employment support to a total annual income of £321,000. It was an administrative challenge to ensure that reporting extracted the appropriate information for each funder without double-counting and without segregating the activities as separate projects in practice.

In anticipation of the end of the Big Lottery grant in 2007, the organisation submitted 29 funding bids but without success. In part, this was due to a lack of expertise and familiarity with the funding environment. More significantly, the public perception of START's work had changed. Refugees were no longer seen as a group Britain was proud to help. Culturally, the public narrative had changed from welcome and integration to antagonism towards immigration in general (Humphries and Hayes, 2004; Cohen, 2006) and we were unable to convince charitable trusts to replace the Big Lottery.

Surviving change: 2007–11

As a painful consequence of losing Big Lottery funding, the annual income was cut by £100,000 and the staff team reduced to three full-time employees who shared management responsibility equally. The proportion of students to staff rose significantly as their labour was vital in meeting START's contractual obligations. Over this period, START was able to attract some funding such as the Migrant Impact Fund and a service-level agreement with the local authority, but these were all central or local government monies and effectively pushed START towards control by state agendas. For example, a successful application to the city's 'Mental Health and Wellbeing – Small Grants Fund' came with the proviso that 'the grant cannot be used to fund services for asylum seekers or people under 18' despite the fact that START works with families. Like the RHSS, this money had to be used in specified ways. It was only by developing sophisticated administrative systems that we were able to use the money for core work in 'open access' services.

A paper published by the Centre for Policy Studies entitled 'Charity: The spectre of over-regulation and state dependency' (Smith and Whittington, 2006) captured the phenomenon we were experiencing. These authors issued a general warning about the potential circumscribing of charities' activities through increased regulation and the contract culture. Their paper warned of the loss of creative spirit and altruistic ambitions of independent charities if the state takes control of all services through contract compliance. In essence, the closer you are to government funding the more likely you are to be forced into working in a way you do not want to. Through Bill Jordan's (2012) critique of contract culture we were alert to the potential dangers of being controlled in this way.

An example of this came in 2008 when START's income was at its lowest and more than 80 per cent of it came from various government sources. The Immigration Service had acknowledged that there were many people with papers lost or mislaid who were waiting for a decision on their asylum claim, sometimes for years, while more recent applications were being processed much more quickly. As part of restructuring to the New Asylum Model (NAM), the Home Office set up the Case Resolution Directorate (GOV.UK, 2010) to deal with the backlog of work either to grant people leave to remain or arrange for deportation. As this was a one-off event to clear the system of the mess left by the previous immigration service (National Asylum Support Service or NASS), it became known as 'Legacy'. It was expected that most of these 'Legacy' families would be allowed to stay. This meant that the local authority could face a sudden increase in referrals as up to 38 families in Plymouth who had been waiting for a decision for years could suddenly be granted leave to remain and have 28 days in which to find accommodation. The RHSS contract was already fully delivered with the existing families and this unexpected spike in numbers was not resourced. Likewise, it would place an enormous pressure on the local authority's housing department and no additional central government funds were forthcoming to meet the need. The housing department identified £25,000 which it offered to START as an RHSS contract variation to acknowledge the additional work. Although pleased to be offered this extra funding, START recognised the danger of being seen to underperform on the main contract if the service was of a lower standard. We also recognised the problem of undermining the contract value if we agreed to provide a similar service for much less income. An important aspect of this period was that we were in danger of simply becoming a government outpost and being made to do more for less. We therefore wrote the following message to the council:

> Regarding the agreed contract variation for £25,000 for 'legacy family' work: as you will be aware, the current RHSS contract is for a total of 70 'cases' over a year and 35 at any time. If the total number of 'legacy' families is 38, a comparable service would cost in excess of £70,000 as it would increase the RHSS work by more than 50%.
>
> As we know that the funding is limited, we have specified a minimum service which will allow for flexibility in response and will support efficient inter-agency working. If you are in agreement with this proposal we would ask that you:
>
> • confirm this in writing so that we can recruit without delay
> • inform all relevant agencies in the city that this service has been initiated enclosing a service description which we will produce.

> We are acutely aware of the need to limit
> expectations so that START and RHSS are not
> seen as failing to provide a service. Your clarity of
> communication about this service is also important
> as this is a sensitive time. We aim to avoid disrupting
> the trust between agencies in the city who are
> increasingly working together. (11 January 2008)

While accepting the reality that the work needed to be covered and that additional funds were not available, START took a position as equal partner in the negotiation, setting out terms for undertaking the contract and acting on the knowledge and experience of the local situation. This included taking account of relationships with other providers who could feel jealous of the organisation being chosen to do the work and, at the same time, ready to be critical of any failure to deliver. On this occasion, START produced a separate service description and appointed a former student to undertake an initial assessment of the needs of each family. The aim was to provide a consistent 'first response' and referral to other agencies. Without this careful and publicly communicated service description, the additional work could have damaged START's reputation and undermined the RHSS contract value. It was essential to re-contract this element of the work in a public way. START had to be nimble-footed, taking the initiative to negotiate what was possible for that amount of money, not least to save its reputation and to protect the value of the original contract, otherwise the argument might have gone: 'If you can do that for that much in the new contract, why are we paying you so much in the old one?' As it was, the Supporting People ring-fenced budget was reduced over time. There was a consistent expectation that costs would be reduced, and the service delivered 'more efficiently'. A change of government in 2010 confirmed the failure of New Labour's 'Third Way', heralding an era of increasing cuts and austerity.

Diversification and expertise: 2011–20

As a ten-year-old charity, we recognised the dangers of contract compliance in threatening to remove the freedom to respond quickly and imaginatively to the changing needs of people without a voice. Many charities find themselves becoming apolitical: what Paolo Freire (1970) refers to as 'domestication'. START, however, is an organisation committed to raising student consciousness of social injustice and how to respond to it. No matter how challenging, we were determined to maintain our commitment and maximise the potential for transformative practice.

We reflected on the difficulty of attracting charitable income and recognised the way in which the public perception of charities has undergone various metamorphoses. With its origins in notions of rich people giving money to poor people, there remains a 'common sense' assumption that money donated should go straight to those we are seeking to help, while administrative costs are seen as diverting funds from beneficiaries. However, even if we accept the spurious notion of 'deserving and undeserving' poor, then someone has to make that judgement and ensure the money is used correctly. Where a charity employs a strengths approach and is determined to act in ways that encourage people's skills, self-esteem and capacity, instead of undermining them with gifts that create dependency, then clearly expertise is required. The NGO sector has become a valid alternative destination for people seeking a career and often the major expenditure of a charity is on staff. Negative publicity about some of the bigger charities' spending on consultants and offering large salaries in order to attract the best people as CEOs has also affected the public perception of charities as lacking integrity, something that has been further compounded by the exploitative behaviour of senior charity personnel in areas of high vulnerability. All of these factors have had a negative influence on whether people see charitable giving as a normal everyday activity. In the context of austerity, in-work poverty and the reduction of living standards for the majority, many charities struggle to maintain a presence.

Every funding application is different and there is a tension between the need for the writer to be embedded in the day-to-day work of the organisation and their knowledge of the world of charitable trusts and foundations. Large national and international charities have whole departments whose principal work is to bring income to the organisation using lotteries, appeals, charity shops and cold-calling (known as 'chugging') to sign up regular donors. We considered different models of managing this interface as a small charity, discussing the relative risks and merits of doing it ourselves at one end of the scale and employing a full-time fundraiser at the other. In 2013 we agreed to apply to the Big Lottery for a second grant and knew we did not have the expertise to maximise our chances of success. We had been told about a local partnership who provide fundraising support commercially and decided to make a single payment to them to prepare our Stage 1 bid. When this was successful, we felt justified in paying them a fee to help us with the Stage 2 bid and were awarded £86,000 per year for five years. This relatively small investment formed the basis of a long-term relationship between START and the partnership (known as Swift Fundraising Limited) that has grown slowly and with substantial mutual benefit. These two local consultants were impressed by the integrity of START's vision, its unusual model and the fact that it actually 'does what it says it does'. They had worked with organisations before whose marketing and rhetoric did not accurately match the reality of the organisation's practice and were delighted to be able to represent START. They offered a contract to seek and apply for funding on our behalf and in line with our activities on a 'no win, no fee' basis. This relationship with professional fundraisers, whose focus is always on the sources of funding, continued on the basis that they received 15 per cent of all funds awarded, until it was converted to a six-monthly retainer contract where they are paid for one or two days per month. Their skill and connections in the world of trusts and other donors has enabled START to achieve a level of financial stability that could, but must not, encourage complacency.

To illustrate START's success, the following information was shared at a trustee strategy day in the form of a quiz and was a surprise to even the most engaged member of the board: in the period from 31 August 2012 (where its income was £195,000) to 31 March 2016, START's income increased by 68 per cent. According to the Directory of Social Change, grants from public bodies nationally declined from £6 billion in 2003 to £2.2 billion in 2013 – a 63 per cent decline.

Careful consideration has been given to the need to plan ahead and secure the organisation financially. A 'reserves policy' has been approved that means the charity aims to have a minimum of six months' running costs in reserve at all times plus the additional costs of closure (redundancy payments, etc). This ensures that START would not be in the same shocking sudden closure position as Kids Company. It is significant that, although the lead-in time for many grants is around six months, a charity that has more than nine months reserves is not seen by charitable foundations as needing funds and one that has less than three months, is too insecure to fund. This is a precarious cliff-edge to negotiate.

We have witnessed the way in which possibilities are influenced by fashions, in particular how funding is responsive to societal changes. We have encountered grants, service level agreements, tendering, contracts and sub-contracts, alliance funding, loans, crowd-funding, income generation, and most recently, competitive prizes. These last few avenues can be understood as a manifestation of the current celebrity culture, exemplified by the BBC programme *Dragon's Den* in which ordinary people are paraded as examples of excellence to an aspirational generation. Applied to the NGO field, this can be seen as an attempt to find examples of good practice that can then be replicated by others. The outstanding projects identified may be compared with existing state welfare provision to show the inadequacies in a service seriously eroded and under-funded by government. This might, in turn, contribute to the privatisation of even more of the welfare state as the success of small-scale initiatives are used in evidence that state services are a poor use of money – wrongly in our view.

In contrast to this short-termism, as ways of seeking funding have diversified, we have recognised the increasing importance of relationships, networking and connection in which the alignment of values and mission is more likely to lead to success than meeting a set of criteria on an anonymous form. This was particularly affirmed by a funder whose offer letter said:

> The trustees were struck by the simplicity of the solutions to the problems created by the support gap for people transitioning from asylum seeker to refugee status that the founders of Students and Refugees

Together came up with. The idea of bringing together the two transient communities of students and refugees is a really clever one where both groups can benefit in multiple ways, learning from each other and building confidence as they exchange skills and the relationship develops. The trustees commented how great it must feel for students to know that they are not only developing the casework skills needed to complete their course but also helping real people find the solutions to the issues facing them.

In a culture where social media networks like Facebook and Instagram provide the illusion of connection with others, the steady development of genuine reciprocal relationships outlined in Chapter 1 (as illustrated by START's work with Swift Fundraising Limited) is more likely to produce results. Swift's understanding of START's history and integrity means they have successfully built longer-term relationships with some charitable foundations, resulting in repeat donations and increasing investment.

Box 5.1 sets out some of the significant factors in START's financial success.

Box 5.1: Significant factors in START's financial success

- **Organisational culture** that espouses a strengths approach and values all contributions offered whatever they are.
- **Values** as a basis for all decision-making ensuring that START does not become a victim of the charity sector contract culture.
- **The student placement model** (set out in Chapter 7) and other non-fiscal resources in the organisation.
- **Preserving a learning environment** with different professional orientations and international students. (The latter are unfamiliar with domestic policy and do not have English as a first language so learn alongside the refugees. They may also bring a much-needed facility with another language.)
- **Welcoming unexpected alliances**: Devon Community Homes residents at Cultural Kitchen; geography and business students;

global health and dental students; creative writing and media studies students; clinical psychology, social archaeology and spatial practice research; Embercombe community; Playback Theatre. (See Chapter 8 for details.)

- **Finding the strengths in other organisations** in order to work with them for the service user's benefit, notably the government-run Job Centre, Plymouth City Council, Home Office, Race Equality Council.
- **A social entrepreneurial approach** that allows opportunities to be realised.
- **Keeping the human** at the centre rather than the money.

Diversification in funding streams

From the very early days, we were conscious that people wanted to categorise START and feel that they understood what it was (Butler, 2005). The danger of being a single-issue organisation, however, is that, although it makes appealing for support more straightforward, it does not reflect the complexity of life or the truth that identity is not fixed (Williams, 1996). This is as true for organisations as it is for individuals and has been an aspect of START's nimble-footed approach to gaining support. An organisation that can describe its activities as refugee integration, social change, professional education, global justice, partnership, research, boundary-crossing, service user-led, employment preparation, building social capital and valuing the environment, for example, is able to position itself to meet the criteria of a wide range of foundations seeking to ensure their money is used effectively. Although social work and occupational therapy have been core to service delivery, no discipline is irrelevant to refugees starting to rebuild their futures from scratch.

Maintaining relationships with contract commissioners is equally important. We frequently encounter potential commissioners querying the precise nature of START's work. This is in spite of numerous documents, contractual agreements, annual reviews, leaflets and a very accessible website and, most recently, a flow-chart showing the relationship between and remit of each organisation in the city with whom START works. These questions are not innocent. They are a precursor to accusations of duplication, inefficiency and waste of resources. There is an assumption that a 'supermarket model' of help (or one-stop shop) is more efficient and more desirable than a range of independents who collaborate and support each other's work – giving individuals a degree of choice in where to get help at any stage of their lives. This fits closely with a culture of amalgamating services to produce economies of scale and consistency. Sadly, we know what results this has had in the health service, for example, with the closure of local hospitals and growth in size of GP health practices, which are now run on a business model. It is increasingly difficult to get an appointment with a GP and the business model of practices means you are unlikely to see one who knows you. In some areas, access is so difficult that increasingly people are consulting their local pharmacist instead. These changes are in spite of the research that shows the health benefits of being seen by a GP who knows you and your family history (Rhodes et al, 2014). Economics and short-term savings triumph over health and long-term benefits. Holding steady to START's principles is not easy in a climate that values financial efficiency and profit above all. However, the strengths approach commits us to arguing for the benefit of a different approach and seeking funding that allows it not to be eroded. A member of the START team said:

> 'My father had a principle and it's one of mine as well. If there's 100 people and 99 are going that way and you think it's this way, so long as you can justify why it's this way, just go that way … even working with funders … if you've done the opposite but we can justify why we did it, so I don't understand the fear. Just tell them. This is the advantage of doing it this way.'

It can be difficult and anxiety-provoking to stand your ground as an organisation, whether this is in relation to government contracts or to other sources of funding. The alternative, however, is to deny the expertise the organisation has developed through learning alongside some of the most disenfranchised people in society. As noted in Chapter 4, if a funder's demands do not fit the organisation, then we should not apply for their money. At the time of writing, START decided not to submit a tender for a new service being commissioned to replace one for which START had the existing contract. The overambitious specification meant it was not deliverable for the organisation without significant contortion. Care was taken to communicate that decision in advance of the deadline and to offer active involvement in the hand-over of work to the new provider. This meant that, when no suitable tenders for the new contract were received, the commissioner came back to START to negotiate a level of service, this time compatible with START's capacity and the service users' needs. Seeking funding needs to be the right thing for the right reason at the right time. Language, and how the work is presented, can be adapted, but only to a point. Not a twist too far!

The process of converting ideas to different narratives that will appeal to funders is complex and time-consuming. It is essential to have good information about all previous applications, what they were for and whether they were successful. Feedback about rejected bids is part of the organisation's accumulated expertise. Whether we are seeking funds from charitable sources or government contracts, it is vital to remember that we are seeking to enter into a mutually beneficial relationship and not one of 'donor and beneficiary'. Even the most philanthropic organisations have targets to meet and reputations to maintain. They need to allocate their funding to organisations that will deliver the outcomes to which they are committed. Looking for enough money is part of the work.

A strengths approach to funding accepts the necessity of this work and how to manage it most effectively. It recognises the environmental conditions prevailing at any particular time and seeks out the convergence of agendas in order to tell stories of possibility, hope and inclusivity.

Learning points

• Reframe competitors or threats as potential resources or allies and work to find points of alignment of purpose.

- Although it is tempting (and normal) to recruit to specific funded projects for clarity of reporting, it is better to invest in complex data management and allow work to be directed by people on the ground.
- The strengths approach is not a 'soft option'. It requires knowledge, openness to learning and long-term commitment.
- Build long-term trusting relationships with funders of every kind.
- Remember that money is the means – not an end in itself.

6

A strengths approach to research

Introduction

Research and practice are inseparable in that each necessarily informs the other. This chapter begins with an exploration of the nature of research and its relationship to practice, illustrated with examples from START. It then focuses specifically on research with refugees, together with the debates and ethical challenges that working with this particular group brings into sharp relief. Undoubtedly these issues are transferable to other groups. Arguably, no one form of research is better than another – or indeed capable of 'telling the truth'. In seeking to 'tell *a* truth' as well as we are able, we acknowledge that all research is itself an intervention. In respect of people who are refugees we have an urgent obligation to ensure that the research process is one that contributes positively to their situations.

A substantial part of this chapter will focus, therefore, on appreciative inquiry as a strengths approach to research. It will introduce the process for those unfamiliar with it and report on work supported by Avril and conducted at START by Kim Embra for her doctoral thesis while studying as a clinical psychology student at Plymouth University.

It concludes with reference to good practice guidance (Temple and Moran, 2011) and the value of a strengths approach lens for judging a research approach.

Research and practice

We cannot do justice to the wealth of scholarship about research that exposes the fallacy of objectivity, the inevitability of context and researcher perspective, and the illusion of binary simplicity (Butler et al, 2007). Traditionally research is judged according to its reliability and validity: features that can be tested by repeating the research in different circumstances and achieving a consistent result. In social sciences (and more mainstream science) these positivist ideas have been challenged and ideas of what constitutes good research extended (May, 1993; Jones, 2012). Jan Fook (2001) argues that there is no one authentic research methodology. She states that all stages of research are complex and interpretive (and therefore biased). These include the selection of the question, methodology and analysis. In her view, authenticity is supported through reflexivity and honesty rather than through a careful adherence to rules. She exposes the inadequacy of binary positions and reflects on the positivist nature of some qualitative research, for example.

Even in the emerging field of practice research, which seeks to relocate research as a discipline within practice, there is a pressure to conform to traditional approaches (Bellinger et al, 2014). Practice research, defined by Beddoe and Harington, is 'inquiring into practice with a view to service improvement' (2012: 87). However, the movement, which has developed significant traction in Nordic countries, interprets 'practice' as research practice as opposed to interventions with service users. It applies conventional measures of reliability and validity (Julkunen, 2011). In a paper exploring the potential for students to contribute to research by theorising about their practice, we state: 'There is an inherent paradox in a movement [practice research] that is open to reflexive disruption and, at the same time, seeks recognition in both academic and practice contexts, reminiscent of the late twentieth century feminist research scholarship' (Bellinger et al, 2014: 61). Writing about our work with one student, we explored the paradigm shift from researchers as experts looking for knowledge to a process in which we co-construct knowledge together.

Shaw, meanwhile, emphasises the importance of social work research being 'distinctively good' (Shaw, 2007: 659). He suggests six benchmarks for assessing this quality in social work research which include 'consistency with broader social work purposes, attention to aspects of the research enterprise that are close to social work, and taking seriously aspects of the research mission that seem on the face of it far from social work' (2007: 659). 'Good' practice pays as much attention to process as outcome in that it values and affirms people's capacity 'to survive and grow' (Nash et al, 2005: 157). Distinctively good research is owned collectively by all concerned.

Within higher education, social work as a discipline is already at some disadvantage as an applied subject. Determination to be accepted by the mainstream can lead researchers to become increasingly obedient to positivist norms. Academic careers are dependent on research outputs being valued within the terms of existing culture. This challenge is certainly evident in the current preoccupation with measuring the impact of research. Initially, 'impact' did not relate to the social difference that an intervention made. Instead, it referred to the extent to which other academics cited the published outcome of the research and the rating of journals in which those citations occurred. Impact was confined to the academic community and its particular concerns. Since 2009, however, major research funding bodies in the UK require applicants to submit an 'impact summary and proposal' with their funding bid while universities are judged on the quantity of research output and on its impact. In this arena, impact relates to the potential social, commercial and policy outcomes of the dissemination of the research, with a particular emphasis on the commercial outcomes. Impact does not relate to the impact of the research activity itself on the individuals, groups or communities who are being researched. The process and product of the research activity are therefore held separately – as if they were disconnected. This separation of research activity and social intervention is like a force field that protects the 'cleanliness' of the research. Even practice research or Participatory Action Research is somehow given a cloak of separation in which the boundaries are policed with concepts of bias and over-involvement.

Without wishing to augment the unhelpful divide between research and practice, the motivation for conducting research within an organisation like START is primarily to discover more about the circumstances, wishes and potential of all participants and so to make the greatest impact possible on their lives. Its aim is to give voice to people who have been silenced and whose public identity has been shaped by political expediency and the media. It is conducted to promote understanding, to counter the hostile myths about the situation and treatment of refugees; it may even save lives (refugeerights.org.uk). As discussed in Chapter 2, refugees are categorised as 'other' by virtue of their legal status or experience of forced migration. Indeed, the definition of 'refugee' in itself is a highly unstable category. When does an individual stop being a refugee? The label conveys almost nothing about their humanity and situation but much about the structures of oppression.

Reflecting on research with disabled people, Michael Oliver rejects 'the research discourse that prioritises investigation over emancipation' (1999: 184). He argues that research is itself a form of production; multiple perspectives and voices are necessary in constructing representations that potentially humanise rather than objectify. Ethics are not simply about ensuring that people are protected from vulnerability and abuse. With refugees in particular, ethics are concerned with research that is a positive intervention in the lives of people forcibly displaced, objectified and misrepresented, often as victims or a problem.

Research conducted by students

Over time, START has attracted the attention of numerous research students and academics from a range of disciplines, including occupational therapy, global health, media and performance, geography, business and social work. Avril has consistently supported clinical psychology students, for example, to complete their doctoral theses, offering academic supervision on a regular basis alongside access to respondents. As other chapters reveal, from the outset, Avril especially has pursued opportunities for research regarding every aspect of START and its operation, much of which is now available on the website (http://www.studentsandrefugeestogether.com/).

On a number of occasions we have not agreed to academics undertaking research with people who use START's services. The study proposals included comparative research into standards of childcare between refugee and British families, a review of newly arrived Syrians' experience in seeking employment, and a questionnaire about attitudes to other ethnic groups and potential causes of extremism. In each case, refusal had more to do with the approach of the researcher than the subject matter. These approaches could be broadly categorised as opportunistic, paying insufficient attention to the people who were the potential objects of the inquiry. In contrast, START has welcomed the involvement of local students and others who have understood the importance of building trust and confidence with both refugees and organisations, and whose research has encouraged the voices of refugees to be heard. We also require research students to share their findings with the research participants in a spirit of care and openness.

An example of such a study is a 'listening project' undertaken by Olivia Fakoussa and Matthew Fish with groups of refugees and support staff to identify the strengths and gaps in mental health provision. It was founded on the acknowledged limitation of a western psychological model as a response to the mental health needs of a diverse population. Refugees are regarded as 'hard to reach' in research terms but the project was enabled by bringing people together into focus groups to talk about existing services: what was valued and what was missing.

The outcome of almost two years' work was a widely disseminated leaflet translated into relevant languages and an article (Fish and Fakoussa, 2018). The findings contributed to a successful funding bid to set up a peer-led support project in the city and, more importantly, strengthened trust between refugees who participated and the agencies supporting them.

Another clinical psychology student, Shreena Ghelani, undertook research regarding the resilience of refugees using the technique of 'Photovoice' (Wang, 1999). In this study, five people from Eritrea were encouraged to take pictures that reflected:

- daily life
- the things that help
- the things that give faith and hope

The photos were printed, and the student met with people to talk about what their photos meant. Together they identified the following themes:

- the link between trauma and resilience
- personal resources and resilience
- connecting to the UK
- remembering home
- connecting with others

These themes reflect the features, identified by Saleebey, of communities that 'amplify individual resilience'. He writes: 'this interaction is complex, recursive and reticulate and always implicated in keeping people well, assisting individuals in regenerating after trauma, and helping individuals and communities survive the impact and aftermath of calamity and ordeal' (1996: 300).

Again, as a student, Shreena spent a substantial amount of time volunteering at Cultural Kitchen (described in Chapter 8), getting to know people and becoming known by them before initiating the research project. Even in these circumstances, the dynamics of 'othering' in both directions described so eloquently by Krumer-Nevo (2002) in her work with Israeli women are almost impossible to avoid. Similarly Kathryn Church's critical autobiography (1995) provides a powerful insight into the difference between a sensitive researcher's perspective and that of a mental health service user. In work with refugees and, indeed, any other group of people, there is always a risk of imposing the researcher's own reality on someone else's situation. Without skilled and open, active listening, we are likely to interpret what we see and hear through our own cultural lens. Taking an ethical position is not a simple or singular event. It is a constantly critically reflexive praxis. We have no control over the long-term consequences of inquiry. Unintended consequences of research may be that findings are used to support discriminatory practices in spite of the researcher's original motivations. In view of this, ethical researchers must give most attention to the dynamics of their relationships and the way those impact on people's lives throughout the process of the inquiry.

Greater public awareness of the situation in Syria has put pressure on the UK government to accept more people who are forcibly displaced. The government initiative (Syrian Vulnerable Persons Resettlement Programme, 2015) was to admit 20,000 Syrians over five years from camps or insecure housing in a third country in collaboration with the United Nations Refugee Agency (UNHCR). This action has continued to fuel public interest in Syrian refugees as a group and highlights the need for research to establish the success of the resettlement programme. Simultaneously it can place these communities at great risk of exploitative and harmful research practices, however unintended such outcomes may be (Hugman et al, 2011). This is borne out by Ravi Kohli's careful explanation of why his research into unaccompanied asylum-seeking young people was conducted with the social workers responsible for their care rather than with the young people themselves (2006).

The START team have always been committed to research in order to improve the service to refugees and the student learning experience. Like all NGOs that must justify funding bids and provide reports to funders, START routinely gathers feedback about people's satisfaction with the service received and explores different approaches to gathering this information that respect the diversity of language and communication skills. For example, a survey was conducted by a business and marketing student in order to discover people's priorities now that they have leave to remain in the UK. Pictures were used to represent issues such as housing, employment, health and education, and respondents were asked to order them in terms of their own priorities. All service users were invited to take part at a specific point in time and the results were displayed at a community event at which individuals' responses were also recorded. This research tested our assumption that people's priorities would align with those of Maslow's hierarchy of needs (1943) as it revealed a strong motivation for finding employment and learning English (Patel, 2012).

As noted, research is intervention. START's approach is to balance the research agenda with the immediate needs and wishes of refugees and always to give precedence to the latter. A research culture that fosters a spirit of curiosity is so much part of the organisation's identity. Inevitably, given the urgency of the work undertaken with refugees, such a culture has taken time to develop and incorporates clarity about what comprises ethical research and what the boundaries are at any particular time. Students' work is particularly valued in this context because they bring a freshness of approach both regarding the questions they address, and the methods used. They can excavate this strengths approach in action and provide insights about how to work more successfully while being supported in their own studies and future careers.

A strengths approach to research: appreciative inquiry

What follows is a more detailed account of a clinical psychology doctoral student's unpublished research regarding the wellbeing of refugees in Plymouth, including START's contribution, using appreciative inquiry.

Appreciative inquiry originates in work done by David Cooperrider in the 1980s. His doctoral thesis in organisational management was based at a teaching hospital where he recognised the energy that accompanied stories of success and good practice. In collaboration with Suresh Srivastva, he developed an approach that 'excavated' the best practice in an organisation and in so doing created conditions for it to increase (Cooperrider and Srivastva, 1987). Appreciative inquiry has underlying principles that can be aligned with the strengths approach.

In the strengths approach:

- all situations are seen as rich with resources;
- people and communities have capacity for change;
- everyone's contribution is valued and needed;
- difficulties, however severe, can also be a source of resilience and creativity;
- we cannot know the potential of others and must not place limits on their aspirations. (Saleebey, 2009)

As discussed in Chapter 1, the strengths approach is concerned with positive change and continued dynamic development towards a better quality of life in a person's own terms. It is not confined to the achievement of specified goals. In contrast to a problem-focused approach, it is not primarily concerned with naming and solving particular difficulties. The strengths approach can best be understood as a dynamic and generative process.

Similarly, appreciative inquiry assumes that:

- in every organisation, whatever its difficulties, something works;
- what we focus on becomes our reality;
- reality is constructed rather than discovered and there are multiple realities;
- people engaged in research are part of constructing that reality;
- language is fundamental to constructing reality;
- asking questions is itself an intervention. (Bellinger and Elliott, 2011)

The purpose of appreciative inquiry is to discover 'what gives life' to an organisation and to increase the conditions in which best practice can occur. As such it does not have an end point, but is owned by all participants. It is concerned with positive and dynamic change in which people are more confident to move to an unknown future because they can take the best of the past with them.

Unlike traditional research methodology, the validity of appreciative inquiry rests on the engagement of as many stakeholders as possible. It has been used in a wide variety of settings ranging from a whole city (Browne, 2004) to a hospital discharge service (Reed et al, 2002); from a network of community organisations (Ludema et al, 2001) to family-run wine producers (Woodfield et al, 2017). The authors' own experience is of using the approach to research the establishment of a new role to support practice learning in social work (Bellinger and Elliott, 2011).

Appreciative inquiry is a cyclical process with a number of elements variously identified as the 4 'D's (Discover, Dream, Design and Deliver) shown in Figure 6.1, or the 4 'I's (Initiate,

Figure 6.1: Stages in appreciative inquiry

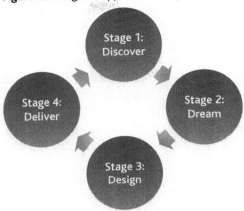

Inquire, Imagine and Innovate) (Coghlan et al, 2003). These elements cannot be simply adopted like a formula, but they provide a broad structure within which each different investigation will develop. Every appreciative inquiry will take shape in accordance with the conditions, context and participation of people concerned. As with all research, it is important to clarify the question or area of interest, limiting the inquiry and defining its terms (Fook, 2001). Clarity of purpose at this stage is essential and can take substantial time and consultation in order to arrive at a consensus (Bellinger and Elliott, 2011).

In the first stage, discovery, stories of best practice are collected from every perspective. This is a careful and detailed excavation of people's experiences of successful organisational delivery using different methods such as semi-structured interviews and focus groups. An almost forensic analysis is needed to identify the conditions in which this practice occurred so that themes can be identified that enable and encourage best practice to occur. In the process of collecting stories of excellence, some people will tell stories of when the organisation has failed them or when their experience has been poor. These stories must be given equal attention with careful questioning about what would have made the experience better, thereby ensuring validity.

In the second stage, dreaming, the researchers explore what the organisation would be like for best practice to happen all the time, and may ask the miracle question: 'If you woke up in the morning and the organisation worked perfectly all the time, how would it be?' This encourages a shift from explaining why things are imperfect to envisaging a theoretical organisation in which best practice is the norm. The stage acts as a counterbalance to the traditional approach of identifying strengths and weaknesses as a product. Research participants are all asked to invest in organisational change in order to improve services in the area of focus.

The third stage of design, in which statements of intention or 'provocative propositions' are written, captures the themes of the research findings and turns them into action-orientated commitments. Stage four, deliver, requires an action plan that carries forward the changes needed to achieve the statements of intention.

It is critical that those with the resources to enable change to happen are full participants in the research process. For example, a statement that all refugees will be given access to legal advice throughout their immigration claim would be unrealistic as the resources for this have been systematically removed by UK government policy. Instead, the area of focus has to be one over which the organisation has control and all those responsible for the organisation are engaged in the process. This can create difficulties for inclusive research that takes time because, with personnel changes, people in influential positions may no longer be in post. The example of the student's work that follows in the next section (Kim's study) accentuates the importance of appreciative inquiry as a continuous process that maintains the momentum of constant change.

Like the strengths approach, appreciative inquiry is wrongly charged with only looking at positives and ignoring difficulties or problems (Graybeal, 2001; Saleebey, 2009). If it is misunderstood in this way then participants are likely to lose confidence and withdraw. Grant and Humphries (2006) give a clear account of this dynamic when they diverted people from telling stories of difficulty. They found that if people's negative stories were not listened to, then they withdrew from the study. They and others have concluded that it is equally important to hear the negative stories in order to explore what would have improved the situation (Carter, 2006).

Such false premises result in accusations of bias and lack of rigour. It is possible to understand this position as defensiveness against a research approach that threatens the beliefs underpinning mainstream traditional methods:

> Like social work, appreciative inquiry is grounded in relationship, context and a determination to collaborate for mutual benefit. It incorporates action and change as an intentional and integral part of the process in parallel with constructive social work processes (Parton and O'Byrne, 2000). It provides a focus on what works whilst not seeking to gloss over what does not, and so rewards and celebrates good practice in a non-competitive environment. (Bellinger and Elliott, 2011: 721)

Appreciative inquiry is an approach to research where people are asked about what is working or supportive *and* what would fill the gaps or improve the situation.

Appreciative inquiry: Kim's study

A clinical psychology doctoral student, Kim Embra conducted her research at START and was co-supervised by Avril. Kim was concerned to explore and contribute to the wellbeing of refugees who had been forcibly dispersed to Plymouth and subsequently granted leave to remain (Embra, 2014). Studies addressing wellbeing and resilience in refugees (Sherwood and Liebling-Kalifani, 2012) argue that refugees are empowered by focusing on strengths rather than pathologising their experiences. Cognitive appraisal or 'positive thinking' and beliefs, including religious beliefs, are highlighted as helpful strategies in promoting resiliency. For many women, a sense of identity through education and employment is imperative, enabling them to provide for their families and feel empowered. Preserving cultural identity also appears to be significant in enhancing wellbeing. Studies highlight that services need to recognise and build upon resilience rather than focus on distress. This supports the critique of refugee research for ignoring resilience and wellbeing (Watters, 2001).

A researcher who does not identify with the participant population can be problematic due to interpretation and representation (Agyeman, 2008). Kim, therefore, made her motivations and assumptions apparent, engaging in reflective conversations and shaping the study collaboratively through consultation between the authors, stakeholders and students. Although the stages of the '4D' cycle overlap, for clarity each stage is presented here separately.

Discovery

Initial consultation involved meetings with stakeholders and informal conversations with refugees. Kim volunteered at Cultural Kitchen and was occasionally present in the START office. Being present, similarly to Whelan et al's description of 'professional loitering' (2002), she built a rapport and trust with people who do not easily respond to research interest. This consultative element clarified research focus and methods of data collection. A semi-structured interview was developed collaboratively, as refugees felt most comfortable with individual interviews. For staff and students, focus groups were more feasible.

Inclusion criteria for the research were that people would be:

* aged 18+;
* a service user at START;
* those who had received refugee status at least one year ago.

Or:

* a staff member or a student at START for at least six months.

Appreciative inquiry is flexible and does not specify a sample size. Approximately 25 people participated throughout the whole process from 'discovery' to 'deliver'. Demographic data for the ten participants interviewed are presented in Table 6.1.

Table 6.1: Demographic data

	Service users	Staff/students
Participants	A, B, C, D, E, F	G, H (Staff) I, J (Social work students)
Age range (approx.)	24–65	Unknown
Years as a refugee in the UK	1–7	n/a
Years lived in the UK	6–12	Unknown
Gender	Four women, two men	Four women
Self-identified country of origin	Democratic Republic of Congo (2), Algeria (1), Iran (1), Middle East (1), unidentified (1)	UK (3), Jamaica (1)

Source: Embra (2014)

Dream

From 'professional loitering' (Whelan et al, 2002) and developing relationships, Kim gradually ascertained people's interest in participating in the interviews. Through a snowballing technique, four individuals self-identified to participate. Additionally, a staff member suggested eight other refugees who fitted the inclusion criteria, using the option to participate via text message; two agreed. Two staff members and two students also agreed to participate through the collaborative process.

Six individual interviews were carried out with refugees; two focus groups were conducted, one with students and one with staff. Refugees were invited to speak about what has assisted them to manage throughout adverse times as a refugee, sharing their experiences of the best (and the worst). Staff and students were invited to identify success stories regarding their work to support refugees and appreciating the best of what START offers. All participants were asked 'the miracle question', that a miracle had happened which enabled support for refugees to go well every time. They then were asked to describe what would be in place and what would happen.

Interviews were recorded and transcribed verbatim. One participant did not consent to recording, so process notes were taken. A timeline was used as a visual map maintaining focus on the timeframe being explored (life as a refugee) and as a non-verbal means of communication. This was done by drawing a line with rough dates about when they came to the UK, when they received leave to remain and discussing that period of time. Interpreters were available but not required as all participants had a conversational level of English. Interviews lasted between 26 and 60 minutes. Participants were offered a copy of their interview transcript to comment on or amend. Data were analysed through thematic analysis (Braun and Clark, 2006), involving multiple readings of the transcripts. The themes developed summarised the breadth of the stories shared. Other stakeholders also read the transcripts and commented on the themes, which were modified accordingly.

Design

Two workshops were held, the first at Cultural Kitchen involving three (interviewed) participants, and a second at a START governance meeting, involving eight individuals including trustees, staff and a student. Themes from the analysis of interview data, plus illustrative quotations, were presented on flip charts and comments were invited. Groups then developed 'provocative propositions', based on the themes, and were encouraged to think creatively, beyond current practice constraints in order to articulate ideal practice. Kim collapsed the statements into 11 propositions, returned them to those at the workshops for consideration, and collaboratively finalised the wording.

Appreciative inquiry findings

Key themes identified were:

1. warm relationships and connections: working together to face challenges;
2. resourcefulness and actively contributing to society;
3. flexible, available and knowledgeable services;
4. managing uncertainty.

These themes, each with two constituent sub-themes, are presented with quotations (where possible from a refugee and a service provider) to offer a broad range of participant views.

1. Warm relationships and connections: working together to face challenges

Working collaboratively with professionals was highlighted as helpful in developing relationships; which in turn assisted with challenges. For most refugees, positive, respectful relationships were the most significant factor in helping them to cope.

1a. Trust, transparency and reciprocity

All participants spoke about the benefits of reciprocal relationships between service users and providers. Trust, transparency and having an emotional investment were key aspects:

> '[S]he's very active ... when I had my degree I brought the photos ... she cried you know ... she said "oh my God you did it" because she knows me well you know ... she was always there for me.' (A)

> '[I]f refugees trust their worker it makes the work happen a lot quicker.' (G and H)

Collaborative working between services was also important:

> '[A] case worker and social services and these kinds of things, and they helped us like going with us to schools and if there was any problem in the school we had to report it to the head teacher.' (E)

One participant highlighted a challenging experience in a service which lacked a relationship:

> '[S]ometimes you go to talk to them, the people in the place they just relate to what is in the computer and

sometimes you even get upset you ask them and it's not a human being it's just information on a computer.' (C)

1b. Belonging in the UK

Some participants spoke about the importance of feeling accepted in society, stressing aspects that have helped them feel as though they belong in the UK:

> 'I can get my citizenship, so I feel I am from this society.' (E)

2. Resourcefulness and actively contributing to society

Drawing upon a number of personal strengths to cope, and actively contributing to society were fundamental for several participants.

2a. Motivation, determination and aspirations to achieve

Personal qualities of motivation, determination and wanting to learn are central in all narratives; helping people to keep going and promoting resiliency:

> 'I said ok I can do anything anyway because I don't want to be on job seekers long.' (A)

> '[B]ecause England does not recognise her qualifications, so she had to go and do another degree for 3 years and end up getting a job as a designer and moved to London.' (G and H)

Staff responses mirrored those of refugees as they also described being motivated and proactive:

> '[I]t's sizably more difficult now than it was when I started because resources have shrunk and there's a lot more obstacles there now than there were, but actually on the whole with most people we still work

alongside them to get to the place that they want to. So when you can see that actually stuff is successful, that's what keeps you going.' (G and H)

Two refugees identified wanting to be role models and providing for their children:

'I wanted to study really and to give also a good example for my kids.' (A)

'I'm especially happy for my son because he has a good life and he's you know, happy.' (F)

Many participants described actively contributing to society, mainly through voluntary work. Two participants also attempted to create a support group, helping others:

'I'm a chef, I cook Fridays, every 2 weeks ... yeah I cooked for 70 people ... I worked for a cancer hospice ... for coffee, tea, cake ... I worked in the shops, the city centre; Save the Children ... I can't stay home all the time, just an old man that is finished, no I don't like that ... I'm looking for a volunteer.' (B)

'[N]ow I can give back to someone, yes it's good ... I like to help, I like to see people be free; for me you have to do everything to be free you don't have to depend on people all the time. You know we even organised like a women's group and we used to meet every 2 weeks.' (C)

2b. Hope, faith and belief

Several participants described how their beliefs, faith and hope are very important components in their identity:

'I've got hope, I've got belief and I believe in God. God saved me from my life there, he will save me here ... we have beliefs in God and we ask God for everything.' (E)

C highlighted her battle with racism and how 'being strong' kept her going:

> '[I]t wasn't easy at all they pushed me a lot, a lot. If I wasn't strong I would have done something ... but I always keep myself calm and I said to them that you can't do nothing you know ... I faced them, I talked to them but I was scared inside.' (C)

Staff and students highlighted 'resilience' as a key factor in the support they offer:

> 'I haven't met anyone yet, any service user that has let it get them down. You can tell that even though they're frustrated about it ... instead of letting it get them down and staying down they really fight to build themselves up.' (I and J)

> 'I think its people's personal strength ... yeah it is they're resilient ... probably the most capable people on the planet they got here, they've gone through huge steps.' (G and H)

3. Flexible, available and knowledgeable services

Participants emphasised the importance of practical services that are needs-led and readily available.

3a. Supportive organisations offering practical assistance

A knowledgeable service that helps practically, meeting people's basic needs was described as imperative, especially when first gaining status. Additionally, friendly, compassionate and available staff allowed refugees to feel relaxed and engaged:

> 'I was struggling with the problems with my benefit, and they know how to get it and how to apply, START helped me. Yeah they filled the form and

phoned them up to see what benefit I can get for because of my son, who's disabled.' (F)

'[A]ll the people are happy, all the people are very nice. All the time you find something, it's no problem to stay, so very nice.' (B)

'[K]nowing that START is there and although we might stop working with them they know that if something goes wrong they can always come back.' (G and H)

Placement students allowed a greater availability and flexibility within the service. They are learning, creating a parallel process which assists with power dynamics and collaborative working.

'[W]e Google it and we say we don't know so we both don't know, us and the service user and then we find out together.' (I and J)

'[W]e've got numbers because of the students, that person can walk down the road with you, go to the job centre ... just having that person there the first few times to kind of work through things I think can be really helpful for people.' (G and H)

3b. Community projects

Several participants described the value of the community projects for meeting people, developing skills and sharing experiences:

'[Y]ou spend time with people, you're not as socially isolated. Finding people that speak their language or same religion or same culture I think is really important.' (I and J)

'I can go to the allotment and dig the ground and put all stress in the ground, this helps of course, this life even with everything we've got, we still think about different things and we get tired, we need something to refresh our brains and we go out there.' (E)

4. Managing uncertainty

Managing uncertainty was a powerful theme, especially ongoing uncertainty through the transition from asylum-seeker status to refugee; constant adaptation and learning processes were described. All refugees felt that being able to communicate was essential for them to manage.

4a. Learning and adapting

Several participants talked about the number of unexpected changes during the transition from asylum seeker to refugee; they felt unprepared:

> '[T]hey often come in really frustrated ... whilst they're an asylum seeker they don't get prepared for if you get given refugee status then this is what's going to happen.' (I and J)

> 'I didn't know anything about being a refugee.' (C)

Many described the uncertainties as an asylum seeker as particularly challenging:

> 'I feel like somebody banned for everything you know?' (F)

> '[W]e can't do anything, we can't work, we can't study and there just was depression and we were waiting for an answer from the Home Office ... they break the door and they took families and put them in the detention centre and they deport them, they force them, and it is a very bad experience for some families. I saw them with children, they suffer deeply, deeply depression.' (E)

Despite ongoing uncertainty, there was a sense of safety, freedom and peace once receiving status. Two participants also highlighted their appreciation:

'I receive money and I have accommodation. I have freedom, I have peace.' (B)

'[A] good country, a lovely country to live in, I like the system, how they deal with people without jobs.' (E)

One participant highlighted the discrimination she faced:

'He knows that there's a language barrier and there are rules and regulations we don't know, he was just playing the game and treating us like animals.' (C)

4b. Language and communication

Having some language to be understood, but also to be able to understand others was vitally important:

'Language barriers and I think that does appear evident in mental health, anxieties.' (G and H)

'When I don't understand a word I read this word and I help myself, it is difficult ... I go to school ... because I live in this country I need to speak English.' (B)

Participants used the themes and illustrative quotes to develop the 'provocative propositions' shown in Table 6.2, collaboratively. Participants were encouraged to think beyond current practice constraints in order to articulate statements of ideal practice based on the themes.

The appreciative inquiry research process alone has been a vital component in empowering and promoting wellbeing for all those involved. This research was set in an environment of constant policy change, continuously presenting challenges but

Table 6.2: Provocative propositions (linked to themes)

Provocative propositions	Key theme
• Every worker will respect, value and celebrate difference and diversity. • Every worker will assist to create new connections and communities for refugees. • Every worker will be compassionate, friendly and always treat others as fellow human beings.	Warm relationships and connections; working together to face challenges
• Everyone will be open to faiths and beliefs of individuals, respecting all people's life experiences. • Everyone will promote and use people's personal strengths and expertise, as well as available community resources.	Resourcefulness and actively contributing to society
• Every worker will be honest about limitations, signposting to people or services who may know. • There will be someone available to physically go with people to new or difficult situations. • There will be support for other workers, for example students, developing their knowledge of systems, services and resources.	Flexible, available and knowledgeable services
• All workers will have an understanding of the complexities involved in having an asylum seeker or refugee identity. • Preparation will be offered to all refugees through being honest about the process and uncertainties. • A variety of communication methods to assist with understanding will be used; language skills will be promoted.	Managing uncertainty

Source: Embra (2014)

also opportunities for refugees and organisations. It highlights the need for partnerships between services to promote wellbeing in refugees and demonstrates the necessity for psychological services to move towards societal models of change adopting community approaches.

Conclusion

These propositions were adopted by START and embedded into the service through policies and practice. They form a reference point for staff, students and volunteers, expressing some of the complex cultural expectations of the largely transitional workforce in the organisation. This emphasises the importance of recognising that appreciative inquiry research is dynamic and not product-orientated, that change is constant, and reality is a construction, not a discovery.

In conclusion, it must be recognised that no research can be perfect, however good the intentions or the scholarship. All research impacts on people's experience and lives. It may have unintended consequences. In that case, unless we assume the same position as Michael Oliver (1999) and undertake no research at all, we must recognise the limitations and adopt a strengths approach. This does not mean dictating the methods or focus of study. It does mean being alert to the well-developed standards in research with refugees (Temple and Moran, 2011) which require researchers to pay close attention to: both approach and methods; being open and honest about the extent to which refugees are participants in the design, data gathering and analysis; appreciating the diversity of worldviews and concerns as well as languages and cultures; appreciating the political and intersectional context of the work; and retaining a focus on the value of the research to refugees themselves.

Learning points

- Good research with any marginalised group means working alongside them as co-constructors of knowledge and co-designers of fields of inquiry.
- Appreciative inquiry as a research approach acknowledges the transient and constructed nature of reality.
- A focus on possibility and success does not limit the capacity to explore difficulties, but allows exploration to happen in an atmosphere of respect for people's achievements and aspirations for the future.

7

A strengths approach
to student learning

> In a time of drastic change it is the learners who inherit
> the future. The learned usually find themselves equipped
> to live in a world that no longer exists.
>
> Hoffer (1973: 22)

In this chapter, we present a model grounded in the strengths
approach which critiques the assumptions about how students
learn in practice. We provide a framework for identifying and
affirming organisations like START that offer a potentially
transformative environment for learning. The framework
is substantiated by previously unpublished research funded
through a university teaching fellowship, undertaken with
14 pioneer students from the first two years of START's
life examining how students learned in that unconventional
setting. Findings from this study are considered in the context
of theorising about the strengths approach, extended by the
experience of working with learners from diverse professional
courses and international students. Fundamental to this
approach are concepts of the learning organisation (Social Care
Institute for Excellence, 2008) and communities of practice
(Wenger, 1998).

We know beyond doubt that students are capable of achieving
the impossible – simply because they do not know that it is. We
have seen them apply their passion for social justice and their life
experience successfully to situations that might have discouraged
an experienced worker. In educating students for the challenges
of the future we want them to bring everything they know from

their lives so far. Similarly, refugees, or indeed anyone seeking help, need to be able to draw on everything *they* know to create the potential for transformation. It is essential for the continued health of the organisation that its two components – service to refugees, and student learning – are held in balance at all times. Emphasis on the interconnection of theory and practice safeguards a learning environment where no one is 'the expert' and everyone is 'an expert' whose contribution is essential. Mutuality is at the core of the strengths approach.

Traditionally, students have learned to practise through placements, whereby a professional practitioner supervises them and gradually passes on their expertise. These apprenticeship models of professional learning can only equip professionals for a future similar to the present. Inevitable changes resulting from the climate emergency, scarcity of natural resources, demographic shifts, global conflicts and their consequences for human populations make that form of future very unlikely. If, as we believe, a profession like social work is a contextual and embodied practice, then it must change with the conditions in which it is found to be necessary.

All the staff at START support students and regard this as equally important as delivering direct services to refugees (see 'charitable objects' outlined in Chapter 3, p 65). They recognise that this investment prepares future professionals to be advocates for refugees in the UK and internationally. They work hard to give students confidence in themselves, knowing that the potential is there, and striving to build on it. In the words of a student supervisor interviewed as she retired:

> 'For me the amazing thing is to see students' confidence grow and I've seen them flourish. I think it's that way of talking, saying "I know you can do it ... If in doubt, let me know" and I let them do it.' (2019)

Putting trust in students in this way needs careful management. Supervisors must express confidence while making what Shulman calls 'a demand for work' (2015: 204) – a demand that is inherent in the strengths approach.

Learning organisations

> Education is the kindling of a flame not the filling of a vessel.

> Socrates

We are struck by the frequency with which students of all disciplines at START say how different this placement is from their expectations. They had anticipated spending much more time observing others, not trusted to work alone with people in need of life-changing support. They talk about the speed at which they are expected to become active team members and express their appreciation of the demands made on them, accompanied by a high level of support. We witness student progression from apprehensive student to autonomous beginning professional, as they realise what they might be capable of:

> 'My time at START has developed my knowledge and given me so many life skills that I can carry with me throughout my personal and professional life. It has enabled me to have the ability to pro-actively adapt my work to meet the needs of the service and service users alike. It has opened my eyes to the many challenges that individuals face when having to deal with the government systems and policies that are in place. It has reiterated the importance of having an effective and supportive multi-disciplinary team as at times it has been essential I get support and also help support my colleagues.' (Placement student, 2016)

They also recognise that, however much knowledge and experience individuals may have, we are all learning. This environment carries the expectation that everyone will need to ask others for help. Boundaries between service users, students and staff are disrupted so that all share ideas of what professional practice can mean when it is not confined by statute or convention and where people's knowledge is not placed in a hierarchy. Learning for professional practice in this environment demands compassion, humanity, philosophy, ethics and values as well as theoretical and technical practice. This purposeful breaking down of traditional barriers is consistent with theories of holistic education (Miller, 2000), which are recognised for their capacity to foster social consciousness and empathy.

Having concluded in Chapter 3 that START is a social innovation, its educational core can best be understood through the lens of learning organisations (Social Care Institute for Excellence, 2008). This framework affirms the importance of regarding all members of an organisation as contributors. It articulates the systems that encourage mutual exchange of knowledge and expertise. A 'no blame' culture in which mistakes are seen as inevitable and as opportunities for learning is key. For this to be practicable, members need to have a high level of trust in each other and relationships need to be as non-hierarchical as possible. Etienne Wenger's work on communities of practice (1998) takes these ideas even further. In such a community, individuals are not necessarily in any line management relationship with each other but, rather, are connected by a passion for their particular subject, sharing and developing practice together. Learning to become a knowledgeable practitioner in a particular discipline is seen as a dynamic interaction between the practice itself, the community with expertise in that practice, the meaning given to that practice and whether individuals are recognised by the community as potential members. In Wenger's early writing, learners were seen as moving from the edge of the community through legitimate peripheral participation and gradually towards the centre. However, in more recent work, he acknowledges the permeability of boundaries around professions, referring instead to the learner's trajectory through a complex and changing landscape (Wenger-Trayner, 2013). Although relationships between students, volunteers and paid staff at START are all articulated in contracts and learning agreements, the practice relationships are as non-hierarchical as can be achieved. Students and volunteers are as likely to give advice and support to new members of the team as to receive it. Through their involvement in the work, participants, including students and refugees who become volunteers, can move from the periphery to the centre of the organisation and its activities. An emphasis on trust and appreciation, humility and collaboration, sharing knowledge and responsibility, learning from mistakes and from successes are all characteristics of learning organisations.

Practice learning in the UK

It is interesting to note that few UK models of practice learning *celebrate* the aspirations and capacity of students to make a difference in the lives of people they meet and in achieving social justice. This is in spite of excellent examples – historically and internationally (Farmaian, 1993; Lam et al, 2007; Pentaraki, 2011). There is increasing concern in the UK, however, about ensuring good quality practice learning across a range of professions. There has been substantial government investment through, for example, the Quality Assurance Agency producing standards for all practice placements in higher education, the Ongoing Quality Monitoring and Enhancement tool developed by the Department of Health, and in social work the high-profile, time-limited Practice Learning Task Force as well as standards introduced by its regulatory body. One such is the regulation that 'each student will have placements in at least two practice settings providing contrasting experiences; and a minimum of one placement taking place within a statutory setting, providing experience of statutory social work tasks involving legal interventions' (Social Work England, 2019: 13).

The particular focus of quality assurance appears to be to ensure students have carefully managed environments that reflect existing state provision with clear processes for accountability. Concern seems to be to minimise risks to students and to universities by defining minimum standards and procedures like 'Health and Safety' together with communication systems for use when there are problems. Moreover, unlike other European countries, social work with refugees is not a service provided in the UK mainstream. UK social workers can graduate without knowing how to work with refugees, or indeed with any other group for whom statutory services have been withdrawn.

Antithetical to the strengths approach, such a focus seems to construct students as vulnerable and in need of protection. It is more in tune with a neoliberal paradigm in which students are simply customers who could resort to litigation if they are not satisfied with the service provided by their courses. In a deficit model, students' lack of experience and short-term relationship position them as inferior to employed staff or even long-term volunteers in that agency. This view is exacerbated by the increasing reliance in local authorities on 'agency workers', and burnout among permanent staff as they try to make relationships with a constantly shifting population. Consequently, practitioners may be less tolerant of students who initially have high needs for support. As the complexity of the work increases and resources decrease, opportunities for student learning are constrained where the work undertaken by staff is seen as too difficult for students. Furthermore statutory agencies can be unwilling to use student labour for preventive work for fear that service user expectations will be raised unrealistically, not least by the amount of time a student might be able to devote to them in contrast to paid staff. Ironically then, the higher the need, the less likely students are to be allowed to meet it.

Service as social action

In a neoliberal environment where services are designed for efficiency and cost-effectiveness it can be challenging to enable students to become critically reflective, social justice-oriented professionals. Like many writers Hugman identifies three options:

- accept the prevailing ideology and confine practice to the competent delivery of services;
- reject the contemporary ideology and instead seek the spaces in which to focus on the macro perspective;
- seek ways of working across a range of contexts, seeing the micro/macro distinction as a continuum in which individual and structural understandings of social need are bridged, combining service delivery with social action. (Hugman, 2009: 1143)

START's intention is to provide students with the challenge and support to take the third option as their professional norm. The strengths approach harnesses their motivation for applying to study their chosen discipline. They are enabled to begin their work of 'making a difference' as they learn to practise alongside people who have been excluded from society. They are seen not as a burden on the professional community, but as potentially high contributors who can be encouraged to realise that potential. As a consequence, many students have transformative experiences at START and retain strong bonds with the organisation after qualification.

Some professions, occupational therapy in particular, recognise the capacity of students to learn from each other. For example, a model of 'collaborative' placements in which the supervisor allocates part of their normal workload to one or more students, uses the time released to support their work and learning. Where there are multiple students, they are found to support each other and make fewer demands on their supervisor (Currens, 2003). This collaborative model, initiated in Canada in 1985, is based on a collegial and constructivist philosophy of learning rather than one that is didactic and expert-centred. Also from the discipline of occupational therapy has developed 'role emerging' placements. These are specifically for final year students who are placed in an agency where there is no tradition of that professional practice. Their role is to create a service where none previously existed (Thew et al, 2008).

A model for learning in practice

However, the resistance in social work especially, to modes of learning that differ from traditional apprenticeship, prompted Avril to develop a theoretical model (Bellinger, 2010). In this model, the quality of the learning environment is not associated with the presence or absence of qualified professionals in the placement setting. In an educational context, the inseparable and dynamic interaction of theory and practice produce a generative space for the co-production of knowledge. The model, represented by Figure 7.1, has a perpendicular axis with

Figure 7.1: A model for learning in practice

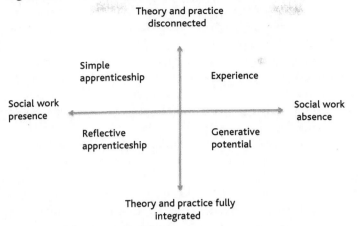

Source: Adapted from Bellinger (2010)

a range in which, at the top, theory and practice are deemed to be separate and even potentially in conflict with each other – hence practitioners who tell students to 'forget the university teaching – you're in the real world now'. In contrast, at the bottom of that axis is the recognition that practice does not exist without theory and vice versa. The students and those supporting their learning are creating knowledge rather than simply applying it.

The horizontal axis represents the diversity of placement sites in which, on the left, qualified and experienced practitioners staff the organisation. On the right, there are no social workers and the work is not included in statutory provision.

Where these two axes are brought together (Figure 7.1), the degree to which placements facilitate student learning in each quadrant can be identified as follows. In the top left quadrant where social workers are present, students learn through a simple apprenticeship model – what used to be referred to as 'sitting by Nellie'. This may produce competent workers where 'Nellie' is an experienced, critically reflective professional who is happy to work with learners. Regrettably, with the high staff turnover and pressures of work already recorded, this is not always the case. In the top right quadrant, where students are unable even to see professionals at work, their experience may or may not result in learning. In both of these quadrants, the separation between theory and practice is significant.

In the lower left quadrant students learn through a reflective apprenticeship. They develop understanding and practice through critical reflection (Brookfield, 2009). Practice educators and other professionals are engaged in learning *with* the student. Teaching received by students is valued by the staff, and together they refine and develop practice. Within this quadrant, it is possible for the student to initiate practice changes and for the practice site to influence future teaching. Finally, in the bottom right quadrant, students may not have professionals to copy but they are in an environment where theory and practice are fully connected. In this situation, as in occupational therapy's role emerging placements (Thew et al, 2008), students are supported to generate professional practice innovations.

As described in Chapter 3, in the first two years at START students were able to develop good practice by attending closely to what service users said they wanted and needed. Drawing on knowledge about values, models, theories and personal experience, and with support, they established professional relationships based on compassion and integrity, sensitive to the responses of those they were seeking to help. This unknown terrain for students, educators and all involved can feel risky in a risk-averse society. The 19th-century settlement movement faced similar challenges (Manthorpe, 2002). But social justice work is not safe or risk-free. By its very nature it is challenging for those involved and also for existing services, as their deficiencies are highlighted. However, working with people who have been excluded from mainstream services is how social work began, with students working in the settlement movement (Attlee, 1920). It is at the core of what it means to be a professional social worker. As the International Federation of Social Workers' definition states: 'Social work is a practice-based profession and an academic discipline that promotes social change and development, social cohesion, and the empowerment and liberation of people. Principles of social justice, human rights, collective responsibility and respect for diversities are central to social work' (IFSW, 2014).

Viewed through the lens of this model in which only the lower two quadrants provide the potential for students to learn to take on professional habitus, an organisation like START can be understood as a rich and potentially transformative placement opportunity. Bernstein (2000) writes that professional habitus comprises an inner dedication to scholarly and professional activity and the accumulation of a distinctive body of knowledge which is engaged in a practical way with the needs of others. It requires a high level of autonomy and initiative based on internal and external motivations (O'Connor, 2007).

> 'In START I have been able to truly and holistically work with the clients, and in an unstructured way, by this I mean being able to work with clients at times that are convenient to them, on issues that really matter to them, opposed to other placements where I have had to work with clients when it is most convenient to the setting, and on issues that are more to do with immediate risk, rather than implementing long-term interventions and plans.'
> (Placement student, 2017)

Both professional practice and educational issues need to be managed with care. Students need regular access to people with current knowledge about local services to ensure they are offering informed, accurate information to the people they work with. Students also need consistently high-quality, strengths-oriented supervision and space for critical reflection about their work to ensure they are not neglecting their professional learning. Indeed, this experience motivates students to seek out research, theories and practical information to help them. It requires engagement in all stages of Kolb's learning cycle (1984) – practising, reflecting, theorising and planning. It demands criticality (Brookfield, 2009) about the wider political context for their work. This learning about the real lives of people 'outside' society is a process described by Paulo Freire (1970) as 'conscientization', which enables students and the people they support to contribute to the knowledge base. In all instances, feedback from service users and their families or trusted networks is of primary importance in measuring a student's performance, lending new weight to the value of service user feedback, to which lip service has sometimes been paid. For example, a service user at START said that they did not want a service from [student] "... because they're lazy". The practice educator asked what the service user's expectation had been and what the student had, or had not, done. The reputations of students and staff are built through the networks of people accessing help and students know that their level of investment will be recognised. The following account of the early days of student placements at START gives an illustration of this model in practice.

Student placements at START: the early years

When we seek transformative learning, we are taking a leap of faith into something unknown. We are changed by new knowledge created with service users, students and others (Butler et al, 2007). When the first three students were introduced to the families they were to support in October 2001, none of us knew what might happen. The preface and introduction describe the beginnings of START and original plan for a placement in the EMAS with support from an off-site practice educator. These expectations were dashed when it became clear that EMAS were not able to accommodate or to be identified as the formal placement agency for the students. At that point, we considered withdrawing and making conventional arrangements for the students. However, motivated by concern for refugee families we formed a steering group and also confirmed that the students were open to the challenge.

With weekly supervision from the EMAS teacher and a referral coordinator in the social services department, we knew that the students would be given tasks to do to support the families. These included making medical appointments and accompanying people to ensure translation services were used, reading Home Office correspondence to avoid missed appointments, working with the Red Cross to locate a pregnant woman's husband in Italy – letting him know when his child was born.

From 2001 to 2003, 14 students from the Diploma, Bachelors and Masters in Social Work programmes provided a service through their first or final assessed placements. They worked with a small number of families each (usually three or four) and, over the two years, provided a needs-led service using a strengths approach to 21 families (35 adults and 68 children) from ten countries of origin, speaking 11 different first languages. Subsequently, the city council provided students with free office accommodation. The university contracted with off-site practice teachers, available to the students by mobile. They met with students weekly to support and assess their learning, and observed their practice. The teacher and referral coordinator allocated work and also met with students for an hour each week but otherwise students had no staff on site. Students *were* the agency and, since the work was so new in the city, there were no role models or instructors.

Without language skills, students improvised. Dictionaries were borrowed and non-verbal communication became the norm using pictures, for example. Without an organisational structure or procedures to follow, students were forced to think carefully about questions of confidentiality, ethical practice and what constituted a professional relationship. In those first two years, there were procedural challenges – to whom do case notes belong and where should they be stored? There were continuity challenges – the service closed for three months in the summer when there were no students on placement. There were relationship challenges – how was it possible to communicate the difference between a professional and a personal relationship to a refugee with no context for understanding social work?

Some university tutors raised particular questions about how the students' health and safety were being protected in the absence of organisational structures. Although all these considerations were valid, each one could be used to prevent a service being offered to people who were at the highest level of risk. Social work that only follows the conventions already established in society is unlikely to challenge the status quo or protect social justice (Hamer, 2006; James et al, 2020). 'Social work is about life, treasuring humanity, building connections, sharing and promoting fairness. It is about creativity, care and love ... we are always in the midst of the messy stuff, finding ways forward' (Allen, 2018: 27). And so, with care and constant discussion, and some trepidation, the placement continued.

Learning from success: the research

All of the students completed their placement successfully and were invited to participate in a piece of funded research summarised in Box 7.1 after the event. The first two years had given us an opportunity to look more deeply into how students learned when there was no qualified practitioner to copy. The outcome was a published paper which presented the findings of an initial survey of the students involved (Butler, 2007). What follows is the subsequent, until now unpublished research, funded through a University of Plymouth Teaching Fellowship, which critically reviewed conventional wisdom about what constitutes 'good learning environments' both in terms of quality assurance frameworks and the literature about teaching and learning.

Each member of the research team brought different strengths. As the originator of START, Avril Butler (now Bellinger) continued to work closely with the organisation throughout the period being investigated. At that time she also had more than 20 years' experience of organising practice learning. Gai Harrison brought with her a substantial practice background in the NGO sector in Australia, was a skilled qualitative researcher and taught social work at the University of Queensland. With a background in psychology and pedagogical research, Caroline Abbey, research assistant, offered an outsider view to social work culture and supported clarity through the process of interviews and analysis. The underpinning epistemological approach recognised the value of social constructivism in seeking the subjective experiences of the students. Narrative approaches were also fundamental to the design and analysis of the data. The exploratory research question was 'How do students learn in the START project?'

Box 7.1: Research synopsis

- **Conceptualisation:** The research question was broken down into its constituent parts. For example, meaningful learning we defined as 'deep embedded learning which becomes a part of who you are, how you function and how you think about the world. It changes how you operate in the future and transforms you. It is not just something you do better.' This definition is allied to that of Mezirow's account of transformational learning (1991).
- **Design:** The design was exploratory and qualitative. We were seeking students' understandings and interpretations of their own learning experiences. Qualitative methodology allowed us to explore meaning at the level of subjective experience.
- **Reflection on past experience:** Social work students are routinely asked to reflect on their practice and their personal experience. As Jan Fook states, 'a reflective approach affirms the importance of experiential and interconnected ways of knowing the world' (1996: 5).
- **Sample:** All 14 students who had undertaken a placement at START in the first two years were invited to participate. Ten completed an initial questionnaire which provided material that informed the interview schedule and eight agreed to be interviewed. Four of the five practice teachers were interviewed and data used to contextualise the student data, not to provide triangulation.
- **Preliminary questionnaires:** Preliminary questionnaires were very open, asking respondents what differences there were in the START placement and what they thought was better or worse. These were anonymous to encourage respondents to be critical.
- **Semi-structured interviews:** Conducted by the research assistant, these interviews pursued respondents' stories and concerns. An outsider to the profession, she was able to query assumptions about social work and the learning framework.
- **Coding and analysis:** All interviews were recorded, transcribed and anonymised. A rigorous coding procedure was used to undertake thematic analysis. All members of the research team read samples, discussed and revised the coding scheme, focusing on convergent and divergent data. This resulted in 19 parent codes and 68 sub-codes for the student data.

- **Limitations**: Not all students participated and it is possible that a more critical perspective would be held by non-respondents. The research also took place at a distance from the experience and would be affected by that. We are also strongly conscious that this process is one of interpretation and that the analysis is from the perspective of the researchers.

Methodology

Findings

Through the analysis, themes emerged that offered a different lens for considering what factors were important in the learning environment. These were particularly in the areas of

- creativity
- autonomy
- confronting racism and making anti-racism real
- accessing support
- transferable learning and
- meaningful learning

Each theme is now discussed.

Creativity

In this placement students only had themselves as resources; there was no funding, no interpreters, no organisational structure. One student described taking a laminated picture of an envelope with her as a way of asking families if they had received any post. Instead of complaining about filling in forms, this student talked about recognising the importance of them:

> '[T]here was nothing particularly written, it was a placement that allowed you to be creative ... and you had to be creative in order to put systems in place, even office systems.' (Student 5)

All students made reference to creativity and the following student comments that this has endured in a more conventional work setting:

> '[B]ecause you're working outside of like statutory boundaries you are having to work in a kind of creative, sort of innovative manner ... I've had experience of that so even though I'm working in a more sort of structured environment now, I can still bring that kind of creativity into it.' (Student 4)

Autonomy

Students also talked about the unusual degree of autonomy they had in this placement. In speaking about her work to advocate for a service user, this student says:

> 'I had to be quite, sort of, firm within, find out a lot about the law and that to ... deal with the situation but also ... really kind of negotiate in an ... effective manner ... that everyone could sort of work with and not ... feel got at. And that was a real learning experience for me ... in terms of my confidence as well and my role.' (Student 4)

The following student worked for two and a half years in a local authority after graduating and then became self-employed. She describes the impact of the START placement:

> 'Actually I'm self-employed, I work for myself [now] so that facet of the placement really suited me ... again no management structure, which is wonderful.' (Student 2)

Confronting racism

The social work programme at the University of Plymouth has a long tradition of seeking to promote student learning about diversity, especially the impact of racism (Butler et al, 2003; Ford, 2012). This has been challenging in what is perceived as a predominantly white, rural area and often students conform to tutor expectations without taking on real learning about the issues. The data revealed a depth of learning in this regard – one student spoke about working with a woman whose change of immigration status had left her with no money or food for herself and her children:

> 'And I just learnt by seeing somebody in that position, I'd never seen anybody in that position before. Umm and I just come away thinking, you know, it changed the way I thought about, you know, making assumptions about people, I don't know, it just had an impact on me.' (Student 2)

Students were confronted with racist responses from members of the public as well as from friends and family who asked why they were working with people who are refugees:

> 'I learnt to challenge, how to challenge appropriately … I learnt huge amounts about discrimination, different faces of discrimination, um such as structural, personal, cultural. It was big learning, very big learning.' (Student 7)

The following student clearly states the level of learning and the lasting nature of it:

> 'You get that grip of what racism and discrimination means, you know. I think that's what stays with you, once you've finished that placement.' (Student 6)

Accessing support

Students were asked what they did when they were not sure what to do. One respondent was clear that it was difficult not to have qualified staff available as role models:

> '[W]hereas I was very aware, that while I was on the refugee project I was, kind of … acting as a

social worker, but hadn't actually ever seen social work, you know, so I was sort of thinking ... "Well I guess what I'm doing is [social work]" you know.' (Student 4)

However, all students were able to give an account of how they would deal with uncertainty and difficulty, illustrating the importance of knowing that support could be available, rather than having staff in the agency:

'I would think about the consequences of things and would reason it out myself, but my practice teacher got me through a lot of issues ... and was at the end of a mobile phone so we had no issues about being left high and dry.' (Student 8)

The student who later became self-employed talked about how she and her fellow-student felt frustrated by being asked simply to be a 'taxi driver' and 'completer of forms'. Their response was to work out together how to use the assessment framework of social work competencies to guide their work:

'[W]e did have some enormous difficulties on that placement and we devised our own way of working, we devised what our work was.' (Student 2)

Transferable learning

The same student speaks of these difficulties as a learning experience:

'So some of the difficulties we had, I think were more valuable than when things went smoothly, for setting you up for decent practice, you know, how to challenge people effectively, how to challenge people professionally, how to accept a differing view and work within that whilst challenging, you know. I think quite possibly that was the better route, so to speak.' (Student 2)

It was also clear that this environment had a politicising effect on students:

> 'It was, kind of a catalyst in … making me more look at things at a much higher, you know, much more of a … political social level than always only at an individual level.' (Student 4)

Meaningful learning

It is important to explore the potential of challenging the taken-for-granted assumptions about what constitutes a good learning environment. This is particularly relevant when the prevailing culture privileges quality assurance and risk reduction at the expense of autonomy, creativity and affirmation:

> 'We were basically self managed. We weren't self managed but up to a point we were. We had our supervision, just to let them know what we were doing, and if they were happy with it, they would let you go with it, so that was quite good, so for me … because of the freedom we had, and we were getting positive feedback, it sort of gave me confidence that perhaps, you know, we were ready after that [placement] … it gave me confidence to actually go into practice because of the freedom we got and the positive feedback we got.' (Student 6)

Meaningful learning cannot be delivered by education alone, it has to be acquired through a process which benefits all concerned. In the words of one of the students, the collaborative nature of that experience is clearly expressed:

> 'Working with refugees and asylum seekers, I found that some of them have touched me and will never leave me, you know, and my experience is that they have taught me an enormous amount, and I did feel very privileged to be allowed to work alongside them.' (Student 8)

The challenge to educators is to provide learning opportunities for students to enable them to undertake learning that transforms both them and the profession that they enter.

What matters in student learning?

Robbins et al (2006) identify three principles of the strengths approach that are aligned with the findings of the research discussed and with the continuing work with students.

- *Understanding empowerment and human strength at the personal and political levels.*
  It is essential that students develop a perspective on their practice that is both personal and political. Through exposure to practice with refugees in this instance, students are confronted by the reality of racism and discrimination that operate routinely in a civilised society. They have to enlist support at the appropriate level whether personal, community or legal.
- *Emphasises the human capacity for resiliency, courage, strength in the face of adversity, ingenuity at accessing and creating resources, and the right of individuals to form their own aspirations and definitions of their situations.*
  Students begin to recognise the difficulties that people seeking help are already managing and to appreciate the strengths and resources they have developed. By appreciating the resources of refugees, they can develop confidence in the knowledge and skills they have developed in their own lives.
- *The assumption that people are most likely able to grow and develop when their strengths are recognised and supported.*
  The availability of support allows students to become increasingly autonomous and to exercise their creativity. An educational environment assumes that everyone will need to seek help from each other and that growth and development are a goal for all – students, refugees and staff. In such an open environment, study skills are no more valuable than the experience of surviving domestic abuse or living in poverty. It is also acknowledged that anyone can make a mistake, and that a mistake is a point for learning which reduces risk to service users and students alike.

START is now 20 years old, having provided learning opportunities for more than 300 students of many disciplines. In a conventional placement, organisational structure, procedures, norms and people to copy and learn from can be very helpful to a student new to a profession. Our experience with START, both in the first two years and subsequently, however, is that the presence of experienced professionals is not the most important factor. Although students may find a conventional environment helpful and reassuring, they could equally 'play safe' by reading the expectations and completing the placement without exposing themselves to transformational learning.

At START, in the first two years there was nothing between the student and service user except, perhaps, the teacher's instructions about the task – and as we could see from student comments under 'Accessing support' earlier – that was not always recognisable as social work. The students had to explore, negotiate and create social work in collaboration with the refugees they worked with, drawing on whatever knowledge, experience and resources they could access, measuring success by the families' responses. In a strengths approach, service users are not 'victims', 'deserving or undeserving', 'criminal' or 'manipulative'. They are people doing their best to manage their lives who can be trusted to find their own solutions, given the opportunity. In the absence of 'experts' in how to practise with refugees, students and colleagues are at the forefront of practice – making social work for the future and transforming their perceptions at the same time:

> 'These four months have been critical to how I see my future as a social worker. The placement has given me confidence and the opportunity to develop my skills and competence as a social worker.' (Placement student, 2016)

> 'START has truly been one of the best placements I have experienced, it has enabled me to develop in many ways as well as ensuring I met all of my learning needs and outcomes. It is a unique organisation with the very core of social work at its heart, and

> provides a platform for students to really get in touch with service users and their needs, with the positive outcome of their independence. An absolutely outstanding learning environment, placement and organisation.' (Placement student, 2017)

Similarly, the range of activities in which students are expected to participate extends their experience from casework to group and community work, aspects of professional practice that are diminishing in the UK and elsewhere.

> 'Now I can't think of another place ... that allows students this much autonomy and this much responsibility in the running of their organisation and as a third year social work student it's been really interesting because I've carried cases but I've also been involved in some quite big things. Other people may not believe that students can take that much on because they are students – but that's what START does really well and it's been going for a long time. It's a success and continues to be so.' (Undergraduate student, 2018)

Conclusion

At START, students are recognised as highly motivated, skilled individuals who also have academic targets to meet. Care is taken to ensure that these requirements are fully understood and that practice learning agreements reflect the individual student's needs. Each student is allocated an experienced supervisor on the staff and is inducted by staff, existing students, refugees and others for the first two weeks. From the beginning, they are encouraged to recognise the capacity of service users and other students; they are brought into the 'community of practice' Wenger (1998) described earlier. Their work is carefully monitored and supervised; student support is regarded as a core activity by all staff. Equally, START's reputation depends on the quality of students' work as accurate and sensitive to refugees' needs. At the same time, students are expected to take responsibility for themselves and to be proactive in critical reflection on their practice, as well as in their use of supervision, so that they and others can learn from both challenges and successes.

Over time, many international students have completed placements at START often through the European Erasmus exchange scheme but sometimes, due to their own efforts, having found START's website. At the time of writing START has provided placements for over 60 students from Germany, France, Norway, Switzerland, Poland and the Czech Republic. They are invaluable in helping UK students and, indeed, the organisation to critically appraise structural factors by providing external lenses on policy and practice. With international students especially, we have noted a shift in supervision from managing relationships, role boundaries and professional integrity to the increasingly urgent concerns of climate change, neoliberalism and global patterns of migration. The strengths approach has encouraged students to look beyond explanations of personal difficulty to incorporate a political and global analysis in their practice.

Learning points

- Students can contribute to knowledge and achieve the impossible if they are supported and allowed to try.
- All aspirations must be respected and taken seriously, not limited by imposing our own beliefs.
- The stronger and more explicit the learning culture is, the more space there is for everyone to discover new possibilities.
- Learning with, and from people affected by problems, directs positive change.
- In the strengths approach, assessment of risk is not ignored but is managed through supervision and critical reflection by all concerned.
- Anyone can make a mistake, and a mistake is a point for learning which reduces risk to everyone.

8

A strengths approach to growing community

If you are coming to help me, you are wasting your time.
But if you are coming because your liberation is bound
with mine, then let us work together.

Aboriginal activists' group Queensland, 1970s

Refugees are people who have been forcibly displaced because of war or persecution and have arrived in a strange land. Imagine you have had to flee for your life. You have left everything you know – friends, family, familiar sounds, sights, smells, objects and everyday activities. You have undergone numerous challenges to reach a place of safety and have been met with suspicion, disbelief and hostility when you arrived (Halpern and Sloan, 2020). You do not need to be treated as a charity case, deprived of your dignity or shamed by the expectation that you should be grateful.

This chapter is about growing community and protecting conditions in which community as a *practice* can thrive. The concepts that inform this chapter are 'community', 'the commons' and 'reciprocity'. Examples follow, from the experience at START and elsewhere, of activities that can facilitate community growth with a particular focus on the way they are informed by a strengths approach. We believe they have wider application. They are offered as a stimulus rather than a recipe!

What is a strengths approach to community?

The literature surrounding community work refers to different models of community relating to:

- profession (Goode, 1957)
- geographical location (Phillips and Pittman, 2014)
- ethnic or cultural allegiance (Breton, 1964)
- interest or practice (Wenger, 1998; Bradshaw, 2008)
- wider society in general, including both human and non-human elements (Dorow and O'Shaughnessy, 2013)

The term *community* remains contested with much of the literature about community work assuming a geographic definition (Stepney and Popple, 2012). A current and popular model of working with community strengths rather than deficits originates in the US with the work of Kretzmann and McKnight (1993; McKnight and Kretzmann, 1996). In a move away from a conflict orientation, they propose a system called 'asset-based community development' (ABCD) that seeks out the strengths and 'assets' of communities in order to affirm, connect and build on them. In affirmation of this more positive paradigm, Mathie and Cunningham describe ABCD as 'an approach, as a set of methods for community mobilization, and as a strategy for community-based development' (2003: 6).

This method has been enthusiastically adopted in the US and is equally promoted to local authorities throughout the UK (McKnight and Russell, 2018; Sutton, 2018; Nesta, 2020). Various websites contain numerous examples of improvement with the adoption of ABCD in the quality of life for older people, people with disabilities, isolated individuals and others in the UK. Graeme Stuart, an experienced community worker in Newcastle, identifies seven principles of a strengths approach to community work. In common with Schwartz's (1971) interactional framework cited in Chapter 1, he asserts that problems are the result of 'interactions between individuals, organisations or structures rather than deficits within individuals, organisations or structures' (Stuart, 2012). It is clear that ABCD is concerned with changing the relationship between local authorities and people in the communities for whom they provide services. We concur that a strengths approach to building community is more concerned with relationship and interaction than systems and structures.

ABCD employs many characteristics of the strengths approach such as positive story-telling or appreciative inquiry. According to Kretzmann and McKnight, communities are supported to 'begin to assemble their strengths into new combinations, new structures of opportunity, new sources of income and control, and new possibilities for production' (1993: 6).

However, it is evident in the positive accounts of ABCD as an alternative to 'needs-based' community development that there is a core purpose of *economic* development. Mathie and Cunningham (2003: 6) cite two key aspects of the process as

- 'mobilizing the community's assets fully for economic development and information sharing purposes'; and
- 'leveraging activities, investments and resources from outside the community to support asset-based, locally defined development'.

This conflation of community development with economic growth betrays the true nature of the practice. In their careful critique of ABCD, MacLeod and Emejulu (2014) place its development and promotion historically in tandem with the neoliberal projects of the US and the UK. While acknowledging its potential for positive outcomes, they caution against its wholesale adoption because it can reconstruct public concerns such as poverty, inequality and deprivation as private. It is, they say, premised on the belief that the welfare state 'breeds a culture of dependency in poor communities and that the best remedy to poverty and inequality is the application of free market principles such as enterprise and entrepreneurship' (2014: 9). Their empirical research in Glasgow with both community development practitioners and officers at a strategic level revealed that, although the stated intention of ABCD is to promote the co-production of services that actually improve people's lives, it could have the effect of simply changing the narrative or even increasing inequalities. 'Shifting the power balance ...

is highly complex and requires a long-term commitment to change. The extent to which the current interest in asset based approaches is motivated by a desire for this change in power, our research suggests, is open for debate' (MacLeod and Emejulu, 2014: 18). These authors express serious reservations about the potential for ABCD to be used as a cost-cutting exercise in areas already seriously underserved by state provision and conclude that 'a hostility to state-sponsored social welfare is the central unacknowledged value embedded within this theory and practice' (2014: 20).

Chapter 1 distinguished between a 'strengths-*based*' approach in which governments colonise aspects of the concept in a 'neoliberal embrace' to serve political agendas, and a strengths approach that infuses the whole system, one that is adopted at every level, and in every aspect of an organisation's functioning. Community is not simply an entity that can be 'asset-mapped' (Field and Miller, 2017) in order to increase its effectiveness. Rather, community is a living system to be nurtured for its own sake, where economic benefit is secondary to the wellbeing of people and planet.

Having repeatedly argued that the strengths approach involves whole systems, it would be inconsistent to seek to limit this notion to a portion of life defined by geography, origin or interest. We define community as a dynamic interaction rather than an entity – one that enables and enhances wellbeing.

Working with refugees who are dispersed without choice to a city in the southwest of England helps us to conceptualise the strengths approach as *growing* community rather than community development. Refugees from countries all over the world have diverse languages, cultures and religions. At START, they learn alongside a constantly changing group of students, also with diverse origins and languages. In the absence of established community groups based on nationality, for example, traditional community development approaches are not applicable. Instead, we conceptualise community *growing* as a process rather than a product. It is a social practice of 'horizontality, networking, transcendence of boundaries and establishment of interconnectivities' (Harvie, 2004: 9). In seeking to represent our conceptualisation of community we have adopted **community**

growing rather than community building or development in order to express its organic rather than static nature. We are indebted to Lucy Holmyard whose work features in Box 8.1 in this chapter, for her clarity about these terms. A concept of community with the strengths approach at its core is local but not boundaried, accepting but not passive; it is curious and brave. It is always a work in progress. It is realised through the apparently random acts of kindness, connection and reciprocation evident through all the activities essential to life. Community is created through history, repetition, relationship and reciprocity.

The commons

In order to conceptualise community as a process, it is important to be clear about the conditions in which it can flourish and for this we now reflect on 'the commons'. The commons can be defined as the space between the market and the state in which neither government structures nor commercial interests are dominant. 'The Commons are resources that are produced and managed collectively by a distinct community of users, according to their rules, and functioning independently of state control or privatisation' (Allan, 2018: 11). The commons refers to all resources, natural and cultural, freely available to all members of a society. These include air, water and land as well as social and cultural spaces that are managed collectively for the benefit of all. The original meaning of the commons as common land is familiar – a resource where animals could be taken to graze, providing an essential support to poorer people with no land of their own, exemplified to this day by places in the UK such as the New Forest. The enclosure of the commons is well recorded by historians who chart the move from a predominantly agricultural way of life to one of increased urbanisation and industrialisation.

Today, public space is increasingly passing into private ownership (Brady, 2011), and the pressures on land to be productive financially are considerable – with unintended consequences. For example, Mary Colwell's (2019) account of travelling across the UK to visit the sites where curlews have been prolific shows the shocking impact of agricultural, industrial and economic interests threatening a common bird with extinction in a very short space of time. Human use of the land is primarily driven by economic or monetary interests – even areas that are designated 'public green or blue spaces' have to pull their economic weight (Jones, 2020). It used to be argued that land enclosure and ownership allowed more careful stewardship of areas. However, it is now understood that the diminishing amount of wilderness has severe consequences for the whole human race and for the planet. The loss of diversity and enclosure of commons are critical aspects of the climate emergency.

Through her clear, practical description of the commons of her rural German childhood, Maria Mies, academic activist and long-term ecofeminist, helps us to appreciate the concept. In her account, the woods and common land are not a 'free for all' (as Hardin's 1968 critique implies) but a treasured resource that requires all who use it to maintain it. This is the reciprocity that connects community and the commons. She describes enclosure as 'piracy, violence, theft, appropriation of what belongs to the people: land, forests, water, rivers, open spaces in cities and villages but also knowledge, culture and language' (Mies, 2014: 108). She also critiques the notion that the internet provides a 'new commons', pointing out its ownership by corporate interests and the high cost to people and planet of gaining access to it. The enclosure of the knowledge, cultural and relational commons has equally devastating effects as that of the natural commons.

To further explore the notion of the commons, David Harvie (2004) uses the concept to identify the neoliberal process of the enclosure of intellectual commons in higher education. In our own careers we have, personally and painfully, experienced the increased regulation and monetisation of academics' time and activity. This enclosure of commons is evident throughout all aspects of life as commercial interests seek to control 'alternative, non-commodified means to fulfil social needs e.g. to obtain social wealth and to organise social production' (De Angelis, 2003, in Harvie, 2004: 3). In higher education, it comprises the systematic timetabling of staff and student time with the effect of severely restricting informal and creative exchange between students and staff, as well as within those groups. Harvie says: 'My departmental community is not constituted through departmental meetings, but through me chatting with a colleague at the photocopier and then that person going for a pint with someone else' (Harvie, 2004: 8). Making the distinction between 'convivial competition' in which the goal is improved practice, and the goal-oriented 'coming first' (or winning bids), he demonstrates the similarity between academia and the NGO sector (Harvie, 2004: 4). For example, at different times agencies in the city (other than START) have gained funding to provide a group for refugee women. In a marketised environment, the existence of more than one women's group for refugees would be seen by funders as duplication and competition for the same 'beneficiaries'. Alternatively, under Harvie's 'convivial competition' frame driven by the strengths approach, organisations collaborate to hold sessions on different days so women can exercise choice and freedom. This is an example of commons where diversity is encouraged and celebrated in contrast to a proprietorial demand for loyalty to particular organisations or cultures.

In summary, there are serious consequences of enclosure of the commons for economic gain. The environmental damage is strongly evident (Duong, 2016; Parker, 2016) resulting in the climate emergency. As serious is the damage done by the enclosure of social and cultural commons. Contemporary constructs of community development for economic outcomes might be understood as a form of enclosure. Creating and protecting commons in contrast comprises a strengths approach to growing community. The strengths approach principle that 'everyone has the capacity for rebound and righting the trajectory of their development in the face of adversity and trauma' (Weick and Saleebey, 1998: 27) provides a foundation for creating a commons where community can grow.

Reciprocity

All refugees have lost home and family and many experience mental health difficulties yet, rather than compassion, they face suspicion and hostility through the immigration process. At all stages of their journeys, refugees can encounter hardship, destitution, poverty, exploitation and racism. These experiences can traumatise even those people who have responded with resilience to forced displacement. Findings from the emergent scholarship in social work about community responses to disaster (Chui and Ford, 2012; Harms et al, 2020) confirm that, beyond immediate safety and shelter, people need meaning and connection. The strengths approach principles are clear that:

- every individual, group, family and community has assets and resources to be used in reconstructing and redirecting their lives;
- every individual and collectivity has the inherent capacity for wholeness, regeneration, healing and transformation;
- every person and group has a fund of innate wisdom and health to draw upon in times of crisis and challenge. (Weick and Saleebey, 1998: 27)

In Chapter 3, we argued that the overwhelming needs of people and planet require social innovation to meet them because traditional approaches have been shown to be inadequate. Healthy communities grow from within and bottom-up rather than top-down (McNally, 2018). The strengths approach responds to problems slowly, gradually and from within. Furthermore, we believe that traditional services unhelpfully demarcate roles of 'donor', 'provider', 'volunteer' and 'beneficiary', restricting people's role identities and their ability to move between them. In contrast, the practice of developing and protecting commons is significant in releasing the potential of refugees and students, for example, to develop and contribute to the organisation in different ways.

Our confidence in people's capacity to make use of such opportunities is borne out by Rutger Bregman's careful work (2020). He provides detailed historical evidence for the view that humans are fundamentally co-operative and loyal – concerned for each other – rather than competitive and individualistic when given the freedom of the commons in the spaces between the market and the state. These spaces may be the result of state failure to respond to the needs of the population. The community response, in contrast, is seen repeatedly in disasters such as London's Grenfell Tower fire of 2017, and through the compassion shown in the town of Frome (Abel and Clarke, 2020). The emergency work of volunteers in the UK such as mountain rescuers and the numerous examples of spontaneous activism recorded in the *Big Issue* magazine during the global pandemic, affirm Bregman's case. It is in stark contrast to media portrayals of humans as intrinsically greedy, selfish and threatening.

Bregman's analysis explains this mismatch in our perceptions as a consequence of separation, distance and enclosure. He accounts for even the most violent behaviours as stemming from the corrupting influence of power on rulers. He attributes the loyalty of ordinary people to their immediate group to belief in the 'just cause' promulgated by those in power in tandem with the media. He is not alone in arguing that the media's determination to feed the public appetite for stories of violence and negativity causes fear and mistrust, providing an opportunity for governments to exert increasing control over their populations (O'Neill, 2002). Creating and protecting the commons in contrast can be seen as a political act to promote social justice.

The examples that follow show how commons can be created and how, in an organisation like START, people can move between the roles of volunteer, service receiver, teacher and student with flexibility and spontaneity. Consistent with the strengths approach, everyone's contribution is regarded as essential and constantly changing. Working to grow community cannot be formulaic. It is contextual and dependent on relationships – human and non-human. In this way, communities are highly original and specific to their time and place. Hilary Cottam's work with community groups shows that even highly successful processes cannot be up-scaled without losing that which gives them life (Cottam, 2019). Similar, but unique, are features of natural complexity. Need is non-linear and so is response.

The strengths approach in action: sharing food

An example of creating commons can be seen in START's Cultural Kitchen. This extraordinary event takes place fortnightly in a church hall on Friday evenings and is a welcoming space for refugees whatever their legal status. On average 80–100 people cook and eat together. The significance of food as a means of growing community is recognised internationally and for diverse groups of people (Whelan et al, 2002; Zavos, 2019). The atmosphere of food provision can vary enormously according to the central purpose such as basic nutrition or social connection. The Cultural Kitchen began in 2003 when a student responded to the despair of a young Muslim man housed in 'Bed and Breakfast' accommodation who had attempted suicide. The student realised that his only hot meal of the day was breakfast with bacon and pork sausage. Working with an interpreter she recognised that chronic hunger and spiritual conflict were major factors. She then identified a number of resources:

- a church hall, recently refurbished and equipped with a catering kitchen which was under-used;
- a trustee of a local NGO supporting people in the asylum system who attended that church;
- a grant of £200 unused by a local charity because it could only be used for 'providing healthy food for refugees';
- a refugee who was a chef.

She developed a proposal for a six-week pilot and the kitchen quickly established a presence in the city. It is a part of START's work that particularly attracts funding and publicity. Maintaining it as a commons is challenging for the organisation because constant risk management is required in an open and free-flowing environment. Everyone is greeted by students or volunteers, invited to contribute a small amount for the meal and to register their name and country of origin. No one is refused entry (unless they are using alcohol) or asked about their status. Anyone not recognised by workers will be approached during the evening to ensure that the commons is not exploited by people unable or unwilling to commit to full participation and reciprocity. Sometimes people come to Cultural Kitchen in the hope of gathering some refugees for their project, whether it is research, an event or to collect images and stories. Where visitors have been willing to invest, develop relationships and take the time for trust to grow, refugees have been able to take part in a wide range of additional activities introduced through the Kitchen, including environmental projects with the British Trust for Conservation Volunteers, and involvement in community arts (Myers, 2006). The guiding principle is that the Cultural Kitchen, like all the START activities, is a safe space for refugees. Every session is different as people arrive in the city and others move on with their lives. While there is a structure and timetable for chopping vegetables, setting out tables and clearing up, it can be challenging to remain open to everyone participating in whatever way they want. The difference between efficient service provision and protecting a space where community can grow is reflected in the skills of the staff and their positive appreciation of participation. The commons gives space for reciprocity and depends upon everyone's need to contribute.

This difference between service and commons can be illustrated by a technique called Creative Capacity Building (CCB) which Avril encountered in Uganda. CCB is a technology-based practice from Massachusetts Institute of Technology Development-Lab using a design cycle as a framework. The process depicted in Figure 8.1, used in rural areas in the global south, begins with a technological problem that a geographical community encounters, such as the labour-intensive process of hulling maize by hand. The practitioner works with people to develop a solution using locally available materials (Childs, 2017). The external expertise is a combination of the design cycle process and developing the community's confidence in managing materials, sawing wood, working with metal, etc. As people's skills in material management increase, they are able to design and develop a prototype by using the ideas and creativity of everyone in the group. The design cycle is then used to refine the prototype, thereby embedding the process in the community. The primary intended outcome of the CCB process is not the product that improves people's day-to-day lives. Avril was corrected when she erroneously concluded that the group could market the product to other villages and make an income. The core philosophy of CCB is

Figure 8.1: Creative capacity building

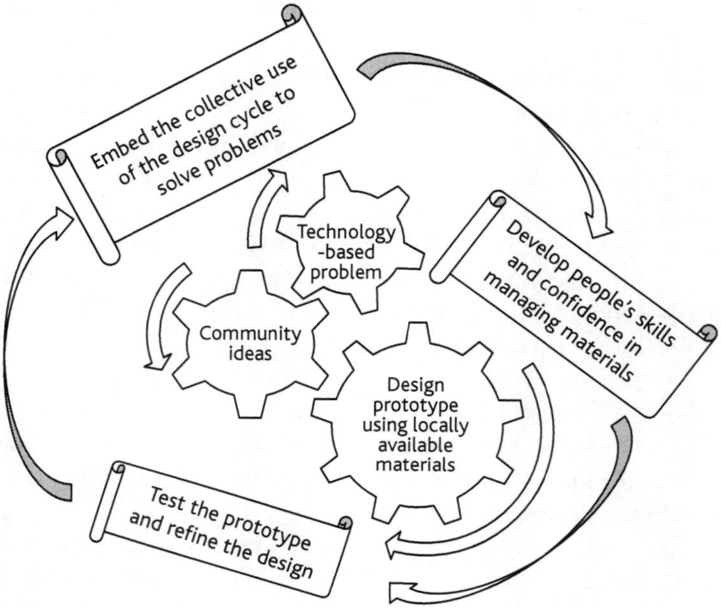

that groups become skilled in using the process themselves with other issues, technical, financial and social.

The key features of CCB are that:

- it uses resources already available;
- everyone contributes – it doesn't ignore anyone or anything;
- it doesn't limit people's aspirations;
- it is self-generating and accumulative, increasing capacity for the future;
- it is founded on the need to trust the people who are worked with and to listen to them and be brave enough to pursue the things that they themselves want to do.

To reiterate, the process is the core and not the outcome. This is what differentiates between providing a service (product) and creating commons (process).

Environmental connection

Connection with the environment is essential to human wellbeing. Lucy Jones (2020) has brought together comprehensive scientific research about the risks to both people and planet of the growing disconnection between the two. Industrialisation, and now global urbanisation, mean that increasing numbers of people are living in artificial environments with limited access to nature. The poorest people are often unable to travel to places that nurture wellbeing and connect them to the environment. A surprising report on children living in Cornwall, a popular UK holiday destination, found that some in relatively poor families had never seen the sea even though it was only six miles away.

One of the responses to this urban environmental deprivation is to promote the use of community green spaces and community gardens. A study in Germany of community gardens registered that their focus is not simply gardening but also they have a function of establishing social networks and developing a sense of community (Rogge and Theesford, 2018). The researchers define community gardens as 'collectively used and self-organised open places, situated in urban areas, where food and non-food plants, and a sense of community is grown, to address diverse local needs and to generate personal and common benefits ... community gardens can be considered to represent new and urban commons' (Rogge and Theesford, 2018: 225).

The START allotments are an example of such an environment where individuals can work on the shared plots or take on a small area of their own. Sheds for storing tools and a polytunnel for delicate plants that can also be used for shelter from the rain make it a convivial space overlooking the city where people can interact as much or little as they want. Regular 'allotment days' are organised where staff, students, volunteers and people receiving help work together and have a barbecue. One of the additional benefits of this particular space is its contribution to student learning – both about agriculture and about interpersonal relationships. One student was cutting dead wood from a currant bush when a refugee who had been difficult to engage held her wrist and said 'Look – alive!' as she pointed to the twig. This is one of many examples where the environment enabled the power relationships between refugee and helper to be disrupted. 'Community gardening offers new ways of social interaction and collective use of urban resources, provides space for recreation, knowledge exchange, social cohesion, and experience in implementing basic democratic principles' (Rogge and Theesford, 2018: 270).

There have been frequent misunderstandings about the purpose of the START allotments as outsiders want to focus on food production, for example, as a measure of its success. As an urban commons space, it is a whole system with a much more complex function. An international social work student who completed her placement at START returned to undertake her dissertation research on the allotments. Using a qualitative approach to focus on environmental justice and social work she found that:

- Social workers can adopt intercultural, inclusive approaches encouraging marginalised or low-income communities to engage in meaningful social participation.
- Bringing people with different forms of knowledge and competences together provides opportunity for them to articulate their interests and talents or to share them.
- What people bring can combine into social and cultural networking capital beyond the limitations of their surroundings, institution, everyday life or professionalism. It can enable access to other groups, networks and worldviews in various ways.
- Such community spaces can lead to interdisciplinary, creative or artistic approaches to complex topics. They can also facilitate non-linear, self-organising processes, through interpersonal exchange and contacts or different communal experience (Gnant, 2019).

Protecting the commons in this case can mean managing the expectations of other city allotment holders, participants, volunteers, the wider public and funding bodies, many of whom may want to enclose the space with regulations and expectations. This tendency is expressed with humour and clarity in the BBC film *Grow Your Own* (Laxton, 2007).

STARTwalking is another activity that connects people with the environment. It was initiated to give refugees confidence to access the beautiful woods, moors, beaches and countryside around the city. The original funding came from a charity promoting language development, who required one output to be a book of walks (Gipetti et al, 2013). In 2012, START brought together creative writing students, English for Speakers of Other Languages students, refugees and others to map and record nine walks. Since then community walks, involving on average 30 refugees, have been a regular feature of START's activities. An example of the delicate balance between managing risk and maintaining shared ownership occurred when the walks were the focus of a BBC (2017) radio series called 'Ramblings'. The presenter, Clare Balding, and producer, Lucy Lunt, joined a group of refugees, students and others in 2017 to record a programme. The walk was carefully planned and shortened to fit with the visitors' schedule. We recall with delight the sight of a group of refugees running down a hill determined to continue on the longer walk which they knew well. We were able to get back on time but this is a small example of the unpredictability of the constant demand for flexibility in growing community. There is a qualitative difference between having to take a number of people on a number of walks to fulfil a funder's criteria and enabling people to do it for themselves. This requires the same degree of technical and theoretical framing as CCB. START brings the knowledge of public transport, footpath guides and weather forecasts, and engages everyone in the process as co-learners in order that people develop their own capacity to enjoy the environment and relate to it as their own. Growing community is about relationships with each other and with the environment.

Income security

As part of the government's austerity measures, the Benefits Agency introduced a new system for everyone who was unemployed. Each claimant was required to sign an agreement that committed them to a specific number of activities to demonstrate they were 'actively looking for work'. Failure to meet this contract would result in sanctions – not receiving any money for at least two weeks, sometimes more. Refugees with limited English language skills were expected to apply for sometimes as many as eight jobs in a week, in an area of high unemployment where ethnic diversity is low. As a result, START was almost overwhelmed by individual requests for help to negotiate these increasingly punitive and complicated rules. Realising that an individualised response was ineffective, START created a 'Job Club', initially provided by students and staff, subsequently by community volunteers (both refugee and white British). This provision was able to attract specific year-on-year funding and, over time, became recognised by the Job Centre as a bona fide 'job-seeking' activity itself which could be written into people's contracts. Positive relationships were built with Job Centre managers to enable START to report unfair or discriminatory practice. In this way, the worst impact of the policy change was mitigated. People were able to avoid sanctions, develop online job-seeking skills, learn about the systems in which they were operating, have support to ensure appointments were not missed (a trigger for automatic sanctions), develop a CV (as in the case example in Chapter 1) and explore the opportunities that might be open to them. The service enabled refugees to help each other, affirming new skills through sharing them with others. It became a forum for collaboration between local concerned citizens, established refugees and organisations wanting to do something to improve the situation.

One such organisation, Embercombe (https://embercombe. org/about-us/), sent representatives to Cultural Kitchen one evening to distribute surplus vegetables they had grown at their community. From this initial approach friendships grew and a relationship developed between START's Job Club and Embercombe, which facilitated opportunities for refugees to develop skills in bread-making, carpentry and building, culminating in a building project at the community. Something that began as an act of charitable giving developed into a mutually beneficial project – a commons.

Numerous other initiatives have grown out of a collaborative spirit. Here we focus on one final example and the research that illustrates the strengths approach to growing community.

Women and self-narration

The experience of forced displacement is gendered (Lenette et al, 2013). A women's group has been in operation for many years because the spaces for any women's voices to be heard are limited by global patriarchy (Mies, 2007). It is essential for women to be able to self-narrate. 'Human understanding operates through storytelling and identity, indeed a sense of self is constructed through the interrelation of life events and the meaning ascribed to the life story' (Butler et al, 2007: 285). One of the principles of the strengths approach is the power of storytelling in transforming lives, as noted in Chapter 1, specifically the belief that: 'All individuals, families, communities, and cultures have rhetorical, metaphorical, narrative tools to refashion and reformulate their understanding and interpretation of their situation and condition' (Weick and Saleebey, 1998: 27).

In 2008, a group of Playback Theatre practitioners approached START and now facilitate popular sessions in the weekly women's group. Playback Theatre is an established technique of inviting stories from participants and using dramatic techniques to play them back (Feldhendler, 2007), checking how accurate the representation is and correcting it where needed. The women who facilitate have practised the particular approach for many years and have an enduring commitment to working with refugees in ways that do not objectify or stereotype (Dennis, 2008). Indeed, research indicates that the relationship between 'performers' and those who attend is fully reciprocal. In 2018, a clinical psychology student, Lucy Holmyard, approached START wanting to undertake her final qualifying research with refugee women. Over a two-year period she joined the women's group and Cultural Kitchen to build relationships and trust. The following extract from her research illustrates the women's group as an example of social and emotional commons in which everyone can access the resources to assist their self-narration and transformation.

Box 8.1: Research extract

Context
A single story of trauma has dominated western psychological meaning making of displaced women's experiences. Although displaced women undoubtedly suffer and experience trauma, a 'problem saturated' narrative risks obfuscating women's strength and growth alongside their suffering, while foregrounding an individualised understanding which does not take account of gendered, socio-cultural and relational contexts.

My research was set within a wider feminist aim of adding to a more nuanced and empowering 'multiplicity of stories'; seeing displaced women as simultaneously suffering, surviving and growing in context. In the context of START's Women's Group, I set out to explore women's strength and growth within multiple relationships: displaced women and their children; displaced women and Playback volunteers; and displaced women and myself as a researcher.

Findings
Reciprocal growth: outside, inside, alongside
Playback volunteer stories and my auto-ethnographic reflections described a process of starting out positioning ourselves as '*outside*' of the displaced women's experiences. One volunteer expressed:

> 'I definitely went there with this sense that, these people ... the "poor refugees" need some help and I'm going to help ... Which now feels so naive really.' (Playback volunteer)

The word 'poor' describes the women as vulnerable or lacking in anything to give. This constructs a one-way relationship in which the 'refugees' are 'receiving' the help and she as a volunteer is the 'giver' of the help.

The stories expressed the discomfort involved as the conception of ourselves as 'outsider helpers' was de-constructed. In my auto-ethnographic interview I express my powerlessness as my expected role is disrupted:

> 'I was from the outside, I was being welcomed in and the women ... were wanting to look after me ... they were bringing me cups of tea ... asking me how I was, they wouldn't let me help.'

For me, as a researcher, de-construction of the 'outsider helper' role was a difficult one. Who I was in relation to the women was not straightforward; I have not fled from a country where my life was in danger, but as I opened myself to the women and their experiences, I began to see my own human experiences reflected back. What I wanted to know from the women felt deeply personal. This was a disturbing realisation, raising anxieties that I had uncovered a position of **'over-identified insideness'** with the women.

As I repeatedly stepped into discomfort, using reflexive spaces to examine the tangly feelings that arose, a space where strength and growth could be shared between myself and the women opened up; I was neither 'outside' or 'inside', but **'alongside'**. There was a growing appreciation of the reciprocity in the research process; I was both seeking meaning and providing a framework for it.

Volunteer stories also de-constructed initial positioning of displaced women as 'other'; coming into empathic connection at the level of womanhood, motherhood and shared suffering. The narratives communicated a process of 'mirroring' and shared meaning making; through witnessing displaced women's strength and growth, the volunteers and I came to represent our own strengths, growth and empowerment through how we saw ourselves reflected in the women's stories. For example, one Playback volunteer expressed:

> 'I have just seen that they have the capacity, even though they have gone through so much, they are continually going through so much ... But despite all that, they have ... this amazing ... inner strength to just still be joyous and appreciating that they have a family and ... they can still ... enjoy life really. So, I think from my point of view ... it just ...

[B sounds tearful] makes me realise the strength that we all have.' (Playback volunteer)

She starts by speaking about '*they*' and the women's '*inner strength*', locating the strength inside the women and separate from herself. In the final sentence, she talks about '*we all*', an emotive recognition of her own strength in the face of adversity, through connecting with the strength in the women. Within the context of the women's group, through the telling and enacting of stories, 'I' became 'we'. Through Playback, meaning making through suffering was constructed at a shared level, generating a sense of community, empowerment and **growing as women together.**

The unique finding of this research was women's and volunteer's co-construction of strength and growth, connecting intra-psychic meaning making to reciprocal relationships and wider community: linking what's 'within' ('I') to what's 'between' ('we'). Consciously paying attention to this reciprocity has empowering connotations for displaced women and those in relationship with them. In the words of one of the displaced women: "I can use what I have been through to plant words of hope and strength like seeds in the minds of others, that can germinate and grow there too."

Source: Holmyard (2020: 86)

Conclusion

If, as Bregman (2020) proposes, we are fundamentally collective beings who are 'hardwired' to care for each other, then it is helpful to revisit the five human givens that Griffin and Tyrrell identify as fundamental to wellbeing (2003: 351). Chapter 1 explored 'the need to give and receive attention'. This is a profoundly two-way process and one that must be acted upon if we are to overcome the existential threats of climate change, for example.

Paying attention to the environment, to ourselves and to each other is essential. START's community activities illustrate how it is possible to respond to the 'need for community and connection beyond the immediate family' through creating commons where everyone's 'need for autonomy or a degree of control' is respected equally. While it is possible to provide shelter and sustenance for others, 'the need for purpose or meaning' can only be discovered by each of us for ourselves in relationship with others. Fear and anxiety undermines our capacity to be fully present – to satisfy 'the need for flow (utter absorption in a worthwhile activity)'. The commons offers a conducive environment for people to gain confidence in themselves and each other – enabling everyone to be open to possibility and to make the most of the potential already there.

We have explored the subtle, but profound, difference between providing services to people – whether food, access to the environment, help with income security, a safe space to meet and share stories with others – and creating commons where people can access these things as contributors and co-producers. In the latter case, we can never know what might happen and must remain open, trusting and willing to learn together as people embedded within a wider growing system. Reciprocity is at the core of the strengths approach to growing community.

Learning points

- Community is a dynamic process not a product.
- Growing community requires attention, knowledge and flexibility.
- The commons is a resource shared by all who are invested in its care. It cannot be regulated or privatised without serious consequences.
- Our relationship with each other and with the planet is one of mutual dependence and reciprocity.
- Growing community is not an alternative to the state's responsibility for the welfare of people and the environment.

9

The strengths approach in practice: how it changes lives

'It is obvious that we cannot play, learn or achieve when we are hungry, weak and homeless.'

Eric

The strengths approach, explored and illustrated throughout these chapters, is one that looks to the future. It is concerned with lives being made rather than looking back on the past, when people became labelled as refugees. The immigration process requires people to tell an unchanging story of their persecution in order to be believed and granted leave to remain. In a media-drenched environment where every detail of people's lives and experiences are shared, it can seem acceptable to ask for the stories of danger and escape. Through media bombardment we are desensitised to the intrusion of satisfying our curiosity. Local volunteers who are new to START have a tendency to ask 'How did you get here?' oblivious to the fact that asking someone to revisit the trauma in this way can be deeply disturbing.

For some people, the opportunity to tell their whole story in their own way can be cathartic and part of the process of building their future. A particularly powerful example is the play *How Not To Drown*, written and performed by Dritan Kastrati who came to England as an unaccompanied, asylum-seeking child aged 11 (Billington, 2019). Similarly, Dina Nayeri's novel (2017) and journalism (2019b) invite the reader to glimpse the complex and nuanced experience of being a refugee. As she writes: 'The refugee story doesn't end at asylum and safety, the moment when many readers look away. It is an endless battle with pride, shame, identity and especially language' (Nayeri, 2019b).

For the majority of people, however, their energy is directed at building their futures rather than examining their past.

Inevitably, not everyone who comes to the organisation is satisfied with the outcome although monitoring consistently gives us confidence in the service. In this chapter we present the positive experiences of five refugees in their own words, using a process described in Box 9.1. The accounts start at the point of their first encounter with START and describe their journeys to the future. In so doing, we hope to show the instability of categories that lock people into stereotypes. The people whose stories are shared here are from Africa and the Middle East. In different ways, they record the human impact of the law and policy changes outlined in Chapter 2. Eric writes in Northern Iraq following his deportation from the UK. As we tried unsuccessfully to stop that deportation process, we learned that he was using his knowledge to help others in the deportation centre and, in some instances, advising them to agree to their deportation so that they could have some control over their specific destination. This example of the strengths approach in the harshest of circumstances celebrates his achievements in subsequently building a family and a school in the area where he now lives.

Themes characteristic of the strengths approach in this book are reflected in these stories. For example, teamwork and learning together where everyone is valued, create commons – a situation that encourages everyone to become the person they want to be. Tesfa and Jokow refer to START as a family, and to the importance of compassion. Feeling safe in an environment that respects diversity is particularly eloquent in Gabriella's account and her poem. Angela talks about hope. As in any group of people subject to categorisation and labelling, these five individuals cannot be representative of a wider group. They each have many identities: as refugees, students, staff, volunteers, participants and teachers who have generously agreed to share their stories.

'Like a powerful arm for a weak person, like a bright and open eye for a blind person, like a light in a dark and long tunnel. This is my definition of START.' (Service user feedback)

Box 9.1: The process of gathering stories

Each person was asked to give a description of themselves and a false name of their choice, and was asked to tell the story of their 'START' experience. A timeline was used to capture the period described and any changes in their relationship to START. The conversations were recorded and transcribed. The stories, presented here, were edited in collaboration with the authors.

Questions
1. How would you describe yourself (age, ethnicity/nationality, religion, gender, qualifications or work background)?
2. When did you first get in touch with START and why? Can you draw a line from then until now and pick out anything significant on the way?
3. Do you know that START works from a strengths approach? From your experience can you say what you think that means?
4. Is there anything else you want to say?

Angela

'I am a 47-year-old black African woman, a Christian and a mum of three and I work as a social worker. After being granted asylum, in 2008 I was referred to START and that's when I received the support to integrate, and when I decided to become a social work student. That's when START played a big role in my journey. 2008–2009 I enrolled on an access course while I was still with START, receiving support from social work students doing their placements there.

I didn't know anything about social work. Where I come from, my background is people and their families, community helping each other. I knew that there were social workers back home, but I was never in contact with them because it was just the community helping and supporting each other, so I didn't know any social workers at all. I was inspired by the students who were on their placement at START.

That's when I thought, "This is what I want to do", to help people and to give back to the community. Because my children at the time were young. When I started my access course, they were only one and a half. It was very difficult as a single mum to twins. Without START I don't think I could have managed. Because I had to know how to apply for benefits, how to apply for student loans or student bursaries when I didn't have a clue. START was able to give advice, to say, "This is what we can apply for. This is what can be helpful. When the boys go to a nursery, this is what you'll be entitled to." So that got me thinking I could do this.

A student was asked to tell me exactly how demanding the course is so I could make an informed decision, to say "Yes I'm willing to go ahead with this." A meeting was arranged with the student who was open and honest and told me that this was not easy. It is a fulfilling and good degree, but it requires a lot, so you have to be mentally and physically strong to be able to go through it. START organised that, to prepare me mentally, so that I couldn't find myself likely to drop off at any time. Support was there from the students who were now towards the end of their course. So when I went ahead, I knew what I was up for. Although it was not what I expected! I had made up my mind. I was lucky with the students that I was allocated to work with me. They really wanted the best in me and the people we were working with. Amazing students in the placement at that time, which inspired me more.

I had to go through the NASS (National Asylum Support Service) system; I had to move houses. No matter how many times I moved, they were there. Even the manager of START offered her car sometimes to help me move, because that's how community-inspired START is. The support was just amazing because at the time the system was completely new to me. With the access course I was up all night having to think about writing and the way of studying here in this country. I just didn't know what I was doing. Some days I didn't sleep at all. But inspiration came from the social work students. I would ask and they would give me advice and say you can keep going, you can do your research from this website, or you can find this book, so I think my journey started from there. I stuck with it even if it was difficult during the access course and I managed to get my UCAS points to be able to go. I did an interview at the university and I was able to get a place in 2009. I graduated in 2012.

While on the course I was still a service user, so I never did a practice placement at START because I was still getting support there at the time.

My son qualified to come and join me from home. He was turning 18 that year and needed support to study. He did media studies. I was receiving my benefits and my student loan. Everything was in place, so I didn't need much support myself, but my son was now the one who was being helped. START managed to get him what he needed. He wanted to apply for a job with young people so he was able to get references.

Then START received an award from SWAP (Higher Education Academy subject centre for Social Policy and Social Work). I, and a Masters student on placement at START, went to receive it in Manchester. It was an amazing experience really for START to be recognised because it was different fields across the nation and the university was recognised for what they were doing in the community. I had been through the journey myself with START and I was going to graduate that year. I went to receive that award and inspired people that we met there by saying "I'm part of this organisation and without this organisation I don't think I would be here receiving this award today."

I think that the job START is doing really helps people in desperate situations whether it is a war-torn country or political issues that people have fled from, and you won't even know anyone throughout that time, relying on the services like START to step in and give people hope. So that's how I felt at the time, that this is giving me hope. Because, how do you even go to the Job Centre on your own? But here you have the students who say, "OK we can meet and go to the

Job Centre." I remember I didn't have any childcare when I wanted to go for an interview to get to college, so the social work student managed to find a child-minder last-minute. So now just that support of saying "I'm going to drop you there, we'll drop the boys to a child-minder." We got into the car and I went for my interview which was really successful. So if I didn't have that support, I don't think I could have even managed to go for that interview. I'd had no one to look after the boys, but they made it happen for me to be able to go and attend the interview, which was the beginning of everything now. I have been qualified since 2012.

The strengths approach covers my journey, really. Because if this approach was not one that underpins START, I think I wouldn't be where I am today. It's given me strength to be the woman that I am today – to be able to raise children as a single mum, and still the boys achieve and do good at school. Because of that strength I am now able to provide for my family. I am emotionally and mentally stable through that support, so it covers everything really, not just for the shorter term, but I think for the longer term. Because that is the foundation that it lays, that whatever happens now, I know how far I have come through that support. This is how we support people to get them to integrate and become who they want to be.

I think the strengths perspective does work. I think it does really work when you put this approach at the centre of everything that we do. It might be difficult decisions that we make along the way, but as long as it underpins everything that we do, I think it changes lives.'

Jokow

'I am 25 years old and I heard of START when I first came, in my first few months in Plymouth City. That was back in 2017. I was still in the asylum process so I heard from someone at Red Cross that he was going to START but I didn't know where START was or what he was doing.

When I was granted my refugee status in January 2018, that's when I first came into contact with START and my experience, I must say, was very, very, very helpful. I met Susie, the first person, and from there it's been always help, yeah. I always received a huge amount of help from START from day one.

We started with the housing, moving from homelessness to temporary and then from temporary to permanent so I could be stable in terms of housing. Initially I didn't even know about tenancy and how to maintain it but through the help of START, yeah. So I transitioned easily from homelessness to full tenancy. Now without the help of START I'm sure it would have been very difficult.

Through the help of people like Kathy who was my caseworker and Abigail who was one of the students, quickly they established my Universal Credit. I stayed with the Job Centre for about a month and then we managed to write a good CV and I got a job offer, within a month. Everything just fell into place really.

That was April 2018. So that was my first taste of a job in a call centre.

It was just receiving calls and also outgoing calls about the products of the company. It was a good experience. Talking to the public, yeah. And once I got the job, I managed to put a month's money and move to get a house. START helped me place the deposit guarantee through PATH (Plymouth Access to Housing). Without START, it would have been hard to do that bit. I moved in in May.

Next contact was volunteering [with START] really. I did volunteer from June, I was doing Job Club and also helping, a bit of interpreting sometime. While I was volunteering, I was working with Hana – she was organising the volunteers, so she informed me about the vacancy [to work at START]. That's when I applied. I did not hesitate when the vacancy came up, I would say, towards the end of November.

Yeah, and I remember START gave me the opportunity to try my skill and also build my skill, so it's really just been one of the best steps in my career and also my personal life. It's changed a huge part of me, I would say the skills have, that came with the work. Also the kind of colleagues. The thing is if you're working with START, you're working as a family, not as just a workplace. You have a lot of support here, it's a learning environment where everybody just learns. Everybody helps each other. If you don't know, you ask, and somebody in the group or team will always help you.

So I've learned a lot of skills that I really didn't know ... casework skills in the beginning, yeah. And I'm hoping I did contribute to the organisation.

And also, to be honest, I think we have good service users that are really very, very, very supportive. They just need our hand and they are eager too. With the help of the team I think I have managed. I would say it's teamwork, it's been very rewarding generally I'd say.

The passion I got from working with refugees, being a refugee itself, and now also to be given an opportunity. It's like somebody trusting in you to be given a chance in life. I'm trying something. In the beginning I had self-doubt and all that because it's not an area of my expertise. But, like I say, through the help of START, now I can say I'm a caseworker, a social worker. I find now I have a deep desire, a passion to help people in need and that is one big character that is in everybody in START, that they are always there to help people who are in need. So that is something that I've taken away and I'm hoping to transfer that wherever I go, definitely.

I think the strengths approach means that every contribution from everyone in the team, from trustees to the students – whatever they say is taken on board, is accepted. Like I say, the environment itself is more like a family. Everyone works hand in hand, helping each other, supporting each other and we listen to each other and what everybody says is welcome. That's what I understand by that. Everyone contributes their small part to the overall organisation objective, which is a rare model and is a very good model, I think. Everybody has their own one or two skills that they bring with them, and if you look at the overall team from trustees to the student or the volunteer, if you put all these skills together that makes the work easy on everyone. So yeah, the organisation is achieving a lot. That's what I think is the strengths approach.

In START if you're part of the team, we look out for each other. Everybody is just ready to help – ready to help in their little way, and you find even students who are new, just come for a week and then they are ready to help. That's a good feeling. It's been a good feeling.

I think the challenges have been overridden by the team support. Maybe the challenges were something to do with limited knowledge in some things, but again I'd always ask. There has to be someone who knows in the team.

To be honest I think the challenges were all overcome because of the team.

That's a big thing that START is built on, the compassion to help, making sure that someone's suffering is abated. So put the person who needs first, that provides the sense of humility. However little the organisation has, then they always want to find a way of helping. Also being part of the team. It's not about individual[s], it's about everybody. Whether you are a volunteer or whether you are staff, you have to know you feel valued and also that people rely on you sometimes, on what you say, so that's a big thing I will take away.

START is more like a family not just an organisation. Everybody is now part of my past, part of my life. I think I would say thank you for the opportunity, that is, as a refugee the journeys people go through are difficult but when, like I say, if you are in START it's an educational environment, you always feel welcome, and I also feel good to know that there's someone who will look out, who will look after you. I always tell my mum when we joke sometimes that I have a lot of mothers in START. Because she says that she's worried about me, but I say that I have a lot of mothers here. Everybody looks out for each other, which is really great, so thank you for the opportunity, the confidence you have shown me, the trust. Going forward I may change my mind and even be a social worker, change from economics, yeah. That has been made possible by my experience and I know this is just a beginning. I think the world is better when everybody is a social worker.'

Tesfa

'I knew about START when I was in Cardiff because people were saying "If you go to Plymouth there is a supportive agency called START and Refugee Council" and so first I went to DCRS (Devon and Cornwall Refugee Support) and then came to START, even before I get my refugee status.

I had to wait a year to become a refugee. And then, even when I was getting support from DCRS, I started voluntary work with START. I was shadowing my caseworker and what she was doing for me. She was really helpful. I carried on doing my voluntary work – DCRS, Refugee Council, everywhere.

I got my status after a year in 2013.

START is locally well known like it's a home for refugees. So that was in my mind and I didn't want to go to somewhere else. The caseworker from PATH [under contract from START] was a student and really nice. She took me to the Job Centre and sorted out my benefit, and my accommodation. They sent me my National Insurance number. I was still doing voluntary work and she was encouraging me: "You're really doing very well. Just carry on doing all the stuff you are doing."

I was working voluntarily at Red Cross and became one of the staff at the Welcome Project – the only lady working with guys welcoming refugees, taking them to the Post Office to get their money, getting them registered with a GP and all sorts of things. They gave me one month paid cover for maternity leave. When I finished that they were still thinking "Which way can we help you to get a job?" Then START advertised this job and I got it because I had voluntary experience, and one month as a paid worker. I have been working in this paid job here for five years.

Working for START is really, really interesting. Every single day you learn a lot – from refugees and your colleagues, because it's teamwork. No one is saying "This is my job. That's yours." Everyone is just sharing ideas and helping each other. And for refugees also, I can understand them because I feel, I passed through this journey and that calms me. That reminds me of my journey and my life. Even if they get angry or anxious, I can understand them because of the situation they passed. START is like home, like a lifesaver.

START is special – special for all of us – special for refugees. Yeah.

It doesn't matter if you speak the language or not. It's respectful for everybody. For example, if they don't speak English, START can provide an interpreter. If they don't have anybody, START can connect them with communities. START is not only getting money from a Job Centre or getting their accommodation. START can help if they want to move city. START is home. Do you understand? For example, this is my home. I don't want to go to anywhere else because I can get whatever I want from my home. START is like that.

Most of the refugees get a job through START because we are supporting them with their CVs, job search and a reference: no one else can give them a reference except START. I mean, to ask START is easier for refugees because they don't know anywhere else – even to get support for their job application. That gives them independence. And through the Job Club we give them a chance to try a computer themselves. Like, that's a chance, for example, for myself even. START always give a chance for people to try. That's something special as well about START. That's why most of the refugees volunteer. They used to start from scratch and then, little by little, they are helping us as well. Yes, and with their family everywhere, like Cultural Kitchen or the allotment or women's group. These are the places for them to be relaxed in, with nothing to worry about. It just feels safe. If people come to START that means they are safe. Everything will be fine. They think "We have this caseworker – we are OK." That's it.

I always say I'm the luckiest person because everyone is giving me ideas or encouraging me: "If you did this, you'll be fine." I am in this place and in the future. I feel really happy with everything and with everybody. I would really like to say thank you for you and for all of START. I didn't know myself before and that I'll be calm, so that's something for me as well.'

Eric

'My name is Eric Hadi. I am a 42-year-old living in Zakho city (Kurdistan region of Iraq). I am the director of Zakho International School. There is nowhere better than home and nothing can be compared to the homeland. Nonetheless, all my dreams and goals are achieved thanks to START and the time I spent in the UK.

I graduated in 1998 with a Diploma in English and in 2018 with a Bachelor degree in English. The first of the class of 38 and with an average of 90 (Outstanding Performance).

I am privileged and honoured to take part and I would love to share my story. I have achieved many goals. I owe much of these achievements to wonderful times and experience gained working and volunteering at START. The knowledge and expertise I acquired working and assisting the team, and the language proficiency have granted and paved the way for me to reach the ultimate and glorious heights I always dreamed of. Therefore, I am obligated to express my utmost appreciation and gratitude to the team at START for standing and supporting us in the most difficult times when there were not many opportunities available for many vulnerable people, including me.

I arrived in the UK and claimed asylum in July 2003. First, I lived in London then was relocated to Stoke-on-Trent under the NASS support system. My application [for asylum] was denied due to the change of address as the Home Office had not noticed the letters I sent informing them about it (later to admit as I was granted an appeal). I was left homeless with no accommodation or support and I was not allowed to have any sort of occupation. I had to face many challenges and obstacles and was left very desperate to seek any sort of support no matter where it was. It is obvious that we cannot play, learn or achieve when we are hungry, weak and homeless. Nonetheless, I was advised to travel to a new city I had never heard of, called Plymouth. There, I was promised to find support, supportive organisations and kind-hearted people that would surely assist my case and help me get back on my feet. (That promise was not a fairy tale and I had the necessary back-up needed.) After I arrived in Plymouth I started a whole new life and for the first time I had the opportunity to interact, communicate and integrate into the community. It gave me the chance to be enrolled in several courses such as Plymouth College of Further Education,

Open Doors (English Language Courses) and a course on IT. Further, to improve my English I joined BTCV [the British Trust for Conservation Volunteers] and worked with YES [Youth Enquiry Service]. However, I was eager to do more and go the farthest to improve my language skills, integrate into the community and repay my debts (voluntarily) to the Great Country that accepted me and given me the chance to breathe some freedom and [to be] treated with respect.

Plymouth had opened new gates of interest, learning and individual gains for me and many more. The Cultural Kitchen managed by START was one of many projects that I really enjoyed. I was always there to take part and do some chores such as preparing and serving food, washing up and cleaning, and keeping children occupied. Every Friday, individuals and families from local communities and different backgrounds from the city and around would gather, cook their favourite and traditional dishes, chat and sing, play games and share memories and meals together. There I had the opportunity to develop more friendships and get to know more people. Gradually as one of many volunteers, I got more involved and participated in extra activities and events organised by START. All these boosted my confidence and contributed to my personal improvement in all aspects of life. The Cultural Kitchen project was a great idea, not only to get people together but also to support people just like me whose weekly allowance only covered 70 per cent of their essential needs. It was a place to enjoy a healthy meal for all members of the family and for children to have fun and do many different activities.

As one of the personal projects to self-develop and improve for my future career, I volunteered to work at START office. Part of my duties was to communicate with people and listen to their issues and concerns. In addition, I had to work with different groups of students and refugee families. This was very necessary for me to build my personality, improve communication skills and build professional relationships – all this still plays a major role in my life until today.

START is an outstanding NGO that is dedicated to bringing people together, building bridges, and supporting vulnerable families and individuals. The strengths approach is in the duties, tasks and obstacles that the START team manage to reveal, expose to all related parties and find practical and lasting solutions; also, by bringing two different groups (students and refugees) together to benefit from each other. The Cultural Kitchen is one example of what the team at START had been searching for to solve the financial allowance issue for asylum seekers and refugee families. Students at START get to understand the lives of refugees, and a closer look into what refugees and asylum seekers face in their daily lives – the problems they have to overcome and the kind of support and assistance they need; not forgetting the communication skills needed to approach them and being extra careful not to harm their feelings or reminding them of the atrocities and suffering they have experienced in their homelands or the journey to safety and starting a new life in a new and strange environment.

Finally, I just feel blessed and fortunate to be chosen to participate in this wonderful book. I would like to express my utmost appreciation and gratitude for the great team working at START and wish them the best and prosperous life and future.'

Gabriella de Souza

'I'm 22 years old, I'm a British citizen now but I came from Angola; I'm training to become a teacher and I've just completed my Master's degree in chemistry.

I don't really remember much from the beginning because I was quite young. What I remember most from when I was a kid is more the feeling. I think about START and remember how happy I was to be there and how it felt like such an important part of my life.

But I have two very vivid memories of the evenings at Cultural Kitchen.

One was showing up really early with my mum and older brother and helping to count the fresh fruit and veg, setting up the tables with the volunteers and then tormenting my mum while she was cooking and wouldn't let five-year-old me into the kitchen. It was a peace-haven, other kids my age who also didn't speak good English, but we had a great time playing. From a young age I was exposed to the beauty of culture and the variety of it, which made me really grow as a person. The volunteers were always happy, and I learnt from them just as much as they learnt from me.

My second vivid memory was clearing up Cultural Kitchen. Of course, five-year-old me was not allowed to help clean the kitchen, so instead I would help by cleaning the tables, putting toys away (I was entrusted with the toy cupboard key, wasn't that exciting?) and then the best bit – running up the hill at full speed with Avril and Deirdre to empty the bins.

I grew up with START, so I went to a fair few walks, picnics, swimming sessions and I can't remember exactly where they were, and exactly who went, but I do remember that these times were some of the happiest of my life. Eventually I was allowed in the kitchen to help cook. This was a big achievement, so I was able to learn all about teamwork even though we couldn't all speak each other's languages. I find that brilliant.

I know that START uses the strengths perspective – from what I know, it's about building up a person/team/community by working to the strengths of these individuals to empower and help build a positive environment.

START has helped many families, mine included, and to this day, I recognise familiar faces. I think that everyone should have the opportunity to experience this, to grow up in a happy, safe and culturally diverse environment.'

Gabriella's poem

In the midst of a sea of hate
Where the word 'refugee'
Brings so much distaste

Where humanity is thin
And almost faded
We stand tall
and wholly create

a place we feel safe
a place we adore one another
a place we call home
no matter the colour.

Here we can love
Here we can grow
Here we unite
And forever we know
To smile
To laugh
To live
To run
We are the future
And we are one.

References

Abel, J. and Clarke, L. (2020) *The Compassion Project*, London: Aster.

Ager, A. and Strang, A. (2004) *The Experience of Integration: A Qualitative Study of Refugee Integration in the Local Communities of Pollockshaws and Islington*, London: Home Office.

Agyeman, G. (2008) 'White researcher – black subjects: Exploring the challenges of researching the marginalised and "invisible"', *The Electronic Journal of Business Research Methods*, 6(1): 77–84.

Allan, T. (2018) 'Inclusion and the commons: exploring the spaces beyond market and the state', discussion paper, Centre for Welfare Reform. Available from: https://www.centreforwelfarereform.org/library/inclusion-and-the-commons.html [Accessed 9 June 2021].

Allen, R. (2018) 'Welcome new social workers: The world really needs you!' *The Agenda*, Professional Social Work Magazine, BASW, September, p 27. Available from: https://www.basw.co.uk/system/files/resources/Welcome%20New%20Social%20Workers.pdf [Accessed 26 October 2020].

APA (American Psychiatric Association) (2013) *Diagnostic and Statistical Manual of Mental Disorders* (5th edn) (DSM-5), Washington, DC: American Psychiatric Publishing.

Armstrong, S. (2017) 'Want, disease, ignorance, squalor and idleness: Are Beveridge's five evils back?', *The Guardian*, [online] 10 October. Available from: https://www.theguardian.com/society/2017/oct/10/beveridge-five-evils-welfare-state [Accessed 7 November 2020].

Attlee, C. (1920) *The Social Worker*, London: G. Bell and Sons.

Baines, D. (2010) ' "If we don't get back to where we were before": Working in the restructured non-profit social services', *British Journal of Social Work*, 40(3): 928–45.

BBC (2017) *Ramblings: Mount Edgcumbe, Plymouth, Series 35*. Available from: https://www.bbc.co.uk/programmes/b08k4bxw [Accessed 8 December 2020].

Beddoe, L. and Harington, P. (2012) 'One step in a thousand-mile journey: Can civic practice be nurtured in practitioner research? Reporting on an innovative project', *British Journal of Social Work*, 42(1): 74–93.

Bellinger, A. (2010) 'Talking about (re)generation: Practice learning as a site of renewal for social work', *British Journal of Social Work*, 40(8): 2450–66.

Bellinger, A. and Elliott, T. (2011) 'What are you looking at? The potential of appreciative inquiry as a research approach for social work', *British Journal of Social Work*, 41(4): 708–25.

Bellinger, A. and Testa, D. (2016) 'Student-led services', in A. Bellinger and D. Ford (eds) *Practice Placement in Social Work: Innovative Approaches for Effective Teaching and Learning*, Bristol: Policy Press, pp 5–19.

Bellinger, A., Bullen, D. and Ford, D. (2014) 'Practice research in practice learning: Students as co-researchers and co-constructors of knowledge', *Nordic Social Work Research*, 4(sup1): 58–69.

Bellinger, A., Ford, D. and Moran, B. (2016) 'Cultivating discretion: Social work education in practice and the academy', in A. Bellinger and D. Ford (eds) *Practice Placement in Social Work: Innovative Approaches for Effective Teaching and Learning*, Bristol: Policy Press, pp 203–14.

Beresford, P., Croft, S. and Adshead, L. (2008) '"We don't see her as a social worker": A service user case study of the importance of the social worker's relationship and humanity', *British Journal of Social Work*, 38(7): 1388–407.

Bernstein, B. (2000) *Pedagogy, Symbolic Control and Identity: Theory, Research and Critique*, Oxford: Rowman & Littlefield.

Bertelli, M. (2019) 'Mediterranean defiant as Italy impounds refugee rescue ship', *Aljazeera*, 13 May. Available from: https://www.aljazeera.com/news/2019/5/13/mediterranea-defiant-as-italy-impounds-refugee-rescue-ship [Accessed 23 November 2020].

Billington, M. (2019) 'How Not to Drown review: An adolescent adventure story of a Kosovan refugee', *The Guardian*, [online] 5 August. Available from: https://www.theguardian.com/stage/2019/aug/05/how-not-to-drown-review-traverse-edinburgh-festival-2019 [Accessed 10 December 2020].

Birrell, I. (2020) 'A shameful failure of decency'. Available from: https://www.ianbirrell.com/a-shameful-failure-of-decency/ [Accessed 13 December 2020].

Blood, I. and Guthrie, L. (2018) *Supporting Older People Using Attainment-Informed and Strengths-Based Approaches*, London: Jessica Kingsley Publishers.

Bovaird, T. (2014) 'Efficiency in third sector partnerships for delivering local government services: The role of economies of scale, scope and learning', *Public Management Review*. Available from: https://www.qub.ac.uk/sites/media/Media,514081,en.pdf [Accessed 7 November 2020].

Bowcott, O. (2015) 'Capita ordered to pay costs over failure to provide interpreters to family courts', *The Guardian*, [online] 2 February. Available from: https://www.theguardian.com/business/2015/feb/02/capita-failure-provide-interpreters-family-courts [Accessed 29 December 2020].

Bradshaw, T. (2008). 'The post-place community: Contributions to the debate about the definition of community', *Community Development*, 39(1): 5–16.

Brady, B. (2011) 'Revealed: The true scale of Britain's woodland sell-off', *The Independent*, [online] 18 December. Available from: https://www.independent.co.uk/news/uk/politics/revealed-true-scale-britain-s-woodland-sell-6278861.html [Accessed 7 December 2020].

Braun, V. and Clarke, V. (2006) 'Using thematic analysis in psychology', *Qualitative Research in Psychology*, 3(2): 77–101.

Braye, S. and Preston-Shoot, M. (2006) 'Broadening the vision: Law teaching, social work and civil society', *International Social Work*, 49(3): 376–89.

Braye, S. and Preston-Shoot, M. (2016) *Legal Literacy: Practice Tool*, Dartington: Research in Practice. Available from: https://www.researchinpractice.org.uk/adults/publications/2016/october/legal-literacy-practice-tool-2016/ [Accessed 13 December 2020].

Braye, S., Preston-Shoot, M. with Cull, L., Johns, R. and Roche, J. (2005) *SCIE Knowledge Review 08: Teaching, Learning and Assessment of Law in Social Work Education*, London: Social Care Institute for Excellence.

Braye, S., Preston-Shoot, M. and Johns, R. (2006) 'Lost in translation? Teaching law to non-lawyers: Reviewing the evidence from social work', *The Law Teacher*, 40(2): 131–50.

Bregman, R. (2020) *Humankind: A Hopeful History*, London: Bloomsbury.

Breton, R. (1964) 'Institutional completeness of ethnic communities and the personal relations of immigrants', *American Journal of Sociology*, 70(2): 193–205.

Brookfield, S. (2009) 'The concept of critical reflection: Promises and contradictions', *European Journal of Social Work*, 12(3): 293–304.

Browne, B. (2004) 'Imagine Chicago: A methodology for cultivating community', *Journal of Community and Applied Social Psychology*, 14(5): 394–405.

Butler, A. (2005) 'A strengths approach to building futures: Students and refugees together', *Community Development Journal*, 40(2): 147–57.

Butler, A. (2007) 'Students and refugees together: Towards a model of student practice learning as service provision', *Social Work Education*, 26(3): 233–46.

Butler, A., Elliot, T. and Stopard, N. (2003) 'Living up to the standards we set: A critical account of the development of anti-racist standards', *Social Work Education*, 22(3): 271–82.

Butler, A., Conceicao, C. and Finch, K. (2006) 'Students and refugees together (START): Inter-professional learning and service innovation', *Irish Journal of Applied Social Studies*, 7(2): 62–75.

Butler, A., Ford, D. and Tregaskis, C. (2007) 'Who do we think we are? Self and reflexivity in social work practice', *Qualitative Social Work*, 6(3): 281–99.

Carey, M. (2003) 'Anatomy of a care manager', *Work, Employment and Society*, 17(1): 121–35.

Carney, M. (2020) *The Reith Lectures*. Available from: https://www.bbc.co.uk/sounds/play/m000q3sp [Accessed 1 January 2021].

Carter, B. (2006) ' "One expertise among many" – working appreciatively to make miracles instead of finding problems: Using appreciative inquiry as a way of reframing research', *Journal of Research in Nursing*, 11(1): 48–63.

Carter, F. (1986) 'Writing our own history: Spend, spend, spent?' *Trouble and Strife*, 8: 51–6.

Carter, M. (2019) *All Together Now? One Man's Walk in Search of his Father and a Lost England*, London: Guardian Faber.

Chapin, R. (1995) 'Social policy development: The strengths perspective', *Social Work*, 40(4): 506–14.

Charity Commission (2010) *Charities and the Economic Downturn*. Available from: https://assets.publishing.service. gov.uk/government/uploads/system/uploads/attachment_ data/file/315540/economic_downturn4.pdf [Accessed 7 November 2020].

Chatterjee, P. and Sarangi, S. (2004) 'Social identity and group lending' (No. 405), DIW Discussion Papers, Berlin: German Institute for Economic Research. Available at: https://www. diw.de/documents/publikationen/73/41263/dp405.pdf [Accessed 29 December 2020].

Chen, I. and Popovich, K. (2003) 'Understanding customer relationship management (CRM)', *Business Process Management Journal*, 9(5): 672–88.

Childs, T. (2017) *Creative Capacity Building in Uganda: Qualitative Research into the Impact of CCB on Individuals and Communities across Uganda*, International Development Innovation Network. Available from: https://www.idin.org/sites/default/ files/resources/CCBUgandaCasesFinal_0.pdf [Accessed 7 December 2020].

Chui, W. and Ford, D. (2012) 'Crisis intervention as common practice', in P. Stepney. and D. Ford (eds) *Social Work Models, Methods and Theories*, Lyme Regis: Russell House Publishing, pp 80–101.

Church, K. (1995) *Forbidden Narratives: Critical Autobiography as Social Science*, Amsterdam: Gordon and Breach Science Publishers.

Clarke, J. and Newman, J. (1997) *The Managerial State*, London: Sage.

Clarke, S. (2000) *Social Work as Community Development: A Management Model for Social Change* (2nd edn), Aldershot: Ashgate.

The Climate Docket (2019) 'Court advisors urge Dutch Supreme Court to uphold historic climate verdict'. Available from: https://www.climatedocket.com/2019/09/13/urgenda-dutch-supreme-court-appeal/ [Accessed 13 December 2020].

Coghlan, A., Preskill, H. and Catsambos, T. (2003) 'An overview of appreciative inquiry in evaluation', *New Directions for Evaluation*, 100: 5–22.

Cohen, S. (2002) 'The local state of immigration controls', *Critical Social Policy*, 22(3): 518–43.

Cohen, S. (2006) *Deportation is Freedom! The Orwellian World of Immigration Controls*, London: Jessica Kingsley Publishers.

Colwell, M. (2019) *Curlew Moon*, London: HarperCollins.

Cooper, C. (2016) 'EU referendum: Immigration and Brexit – what lies have been spread?' *The Independent*, [online] 20 June. Available from: https://www.independent.co.uk/news/uk/politics/eu-referendum-immigration-and-brexit-what-lies-have-been-spread-a7092521.html [Accessed 9 December 2020].

Cooperrider, D. and Srivastva, S. (1987) 'Appreciative inquiry in organisational life', *Research in Organisational Change and Development*, 1: 129–69.

Corradi, S. (2020) *Sitting in Limbo*, London: Left Bank Pictures, BBC.

Cottam, H. (2019) *Radical Help: How We Can Remake the Relationships Between Us and Revolutionise the Welfare State*, London: Virago.

Craston, M., Balfour, R., Henley, M., Baxendale, J. and Fullick, S. (2020) *Process Evaluation of the Violence Reduction Units*, London: Home Office.

Currens, J. (2003) 'The 2:1 clinical placement model', *Physiotherapy*, 89(9): 540–54.

Dalrymple, J. and Burke, B. (2006) *Anti-Oppressive Practice: Social Care and the Law*, Maidenhead: Open University Press.

Darling, J. and Passarlay, G. (2017) *A Shared Britain: Refugee Policy for 2017*. Available from: http://blog.policy.manchester.ac.uk/posts/2017/01/refugeepolicy2017/ [Accessed 9 December 2020].

Davys, A. and Beddoe, L. (2021) *Best Practice in Professional Supervision: A Guide for the Helping Professions* (2nd edn), London: Jessica Kingsley Publishers.

De Angelis, M. (2003) 'Reflections on alternatives, commons and communities, or, building a new world from the bottom up', *The Commoner*, 6. Available from: https://thecommoner. org/wp-content/uploads/2020/06/Massimo-de-Angelis-Reflections-on-Alternatives-Commons-and-Communities. pdf [Accessed 16 December 2020].

Dees, J. (1998) *The Meaning of Social Entrepreneurship*, Kansas City: Kauffman Institute and Stanford University.

Dennis, R. (2008) 'Refugee performance: Aesthetic representation and accountability in playback theatre', *Research in Drama Education*, 13(2): 211–15.

Department of Health and Social Care (2016) *Department of Health Strategic Statement for Social Work with Adults in England 2016–2020*. Available from: https://www.gov.uk/ government/publications/vision-for-adult-social-work-in-england [Accessed 13 December 2020].

Dhalech, M. (1999) *Challenging Racism in the Rural Idyll: Final Report of the Rural Race Equality Project Cornwall, Devon and Somerset 1996–1998*, Exeter: NACAB.

Dorow, S. and O'Shaughnessy, S. (2013) 'Fort McMurray, Wood Buffalo, and the oil/tar sands: Revisiting the sociology of "community"', *Canadian Journal of Sociology*, 38(2): 121–40.

Dunn, W., Koenig, K., Cox, J., Sabata, D., Pope, E., Foster, L. and Blackwell, A. (2013) 'Harnessing strengths: Daring to celebrate EVERYONE'S unique contributions, Part 1', *Developmental Disabilities*, 36(1): 1–3.

Duong, T. (2016) 'Amazon Rainforest will collapse by 2064, new study predicts', *EcoWatch*. Available from: https://www. ecowatch.com/amazon-rainforest-collapse-2649776959. html?rebelltitem=6#toggle-gdpr [Accessed 6 August 2021].

Eggers, D. (2006) *What is the What: The Autobiography of Valentino Achak Deng*, London: Penguin Books.

Embra, K. (2014) 'The well-being of refugees in the UK: Living in peace. An appreciative inquiry study', PhD thesis, Plymouth University.

Engelbrecht, L. (2010) 'A strengths perspective on supervision of social workers: An alternative management paradigm within a social development context', *Social Work and Social Sciences Review*, 14(1): 47–58.

Evans, T. (2010) *Professional Discretion in Welfare Services: Beyond Street-Level Bureaucracy*, Abingdon: Ashgate.

Farmaian, S. (1993) *Daughter of Persia: A Woman's Journey from Her Father's Harem Through the Islamic Revolution*, New York: Anchor Books/Doubleday.

Feldhendler, D. (2007) 'Playback theatre: A method for intercultural dialogue', *Scenario*, 1(2): 46–55.

Field, R. and Miller, C. (2017) *Asset-based Commissioning*, Bournemouth: Bournemouth University.

Fish, M. and Fakoussa, O. (2018) 'Towards culturally inclusive mental health: Learning from focus groups with those with refugee and asylum seeker status in Plymouth', *International Journal of Migration, Health and Social Care*, 14(4): 361–76.

Fook, J. (1996) *The Reflective Researcher: Social Workers' Theories of Practice Research*, London: Allen & Unwin.

Fook, J. (2001) 'Identifying expert social work: Qualitative practitioner research', in I. Shaw and N. Gould (eds) *Qualitative Research in Social Work*, Thousand Oaks: Sage, pp 116–31.

Ford, D. (2012) 'Anti-racism and social work', in P. Stepney and D. Ford (eds) *Social Work Models, Methods and Theories: A Framework for Practice* (2nd edn), Lyme Regis: Russell House Publishing, pp 51–61.

Ford, D. and Nosowska, G. (2020) 'Supervision for social work in disasters'. Available from: https://www.researchinpractice.org.uk/all/news-views/2020/may/supervision-for-social-work-in-disasters/ [Accessed 2 January 2021].

Ford, P., Johnston, B., Brumfit, C., Mitchell, R. and Myles, F. (2005) 'Practice learning and the development of students as critical practitioners: Some findings from research', *Social Work Education*, 24(4): 391–407.

Freire, P. (1970) *Pedagogy of the Oppressed*, London: Bloomsbury.

Friedman, M. (2005) *Trying Hard is Not Good Enough: How to Produce Measurable Improvements for Customers and Communities*, Victoria, Canada: Trafford Publishing.

Gawande, A. (2010) *The Checklist Manifesto: How to Get Things Right*, London: Profile Books.

Gawande, A. (2012) 'Daily comment: Something wicked this way comes', *The New Yorker*, 28 June. Available from: https://www.newyorker.com/news/daily-comment/something-wicked-this-way-comes [Accessed 18 April 2021].

Gayle, D. (2018) 'Oxfam sexual exploitation scandal in Haiti', *The Guardian*, [online] 15 June. Available from: https://www.theguardian.com/world/2018/jun/15/timeline-oxfam-sexual-exploitation-scandal-in-haiti [Accessed 5 November 2020].

GDPR (2018) *Guide to the General Data Protection Regulation*, Information Commissioners Office, 25 May. Available from: https://www.gov.uk/government/publications/guide-to-the-general-data-protection-regulation [Accessed 7 November 2020].

Gentleman, A. (2019) *The Windrush Betrayal: Exposing the Hostile Environment*, London: Guardian Faber Publishing.

Gill, R. (2009) 'Breaking the silence: The hidden injuries of neo-liberal academia', in R. Flood and R. Gill (eds) *Secrecy and Silence in the Research Process: Feminist Reflections*, London: Routledge, pp 228–44.

Gipetti, R., Lloyd, Y., Greathead, H., Chaplin, D., Locke, M. and Smith, P. (2013) *STARTwalking*, Plymouth: Truffle Hog. Available from: http://www.studentsandrefugeestogether.com/publications/swfb.pdf [Accessed 8 December 2020].

Giroux, H. (2014) *Neoliberalism's War on Higher Education*, Chicago: Haymarket Books.

Glasby, J., Miller, R. and Lynch, J. (2013) *Turning the Welfare State Upside Down? Developing a New Adult Social Care Offer*, Birmingham: Health Services Management Centre, University of Birmingham.

Gnant, E. (2018) 'Practical placement reflection: Support work with refugees', unpublished report for International Social Work (Dual Award) Degree, Protestant University of Applied Sciences Ludwigsburg, Germany and Newman University Birmingham, United Kingdom.

Gnant, E. (2019) 'Social work approaches to environmental justice', BA Dissertation, International Social Work, Protestant University of Applied Sciences Ludwigsburg, Germany and Newman University Birmingham, United Kingdom.

Goldsworthy, J. (2002) 'Resurrecting a model of integrating individual work with community development and social action', *Community Development Journal*, 37(4): 327–37.

Goode, W. (1957) 'Community within a community: The professions', *American Sociological Review*, 22(2): 194–200.

Gorman, H. and Postle, K. (2003) *Transforming Community Care: A Distorted Vision?* Birmingham: Venture Press.

GOV.UK (2010) *17011 Case Resolution Directorate, FOI Release*, 22 December, London: Home Office.

GOV.UK (2017) *Keeping Kids Company: Intention to Commence Company Director Disqualification Proceedings Advised*, 31 July, The Insolvency Service.

Grant, S. and Humphries, M. (2006) 'Critical evaluation of appreciative inquiry: Bridging an apparent paradox', *Action Research*, 4(4): 401–18.

Gray, M. (2011) 'Back to basics: A critique of the strengths perspective in social work', *Families in Society*, 92(1): 5–11.

Graybeal, C. (2001) 'Strengths-based social work assessment: Transforming the dominant paradigm', *Families in Society: The Journal of Contemporary Human Services*, 82(3): 233–42.

Green, B. (2020) 'Drowning in neoliberal lies: State responses towards people seeking asylum', *British Journal of Social Work*, 50(3): 908–25.

Green, F. (2004) 'Work intensification, discretion, and the decline in well-being at work', *Eastern Economic Journal*, 30(4): 615–25.

Griffin, J. and Tyrrell, J. (2003) *Human Givens: A New Approach to Emotional Health and Clear Thinking*, Chalvington: Human Givens Publishing.

Halliday, J. (2020) 'Boris Johnson was warned over Covid "moonshot" testing programme', *The Guardian*, [online] 15 September. Available from: https://www.theguardian.com/world/2020/sep/15/boris-johnson-was-warned-over-covid-moonshot-testing-plan [Accessed 1 January 2021].

Halpern, J. and Sloan, M. (2020) *Welcome to the New World*, London: Bloomsbury.

Ham, C. and Tuddenham, R. (2020) 'Testing and contact tracing: A role for local leaders', HSJ. Available from: https://www.hsj.co.uk/technology-and-innovation/testing-and-contact-tracing-a-role-for-local-leaders/7027567.article [Accessed 29 December 2020].

Hamer, M. (2006) *The Barefoot Helper: Mindfulness and Creativity in Social Work and the Caring Professions*, Lyme Regis: Russell House Publishing.

Hardin, G. (1968) 'The tragedy of the commons', *Science*, 162: 1243–8.

Harms, L., Boddy, J., Hickey, L., Hay, K., Alexander, M., Briggs, L., Cooper, L., Alston, M., Fronek, P., Howard, A., Adamson, C. and Hazeleger, T. (2020) 'Post-disaster social work research: A scoping review of the evidence for practice', *International Social Work*. Available from: https://doi.org/10.1177/0020872820904135 [Accessed 9 June 2021].

Harrell-Bond, B. (1986) *Imposing Aid: Emergency Assistance to Refugees*, Oxford: Oxford University Press.

Harvie, D. (2004) 'Commons and communities in the university: Some notes and some examples', *The Commoner*, Autumn/Winter, 1–10. Available from: https://thecommoner.org/wp-content/uploads/2020/06/David-Harvie-Commons-and-Communities-in-the-University.pdf [Accessed 10 May 2021].

Hill, A. (2018) 'Home Office "wrongly tried to deport 300 skilled migrants"', *The Guardian*, 23 November. Available from: https://www.theguardian.com/uk-news/2018/nov/23/home-office-tried-to-deport-300-skilled-migrants-under-terrorism-law [Accessed 9 December, 2020].

Hingley-Jones, H. and Ruch, G. (2016) 'Stumbling through? Relationship-based social work practice in austere times', *Journal of Social Work Practice*, 30(3): 235–48.

Hoffer, E. (1973) *Reflections on the Human Condition*, New York: Harper & Row.

Hollis, F. (1964) *Casework: A Psychosocial Therapy*, New York: Random House.

Holman, B. (2001) 'Forming solid relationships should be a priority', *The Guardian*, 12 July.

Holmyard, L. (2020) 'Women's strengths and growth in reciprocal relationship in the context of forced displacement', Doctoral Thesis, University of Exeter.

Hood, C. (1991) 'A public management for all seasons?', *Public Administration*, 69(1): 3–19.

Hood, C. (1995) 'The "New Public Management" in the 1980s: Variations on a theme', *Accounting, Organisations and Society*, 20(2/3): 93–109.

Horton, V. (2018) *Report on Kulika Uganda Microfinance Loan Programmes*, Kampala: Kulika Uganda (unpublished).

Howe, D. (1991) 'Knowledge, power and the shape of social work practice', in M. Davies (ed) *The Sociology of Social Work*, London: Routledge, pp 202–220.

Howe, D. (1992) *An Introduction to Social Work Theory: Making Sense in Practice*, London: Wildwood House.

Hugman, R. (2009) 'But is it social work? Some reflection on mistaken identities', *British Journal of Social Work*, 39(6): 1138–53.

Hugman, R., Pittaway, E. and Bartolomei, L. (2011) 'When "do no harm" is not enough: The ethics of research with refugees and other vulnerable groups', *British Journal of Social Work*, 41(7): 1271–87.

Humphries, B. (2004) 'An unacceptable role for social work: Implementing immigration policy', *British Journal of Social Work*, 34(1): 93–107.

Humphries, B. and Hayes, D. (eds) (2004) *Social Work, Immigration and Asylum: Debates, Dilemmas and Ethical Issues for Social Work and Social Care Practice*, London: Jessica Kingsley Publishing.

IFSW (2012) *Global Social Work Statement of Ethical Principles*. Available from: https://www.ifsw.org/global-social-work-statement-of-ethical-principles/ [Accessed 11 May 2021].

IFSW (2014) 'Global definition of social work', International Federation of Social Workers. Available from: https://www.ifsw.org/what-is-social-work/global-definition-of-social-work/ [Accessed 2 June 2021].

James, E., Mitchell, R. and Morgan, H. (2020) *Social Work, Cats and Rocket Science: Stories of Making a Difference in Social Work with Adults*, London: Jessica Kingsley Publishers.

Jarrett, T. (2012) *The Supporting People Programme*, Research Paper 12/40, London: House of Commons Library.

Jay, E. (1992) *Keep Them in Birmingham: Challenging Racism in South West England*, London: Commission for Racial Equality.

Johnstone, R. (2018) 'Carillion collapse: Cabinet Office sets out plans to maintain public services run by contractor', *Civil Service World*, 1, 5 January. Available from: https://www.civilserviceworld.com/professions/article/cabinet-office-sets-out-plan-to-rebuild-trust-in-private-providers-after-carillion-collapse [Accessed 29 December 2020].

Jones, L. (2020) *Losing Eden: Why Our Minds Need the Wild*, London: Allen Lane.

Jones, M. (2012) 'Research minded practice in social work', in P. Stepney and D. Ford (eds) *Social Work: Models, Methods and Theories*, Lyme Regis: Russell House Publishing, pp 272–86.

Jordan, B. (2012) 'Making sense of the "Big Society": Social work and the moral order', *Journal of Social Work*, 12(6): 630–46.

Jordan, B. with Jordan, C. (2000) *Social Work and the Third Way: Tough Love as Social Policy*, London: Sage.

Judiciary UK (2021) *Official Receiver -v- Batmanghelidjh & others judgment*. Available from: https://www.judiciary.uk/wp-content/uploads/2021/02/Official-Receiver-v-Batmanghelidjh-judgment-120221.pdf [Accessed 18 May 2021].

Julkunen, I. (2011) 'Critical elements in evaluating and developing practice in social work', *Social Work and Social Sciences Review*, 15(1): 74–91.

Kaplan, C. (2002) 'An early example of brief strengths-based practice: Bertha Reynolds at the National Maritime Union, 1943–1947', *Smith College Studies in Social Work*, 72(3): 403–16.

Kavanagh, J. (2012) *Small Change, Big Deal: Money as if People Mattered*, Arlesford: John Hunt Publishing.

Keevers, L., Treleaven, L., Sykes, C. and Darcy, M. (2012) 'Made to measure: Taming practices with results-based accountability', *Organization Studies*, 33(1): 97–120.

Kenny, S. (2002) 'Tensions and dilemmas in community development: New discourses, new Trojans?', *Community Development Journal*, 37(4): 284–99.

Kitwood, T. (1997) *Dementia Reconsidered: The Person Comes First*, Buckingham: Open University Press.

Kivnick, H. and Stoffel, S. (2005) 'Vital involvement practice', *Journal of Gerontological Social Work*, 46(2): 85–116.

Koerin, B. (2003) 'The settlement house tradition: Current trends and future concerns', *Journal of Society and Social Welfare*, 30(2): 53–68.

Kohli, R. (2006) *Social Work with Unaccompanied Asylum-Seeking Children*, Houndmills: Palgrave.

Kolb, D. (1984) *Experiential Learning Experience as the Source of Learning and Development*, Englewood Cliffs: Prentice Hall.

Kondrat, D. (2010) 'The strengths perspective', in B. Teater (ed) *An Introduction to Applying Social Work Theories and Methods*, Maidenhead: Open University Press, pp 38–53.

Kretzmann, J. and McKnight, J. (1993) *Building Communities from the Inside Out: A Path toward Finding and Mobilizing a Community's Assets*, Chicago: ACTA Publications.

Krumer-Nevo, M. (2002) 'The arena of othering: A life-story study with women living in poverty and social marginality', *Qualitative Social Work*, 1(3): 303–18.

Kumar, S. (2019) *Elegant Simplicity*, Gabriola Island, Canada: New Society Publishers.

Laird, J. (1989) 'Women and stories: Restorying women's self-constructions', in M. McGoldrick, C. Anderson and F. Walsh (eds) *Women in Families: A Framework for Family Therapy*, London: Norton, pp 427–50.

Lam, C., Wong, H. and Leung, T. (2007) 'An unfinished reflexive journey: Social work students' reflection on their placement experiences', *British Journal of Social Work*, 37(1): 91–105.

Laxton, R. (2007) *Grow Your Own*, London: BBC film.

Lenette, C., Brough, M. and Cox, L. (2013) 'Everyday resilience: Narratives of single refugee women with children', *Qualitative Social Work*, 12(5): 637–53.

Leung, Z. (2009) 'Knowledge management in social work: Types and processes of knowledge sharing in social services organisations', *British Journal of Social Work*, 39(4): 693–709.

Lieberman, A. (2014) 'School of Social Work marks anniversary of the strengths perspective', The University of Kansas. Available from: https://news.ku.edu/2014/02/19/ku-school-social-welfare-marks-25th-anniversary-revolutionizing-social-work-practice-and [Accessed 11 May 2021].

Lietz, C. (2009) 'Establishing evidence for strengths-based interventions? Reflections from social work's research conference', *Social Work*, 54(1): 85–87.

Lipsky, M. (1980) *Street-Level Bureaucracy: Dilemmas of the Individual in Public Service*, Manhattan: Russell Sage Foundation.

Littlejohn, P. (2014) *Kids Company: Review of Financial and Governance Controls*, London: PKF Littlejohn. Available from: https://assets.publishing.service.gov.uk/government/uploads/system/uploads/attachment_data/file/455609/Kids_Company_Review_2014.pdf [Accessed 18 May 2021].

Loach, K. and Obiols, L. (2016) *I, Daniel Blake*, Film, Sundance Selects.

Lorde, A. (1984) *Sister Outsider*, Freedom, CA: The Crossing Press.

Ludema, J., Cooperrider, D. and Barrett, F. (2001) 'Appreciative inquiry: The power of the unconditional positive question', in P. Reason and H. Bradbury (eds) *Handbook of Action Research*, London: Sage, pp 189–99.

Macdonald, K. and Morgan, H. (2020) 'The impact of austerity on disabled, elderly and immigrants in the United Kingdom: A literature review', *Disability & Society*. Available from: DOI: 10.1080/09687599.2020.1779036 [Accessed 9 June 2021].

MacKinnon, C. (2010) 'Engaged scholarship as method and vocation', *Yale Journal of Law and Feminism*, 22(2): 193–205.

MacLeod, M. and Emejulu, A. (2014) 'Neoliberalism with a community face? A critical analysis of asset-based community development in Scotland', *Journal of Community Practice*, 22(4): 430–50.

Malik, K. (2020) 'For all its sophistication AI is not fit to make life-and-death decisions', *The Guardian*, 16 May. Available from: https://www.theguardian.com/commentisfree/2020/may/16/for-all-its-sophistication-ai-isnt-fit-to-make-life-or-death-decisions-for-us [Accessed 5 November 2020].

Manthey, T., Knowles, B., Asher, D. and Wahab, S. (2011) 'Strengths-based practice and motivational interviewing', *Advances in Social Work*, 12(2): 126–51.

Manthorpe, J. (2002) 'Settlements and social work education: Absorption and accommodation', *Social Work Education*, 21(4): 409–19.

Marlowe, J. (2010) 'Beyond the discourse of trauma: Shifting the focus on Sudanese refugees', *Journal of Refugee Studies*, 23(2): 183–98.

Marmot, M. (2010) *Fair Society, Healthy Lives: The Marmot Review: Strategic Review of Health Inequalities in England Post-2010*, London: The Marmot Review.

Martin, R. and Osberg, S. (2007) 'Social entrepreneurship: The case for definition', *Stanford Social Innovation Review*, Spring, 5: 29–34.

Maslow, A. (1943) 'A theory of human motivation', *Psychological Review*, 50(4): 370–96.

Mathie, A. and Cunningham, G. (2003) 'From clients to citizens: Asset-based community development as a strategy for community-driven development', *Development in Practice*, 13(5): 474–86.

May, T. (1993) 'Feelings matter: Inverting the hidden equation', in D. Hobbs and T. May (eds) *Interpreting the Field: Accounts of Ethnography*, Oxford: Clarendon Press, pp 69–97.

McFadden, P. (2015) 'Measuring burnout among UK social workers: A Community Care study'. Available from: https://www.qub.ac.uk/sites/media/Media,514081,en.pdf [Accessed 7 November 2020].

McKnight, J. and Kretzmann, J. (1996) *Mapping Community Capacity*, Evanston: Institute for Policy Research, Northwestern University.

McKnight, J. and Russell, C. (2018) 'What is distinctive about an abcd process: Four essential elements' [Blog]. Available from: https://www.nurturedevelopment.org/blog/abcd-practice/what-is-distinctive-about-an-abcd-process-four-essential-elements/ [Accessed 7 December 2020].

McNally, P. (2018) 'Development of a qualitative research framework to define social innovation', MSc Dissertation, Plymouth University. Available from: http://www.studentsandrefugeestogether. com/publications/DevelopmentofaSocialEnterprise ResearchFrameworkSTART.pdf [Accessed 7 November 2020].

McNally, P., Apostolopoulos, N. and Al-Dajani, H. (2020) 'Social innovation in refugee support: Investigating prerequisites towards a conceptual framework', in V. Ratten (ed) *Technological Progress, Inequality and Entrepreneurship*, New York: Springer Nature, pp 123–38.

Meade, A. (2016) 'The charity sector reacts to the BBC Kids Company documentary', *The Guardian*, [online] 4 February. Available from: https://www.theguardian. com/voluntary-sector-network/2016/feb/04/bbc-kids-company-documentary-charity-sector-tweets [Accessed 5 November 2020].

Meadows, D. (2002) 'Just so much, and no more', *Resurgence*, 210, January/February.

Merrick, J. (2020) 'Track and trace: Why Labour is calling for local-led COVID-19 contact tracing', *The Independent*, 14 October. Available from: https://inews.co.uk/news/politics/ track-and-trace-labour-covid-19-contact-tracing-local-coronavirus-nhs-715436 [Accessed 29 December 2020].

Mezirow, J. (1991) *Transformative Dimensions of Adult Learning*, San Francisco: Jossey-Bass.

Mies, M. (2007) 'Patriarchy and accumulation on a world scale – revisited (Keynote lecture at the Green Economics Institute, Reading, 29 October 2005)', *International Journal of Green Economics*, 1(3/4): 268–75.

Mies, M. (2014) 'No commons without community', *Community Development Journal*, 49(S1): i106–i17.

Miller, J. (2000) *The Holistic Curriculum*, Toronto: OISE.

Morris, S. (2016) 'Poppy seller who killed herself got over 3,000 requests for donations a year', *The Guardian*, [online] 20 January. Available from: https://www.theguardian.com/ society/2016/jan/20/poppy-seller-who-killed-herself-got-up-to-3000-charity-mailings-a-year [Accessed 5 November 2020].

Morrison, T. and Wonnacott, J. (2010) *Supervision: Now or Never Reclaiming Reflective Supervision in Social Work*, London: Social Work Reform Board.

Munro, E. (2004) 'The impact of audit on social work practice', *British Journal of Social Work*, 34(8): 1075–95.

Munro, E. (2010) 'Learning to reduce risk in child protection', *British Journal of Social Work*, 40(4): 1135–51.

Munro, E. (2011) *The Munro Review of Child Protection: Final Report*. Available from: https://assets.publishing.service.gov.uk/government/uploads/system/uploads/attachment_data/file/175391/Munro-Review.pdf [Accessed 9 June 2021].

MVP (2020) *Mentors in Violence Prevention: An Overview*, Education Scotland, National Improvement Hub. Available from: https://education.gov.scot/improvement/practice-exemplars/mentors-for-violence-prevention-mvp-an-overview [Accessed 7 November 2020].

Myers, M. (2006) 'Along the way', *The International Journal of the Arts in Society*, 1(2): 1–6.

Naess, A. (1973) 'The shallow and the deep, long-range ecology movement: A summary', *Inquiry*, 16(1–4): 95–100.

Nash, M., Munford, R. and O'Donoghue, K. (eds) (2005) *Social Work Theories in Action*, London: Jessica Kingsley Publishers.

National Audit Office (2015) 'Investigation: The government's funding of Kids Company', December 2015, London, National Audit Office Press. Available from: https://www.nao.org.uk/wp-content/uploads/2015/10/Investigation-the-governments-funding-of-Kids-Company-Summary.pdf [Accessed 18 May 2021].

National Audit Office (2018) *Rolling Out Universal Credit*, London: National Audit Office Press.

Nayeri, D. (2017) *Refuge*, Edinburgh: Prentice Hall.

Nayeri, D. (2019a) 'Pride and prejudice: The best books on the refugee experience', *The Guardian*, [online] 30 September. Available from: https://www.theguardian.com/books/2019/sep/30/refugee-stories-books-exile-asylum-further-reading [Accessed 11 December 2020].

Nayeri, D. (2019b) *The Ungrateful Refugee*, Edinburgh: Canongate.

Neal, J. (2018) 'The mental health continuum: Spreading the message', *Human Givens Journal*, 25(1): 16–21.

Nesta (2020) *Asset-based Community Development for Local Authorities*. Available from: https://www.nesta.org.uk/report/asset-based-community-development-local-authorities/ [Accessed 13 December 2020].

O'Connor, R. (2020) 'Comic Relief scraps celebrity Africa trips after "white saviour" criticism', *The Independent*, 28 October. Available from: https://www.independent.co.uk/arts-entertainment/tv/news/comic-relief-bbc-africa-celebrities-stacey-dooley-ed-sheeran-lenny-henry-b1392527.html [Accessed 5 November 2020].

O'Connor, S. (2007) 'Developing professional habitus: A Bernsteinian analysis of the modern nurse apprenticeship', *Nurse Education Today*, 27: 748–54.

O'Neill, O. (2002) *A Question of Trust: The BBC Reith Lectures 2002*, Cambridge: Cambridge University Press.

Oddie, D. (1997) *The Barefoot Actor*, Plymouth: The Barefoot Project, The University College of St Mark and St John.

Oliver, M. (1990) 'The summer day', in *The House of Light*, Boston, MA: Beacon Press, p 60.

Oliver, M. (1999) 'Final accounts and the parasite people', in M. Corker and S. French (eds) *Disability Discourse*, Buckingham: Open University Press, pp 183–91.

Olusoga, D. (2019) *The Unwanted: The Secret Windrush Files*, BBC. Available from: https://www.bbc.co.uk/programmes/m00068sk [Accessed 18 April 2021].

Parker, L. (2016) 'What you need to know about the world's water wars', *National Geographic*, 14 July. Available from: https://www.nationalgeographic.com/news/2016/07/world-aquifers-water-wars/ [Accessed 7 December 2020].

Parton, N. and O'Byrne, P. (2000) *Constructive Social Work: Towards a New Practice*, London: Macmillan.

Patel, A. (2012) 'START Community research: Priority of needs'. Available from: http://www.studentsandrefugeestogether.com/publications/START%20Community%20Research%20-Priority%20of%20Needs%202012.pdf [Accessed 26 May 2021].

References

Pentaraki, M. (2011) 'Grassroots community organising in a post-disaster context: Lessons for social work education from Ilias, Greece', in M. Lavalette and V. Ioakimidis (eds) *Social Work in Extremis: Lessons for Social Work Internationally*, Bristol: Policy Press, pp 51–64.

Perlman, H. (1957) *Social Casework: A Problem-solving Process*, Illinois: University of Chicago Press.

Peston, R. (2017) *WTF?* London: Hodder & Stoughton.

Pettifor, A. (2019) *The Case for the Green New Deal*, London: Verso.

Phillips, R. and Pittman, R. (eds) (2014) *An Introduction to Community Development*, Abingdon: Routledge.

Powell, E. (1968) 'Rivers of blood' [speech]. Available from: https://anth1001.files.wordpress.com/2014/04/enoch-powell_speech.pdf [Accessed 12 December 2020].

Power, M. (1997) *The Audit Society: Rituals of Verification*, Oxford: Oxford University Press.

Rankin, J., Smith, H., Connolly, K. and McKernan, B. (2020) 'Refugees told "Europe is closed" as tensions rise at Greece-Turkey border', *The Guardian*, [online] 6 March. Available from: https://www.theguardian.com/world/2020/mar/06/refugees-europe-closed-tensions-greece-turkey-border [Accessed 23 November 2020].

Rapp, C. and Sullivan, P. (2014) 'The strengths model: Birth to toddlerhood', *Advances in Social Work*, 15(1): 129–42.

Rapp, C., Saleebey, D. and Sullivan, W. (2005) 'The future of strengths-based social work', *Advances in Social Work*, 6(1): 79–90.

Reed, J., Pearson, P., Douglas, B., Swinburne, S. and Wilding, H. (2002) 'Going home from hospital: An appreciative inquiry study', *Health and Social Care in the Community*, 10(1): 36–45.

Refugee Action (2021) *Facts about Refugees*. Available at: https://www.refugee-action.org.uk/about/facts-about-refugees/ [Accessed 11 May 2021].

Reynolds, B. (1951) *Social Work and Social Living: Explorations in Philosophy and Practice*, Silver Spring: NASW Press.

Rhodes, P., Sanders, C. and Campbell, S. (2014) 'Relationship continuity: When and why do primary care patients think it is safer?' *British Journal of General Practice*, 64(629): 758–64.

Richmond, M. (1922) *What is Social Casework? An Introductory Description*, New York: Russell Sage Foundation.

Robbins, S., Chatterjee, P. and Canda, E. (2006) *Contemporary Human Behavior Theory* (2nd edn), Boston: Pearson.

Rogge, N. and Theesford, I. (2018) 'Categorizing urban commons: Community gardens in the Rhine-Ruhr agglomeration', *International Journal of the Commons*, 12(2): 251–74.

Romeo, L. (2017) *Strengths-based Social Work Practice with Adults: Roundtable Report*, London: Department of Health.

Royal College of Occupational Therapists (2017) *Professional Standards for Occupational Therapy Practice*, London: RCOT.

Ruch, G., Turney, D. and Ward, A. (2010) *Relationship-based Social Work: Getting to the Heart of Practice*, London: Jessica Kingsley Publishers.

Saffer, J., Nolte, L. and Duffy, S. (2018) 'Living on a knife edge: The responses of people with physical health conditions to changes in disability benefits', *Disability & Society*, 33(10): 1555–78.

Salamon, L. and Anheier, H. (1996) *The International Classification of Nonprofit Organizations: ICNPO-Revision 1, 1996*, Baltimore: Johns Hopkins University Institute for Policy Studies.

Saleebey, D. (1994) 'Culture, theory and narrative: The intersection of meanings in practice', *Social Work*, 39(4): 351–9.

Saleebey, D. (1996) 'The strengths perspective in social work practice: Extensions and cautions', *Social Work*, 41(3): 296–305.

Saleebey, D. (ed) (2009) *The Strengths Perspective in Social Work Practice* (5th edn), Boston: Pearson Allyn and Bacon.

Sayer, A. (2016) 'Responding to the Troubled Families Programme: Framing the injuries of inequality', *Social Policy and Society*, 16(1): 155–64.

Scerra, N. (2011) *Strengths-based Practice: The Evidence: A Discussion Paper*, Canberra: UnitingCare.

Schön, D. (1991) *The Reflective Practitioner: How Professionals Think in Action*, Abingdon: Routledge.

Schwartz, W. (1971) 'On the use of groups in social work practice', in W. Schwartz and S. Zalba (eds) *The Practice of Group Work*, New York: Columbia University Press, pp 3–24.

References

Scottish Government (2018) *New Scots Refugee Integration Strategy 2018 – 2022*. Available from: https://www.gov.scot/publications/new-scots-refugee-integration-strategy-2018-2022/ [Accessed 11 May 2021].

Shaw, I. (2007) 'Is social work research distinctive?', *Social Work Education*, 26(7): 659–69.

Sherwood, K. and Liebling-Kalfani, H. (2012) 'A grounded theory investigation into the experiences of African women refugees: Effects on resilience and identity and implications for service provision', *Journal of International Women's Studies*, 13(1): 86–108.

Shulman, L. (1978) 'A study of practice skills', *Social Work*, 23(4): 274–80.

Shulman, L. (1993) 'Developing and testing a practice theory: An interactional approach', *Social Work*, 38(1): 91–7.

Shulman, L. (2015) *The Skills of Helping Individuals, Families, Groups and Communities* (8th edn), Boston: Cengage Learning.

Singh Watson, G. (2018) 'Guy's news: An experiment in benign neglect'. Available from: https://wickedleeks.riverford.co.uk/opinion/farming-news-farm/guys-news-experiment-benign-neglect [Accessed 5 November 2020].

Smith, R. and Whittington, P. (2006) 'Charity: The spectre of over-regulation and state dependency', London: Centre for Policy Studies. Available from: https://www.cps.org.uk/research/charity-the-spectre-of-over-regulation-and-state-dependency/ [Accessed 7 November 2020].

Social Care Institute for Excellence (2008) 'Learning organisations: Knowledge about Learning Organisations'. Available from: https://www.scie.org.uk/publications/learningorgs/know/ [Accessed 26 October 2020].

Social Care Institute for Excellence (2015) *Care Act Guidance on Strengths-based Approaches*. Available from: https://www.scie.org.uk/strengths-based-approaches/guidance [Accessed 11 May 2021].

Social Work England (2019) *Qualifying Education and Training Standards 2019*. Available from: https://www.socialworkengland.org.uk/media/1641/socialworkengland_ed-training-standards-2019_final.pdf [Accessed 2 June 2021].

Solnit, R. (2005) *Hope in the Dark: The Untold History of People Power*, Edinburgh: Canongate Books.

Sontag, S. (2004) *Regarding the Pain of Others*, London: Penguin Books.

Sorensen, S. (2015) 'Privileged glimpses 11: Risk-free is impossible' [blog published 26 March]. Available from: https://mindthecaretraining.com/2015/03/26/privileged-glimpses-11-risk-free-is-impossible [Accessed 7 November 2020].

Stepney, P. and Popple, K. (2012) 'Community social work', in P. Stepney and D. Ford (eds) *Social Work Models, Methods and Theories*, Lyme Regis: Russell House Publishing, pp 181–200.

Stone, J. (2015) 'The refugee crisis is actually having "sizable" economic benefits in European countries, EU says', *The Independent*, 5 November. Available from: https://www.independent.co.uk/news/world/europe/refugee-crisis-will-actually-have-sizable-positive-economic-impact-european-countries-eu-says-a6722396.html [Accessed 9 June 2021].

Stone, J. (2016) 'Plans to replace Human Rights Act with British Bill of Rights will go ahead, Justice Secretary confirms', *The Independent*, 23 August. Available from: https://www.independent.co.uk/news/uk/politics/scrap-human-rights-act-british-bill-rights-theresa-may-justice-secretary-liz-truss-a7204256.html [Accessed 9 December, 2020].

Stott, N. and Tracey, P. (2018) 'Organizing and innovating in poor places', *Innovation*, 20(1): 1–17.

Stuart, G. (2012) 'What is the strengths perspective?' [Blog], Sustaining Community. Available from: https://sustainingcommunity.wordpress.com/2012/05/30/what-is-the-strengths-perspective/ [Accessed 7 December 2020].

Suguna, B. (2006) *Empowerment of Rural Women Through Self Help Groups*, Durham: Discovery Publishing House.

Sullivan, W. and Rapp, C. (1994) 'Breaking away: The potential and promise of a strengths-based approach to social work practice', in R. Meinert, J. Pardeck and W. Sullivan (eds) *Issues in Social Work: A Critical Analysis*, Westport, CT: Auburn House, pp 83–104.

Sumption, J. (1999) *The Reith Lectures: Law and the Decline of Politics: Lecture 1: Law's Expanding Empire*, London: BBC.

Sutton, J. (2018) *Asset-based Work with Communities*, Dartington: Research in Practice for Adults.

Syrian Vulnerable Persons Resettlement Programme (2015) HM Government, UK. Available from: https://www.gov.uk/government/publications/syrian-vulnerable-person-resettlement-programme-fact-sheet [Accessed 26 October 2020].

Taylor, B. (2018) 'Worse than prison: Life inside Britain's 10 deportation centres', *The Guardian*, [online] 11 October. Available from: https://www.theguardian.com/uk-news/2018/oct/11/life-in-a-uk-immigration-removal-centre-worse-than-prison-as-criminal-sentence [Accessed 9 December 2020].

Taylor, D. (2020) 'Serco wins COVID-19 test-and-trace contract despite £1m fine', *The Observer*, 6 June. Available from: https://www.theguardian.com/world/2020/jun/06/serco-wins-covid-19-test-and-trace-contract-despite-1m-fine [Accessed 29 December 2020].

Temple, B. and Moran, R. (eds) (2011) *Doing Research with Refugees: Issues and Guidelines*, Bristol: Policy Press.

Thew, M., Hargreaves, A. and Cronin-Davis, J. (2008) 'An evaluation of a role-emerging practice placement model for a full cohort of occupational therapy students', *British Journal of Occupational Therapy*, 71(8): 348–53.

Tomlinson, J. (2018) 'What happens to empathy in medical education?' [Blog] 9 February. Available from: https://abetternhs.net/ [Accessed 5 November 2020].

Tree, I. (2018) *Wilding: The Return of Nature to a British Farm*, Basingstoke: Picador.

Tse, S., Tsoi, E., Hamilton, B., O'Hagan, M., Shepherd, G., Slade, M., Whitley, R. and Petrakis, M. (2016) 'Uses of strength-based interventions for people with serious mental illness: A critical review', *International Journal of Social Work*, 62(3): 281–91.

Unison (2020) 'Unison responds to COVID testing plans for English schools'. Available from: https://www.unison.org.uk/news/article/2020/12/unison-responds-covid-testing-plans-english-schools/ [Accessed 29 December 2020].

Van Thiel, S. and Leeuw, F. (2002) 'The performance paradox in the public sector', *Public Performance & Management Review*, 25(3): 267–81.

Van Til, J. (2000) *Growing Civil Society: From Nonprofit Sector to Third Space*, Bloomington: Indiana University Press.

Vare, P. (2008) 'From practice to theory: Participation as learning in the context of sustainable development projects', in A. Reid, B. Jensen, J. Nikel and V. Simovska (eds) *Participation and Learning*, Dordrecht: Springer, pp 128–43.

Wang, C. (1999) 'Photovoice: A participatory action research strategy applied to women's health', *Journal of Women's Health*, 8(2): 185–92.

Wasserman, H. (1983) 'American born and reborn', in J. Speake (ed) *Oxford Dictionary of Proverbs* (6th edn; 2015), Oxford: Oxford University Press, p 176.

Watters, C. (2001) 'Emerging paradigms in the mental health care of refugees', *Social Science and Medicine*, 52: 1709–18.

Weick, A. (1994) 'Reconstructing social work education', *Journal of Teaching in Social Work*, 8(1–2): 11–30.

Weick, A. and Saleebey, D. (1998) 'Postmodern perspectives for social work', *Social Thought: Journal of Religion in the Social Services*, 18(3): 21–40.

Weick, A., Rapp, C., Sullivan, P. and Kisthardt, W. (1989) 'A strengths perspective for social work practice', *Social Work*, 34(4): 350–4.

Weisbrod, B. (ed) (1998) *To Profit or Not to Profit: The Commercial Transformation of the Nonprofit Sector*, Cambridge: Cambridge University Press.

Wenger, E. (1998) *Communities of Practice: Learning, Meaning and Identity*, Cambridge: Cambridge University Press.

Wenger-Trayner, E. (2013) 'The practice of theory: Confessions of a social learning theorist', in V. Farnsworth and Y. Solomon (eds) *Reframing Educational Research: Resisting the 'What Works' Agenda*, London: Routledge, pp 105–118.

Western, S. (2019) *Leadership: A Critical Text*, London: SAGE Publications.

Whelan, J., Swallow, M., Peschar, P. and Dunne, A. (2002) 'From counselling to community work: Developing a framework for social work practice with displaced persons', *Australian Social Work*, 55(1): 13–23.

White, M. and Epston, D. (1990) *Narrative Means to Therapeutic Ends*, New York: W.W. Norton.

Whiteford, A. (2016) 'Agency and alliance in the Anthropocene: Implications for practice, education and enquiry in social work', MA thesis, Plymouth Institute of Education, University of Plymouth.

Williams, F. (1996) 'Postmodernism, feminism and the question of difference', in N. Parton (ed) *Social Theory, Social Change and Social Work*, London: Routledge, pp 61–76.

Williams, J. (2004) 'Social work, liberty and law', *British Journal of Social Work*, 34(1): 37–52.

Woodfield, P., Woods, C. and Shepherd, D. (2017) 'Appreciating entrepreneurship: A new approach for field research', *Entrepreneurship Research Journal*, 7(2). Available from: https://www.degruyter.com/view/journals/erj/7/2/article-20160027.xml?language=en [Accessed 2 June 2021].

Woolford, A. and Curran, A. (2012) 'Neoliberal restructuring, limited autonomy, and relational distance in Manitoba's nonprofit field', *Critical Social Policy*, 31(4): 583–606.

Yuval-Davis, N., Wemyss, G. and Cassidy, K. (2019) *Bordering*, Cambridge: Polity Press.

Zavos, J. (2019) 'Ethical narratives, street kitchens and doing religious difference amongst post-migrant communities in contemporary Britain', *Culture and Religion*, 20(1): 39–64.

Zorn, J. (2005) 'Ethnic citizenship in the Slovenian state', *Citizenship Studies*, 9(2): 135–52.

Index

References to figures appear in *italic* type;
those in **bold** type refer to tables.